Creating a Christian Lifestyle

Katie McKenna

Nihil Obstat: Rev. Jack L. Krough
               Censor Deputatus
               7 March 1995

Imprimatur: †Most Rev. John G. Vlazny, DD
               Bishop of Winona
               14 March 1995

The nihil obstat and imprimatur are official declarations that a book or pamphlet is free of doctrinal or moral error. No implication is contained therein that those who have granted the nihil obstat or imprimatur agree with the contents, opinions, or statements expressed.

The publishing team included Barbara Allaire, development editor; Stephan Nagel, Robert Smith, and Michael Wilt, consulting editors; Rebecca Fairbank, copy editor; Gary J. Boisvert, page designer, typesetter, and production editor; Maurine Twait, art director; Penny Koehler, photo researcher; Tom Wright, cartoonist and photographer for cover and chapter openers; and Alan M. Greenberg, Integrity Indexing, indexer.

The acknowledgments continue on page 316.

Printed in the United States of America

1125 (PO3190)

ISBN 978-0-88489-358-5

Creating a Christian Lifestyle

Carl Koch

saint mary's press

Contents

Creating You

Creating Your Relationships

Creating Your
Life Path

1
Changes Ahead:
Your Life Takes New Directions

New Horizons

This course is about living fully, becoming all that you can be as a person. Life is a rich adventure if we know how to be attentive to it, value it, and enter into it with our whole being.

Transition: Hazard and Opportunity

Right now you are at a great turning point in your life: finishing high school, moving into legal adulthood, facing the new challenges of college or career training or a job. Life is full of promise, but you may be fraught with anxiety about what is ahead. The following cases illustrate the kinds of situations in which many seniors find themselves.

Marisa

Marisa finishes the last bit of her calculus homework. She smiles contentedly because she likes mathematics and, just as important, is very good at it. Tossing her books and papers into her book bag, she takes out the catalog from the university she wants to attend and flips to the section on electrical engineering. Although she knows that engineering is a tough major, she feels excited about it.

Unfortunately, two clouds hover over Marisa's plans. She wonders if she will encounter the kind of prejudice that she has felt in some of the advanced math classes in high school. She overheard two guys making a sarcastic remark about another Hispanic student in the same class. Disturbed, Marisa summarized the remark to the teacher: "They basically said, 'What's she doing in calculus? All she needs to know is how to count beans.'" Marisa's fury at their ridiculous prejudice is only partially able to overcome some of her self-doubts.

The bigger problem is money. Her mother's small salary barely covers necessities, and Marisa's father has sworn he will cut off child support when she turns eighteen. Marisa is sure she can get some kind of loan, but she still needs a well-paying summer job if she is going to make ends meet. What if she can't earn enough money? With the tight job market, finding any summer work at all could be tough.

Joe

Joe sits at the dinner table, staring out the window into the night sky.

"Well, Joe, what do you think? Have you decided yet?" his father asks.

"I don't know. I just don't know yet," Joe answers, irritated.

His father's look is not unkind, but he adds, "You have to make up your mind one of these days."

"Yeah, I know."

After supper, Joe returns to his room, puts on his headphones, and cranks up his stereo. He opens the drawer that holds his catalogs—catalogs for the Navy, a local community college, and an area technical school. Each catalog makes promises for a full, successful future.

However, Joe's thoughts always take him in a different direction. He imagines himself having his own apartment, a car that he really wants, and enough time to hunt, ski, and fish. Further schooling and a stint in the Navy seem to be only more delays. **1**

A Time to Stretch and Grow

A **transition**—a crossing or a passage—such as leaving high school and moving on in the world can be understood as a crisis of sorts. However, the word *crisis* need not be thought of as totally, or

1

Using the stories of Marisa and Joe as examples, write a brief description of the situation you are in right now as a senior, including some of the details requiring decisions.

even mostly, negative. The Chinese character for *crisis* is composed of two other Chinese characters—one for *danger* and the other for *opportunity*. Now crossing the Golden Gate Bridge into San Francisco by car can be dangerous: the bridge could collapse, you could hit another car if the fog is thick, or your car could break down in the middle. But San Francisco, with all its attractions and opportunities, waits on the other side. Finishing high school—crossing into a new world—confronts us with both dangers and opportunities, just as crossing the Golden Gate Bridge does.

Despite the tensions, pressures, and hazards, a transition may encourage us to ask more questions about life. These questions can lead to an honest process of self-discovery that brings about growth in us. Think about Marisa and Joe as they look ahead to life beyond high school. Marisa is already asking herself how she will handle the challenges of college, both in others' attitudes toward her and in financial demands. Joe has not yet focused on a goal, and the process of discovering where he wants to go and what he wants to do will require a lot more reflection than perhaps he has ever done. Both Marisa and Joe will surely be stretched and at times they will no doubt feel uncomfortable. **2**

A Call to Be Fully Alive

Going through a transition enables us to keep growing. Growth comes naturally to all living things. Given some water and halfway decent soil, a potato sprout will grow into an edible spud. Given nurture, human beings can become fully alive too. A big difference between a potato and us, of course, is that we have a conscious part in making

2
Think of one transition that you have already been through. List and describe the painful or hazardous elements and the opportunities of this experience of transition. Overall, are you better off now, after the change?

Student art: "Building Bridges," linocut by Brooke Prudhomme, St. Agnes Academy, Memphis, Tennessee

our own growth happen. The person you will be at age eighty is, to a great extent, the person you are forming right now.

The Gift of the Present Moment

The only life we have is the one we are living right now. Dr. Jon Kabat-Zinn, who works with chronic pain sufferers and those with terminal illnesses, teaches his patients meditation. He sums up his reason for doing so this way: "Your life is the sum of your present moments, so if you're missing lots of them, you may actually miss much of your [life]."

The gift of our life is the accumulation of present moments. If we always look into the future for living, we can get into a pattern of "Wait until . . ." thinking. Life will be good when we have accomplished *X, Y,* or *Z.* "Wait until I have my degree, then . . ." "Wait until I find the right job, then I'll really live," and on and on. People who know how to live fully, however, cherish each day and each moment as a gift. **3**

Our Own Adventure

Being fully alive is also something we have to do for ourselves. No one else can make it happen for us. A little story about an explorer of the Amazon jungles makes the point:

The explorer returned to his people, who were eager to know about the Amazon. But how could he ever put into words the feelings that flooded his heart when he saw exotic flowers and heard the night-sounds of the forest; when he sensed the danger of wild beasts or paddled his canoe over treacherous rapids?

He said, "Go and find out for yourselves." To guide them he drew a map of the river.

They pounced upon the map. They framed it in their town hall. They made copies of it for themselves. And all who had a copy considered themselves experts on the river, for did they not know its every turn and bend, how broad it was and how deep, where the rapids were and where the falls? (De Mello, *The Song of the Bird,* pages 32–33)

In order to be fully alive, we have to explore life ourselves—to see, listen, act, and take our own risks. This adventure does not necessarily require traveling long distances, doing dangerous deeds, or being a "lone ranger." We embark on the great adventure of living fully as we go through the process of becoming who and what we are called to be.

3
Write some notes in response to this statement: *For me, happiness cannot be found living in the present; it's out in the future somewhere.*

Jesus, Model of Living Fully

For Christians, **Jesus** is the model of **living fully**, and he calls us to that same kind of life. He beckons his followers to fulfill their complete potential, which for every human being is to love and be loved.

God sent Jesus, his Son, to show humans how much they are loved by God and how they in turn can love others. Jesus went about healing, feeding hungry people, listening, and reminding people how valuable and beloved by God they are. Jesus summarized his desire for full life for all people in these two great commandments:

"'You shall love the Lord your God with all your heart, and with all your soul, and with all your mind.' This is the greatest and first commandment. And a second is like it: 'You shall love your neighbor as yourself.'" (Matthew 22:37–39)

Christians through the ages have understood that love builds on itself and leads to full life. As Saint Paul told the people of Ephesus:

I pray that . . . [God] may grant that you may be strengthened in your inner being with power through his Spirit, and that Christ may dwell in your hearts through faith, as you are being rooted and grounded in love. I pray that you may have the power to comprehend, with all the saints, what is the breadth and length and height and depth, and to know the love of Christ that surpasses knowledge, so that you may be filled with all the fullness of God. (Ephesians 3:16–19)

Love leads to power and strength and understanding—all essential to living fully. Love gives us the energy and desire to become completely what we are capable of being. It draws us to learn new skills and develop our talents, and to cope and grow through all the changes and stages of our life.

Taking Life in Stages

Psychologists who have studied human development have outlined the **stages** of a person's life and growth in a variety of ways.

Eight Stages with Transitions

A typical outline of how a human life develops includes eight stages:

1. infancy
2. early childhood
3. play age
4. school age
5. adolescence
6. young adulthood
7. adulthood
8. mature adulthood

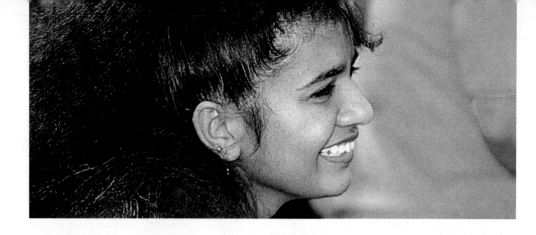

Any description of life stages is, of course, somewhat dependent on a people's culture. For instance, different cultures hold different norms for when adulthood actually begins. In some cultures adolescence is virtually nonexistent; a person passes from childhood to adulthood as soon as puberty begins. In North American society the move to adulthood takes a long time. A **transitional period**, lasting from about ages seventeen to twenty-two, leads a person out of adolescence and into young adulthood. Like any transitional phase, this one is full of challenges but essential to the process of growth. **4**

Lots to Do!
The Passage to Young Adulthood

During the present transition in your life, you will be challenged to take on **developmental tasks** in about eleven areas. If you are aware of these tasks, you will be better equipped to understand some of the feelings and dilemmas you are having. This course will help you look at these eleven tasks:

1. developing a sense of identity
2. growing in autonomy
3. renewing oneself by learning and creating
4. gaining competencies
5. selecting a career and taking an adult job
6. constructing and living out a value system
7. integrating sexuality into one's life
8. making friends and living with intimacy
9. making loving commitments
10. reflecting on religion
11. taking part in the larger community

Clearly a person does not move through these tasks in order, nor complete them once and for all between ages seventeen and twenty-two! For instance, all through life, not just at this transition phase, people move in and out of friendships, learning more and more about how to be intimate with others. But these eleven tasks have particular prominence and importance during the phase you are in now. **5**

In this chapter we will begin looking at these significant tasks by considering what it means to develop a sense of identity and to grow in autonomy.

For Review

- In what sense can a transition such as leaving high school be understood as a crisis?
- What lesson about living fully can be learned from the story of the explorer in the Amazon?
- For Jesus, what did it mean to live fully?
- List the eleven developmental tasks of the transitional stage from adolescence to young adulthood.

4
Agree or disagree with this statement, and explain your reasons in writing: *If I had my choice, I'd rather have a prolonged adolescence than none at all.*

5
Of the eleven tasks, which one are you most eager to work on? Which one are you most anxious about? Explain your choices in writing.

Identity:
A Sense of Who You Are

In this process of becoming fully alive, as persons who can love and be loved, we need to gain a sense of who we are—a sense of identity. We need to be able to name, claim, and honor the complex person we are at any one time. We will never have a *total* grip on our identity because we keep changing and are always more than we can imagine. But having some sense of who we are helps us to make better decisions, to develop enriching relationships, and to live in greater appreciation of ourselves.

Consider this story about someone in the process of finding his own sense of identity:

Zack sat at the end of the cafeteria table, eating his ham and cheese on rye. The conversation about the coming weekend surged ahead without him. Zack's position at the table defined his role with these guys: he was at the end, on the fringe.

When the bell rang at the end of the lunch period, the group split up and headed for different classes. Zack threw his garbage into a wastebasket and walked alone down the hall. "Why didn't I say something, *anything?* All I do is just sit like a lump. What a dope!" he thought.

After Zack sat down in economics class, he flipped open his textbook to the page marked by a letter. He unfolded his letter of acceptance to the state university. Everyone else had been talking at lunch about college applications, but Zack had never found an opening to mention his own good news. "Maybe I can get involved more at the U." This was half question and half hope, spoken only in Zack's mind.

Meanwhile, down the hallway, a conversation was in progress. "Are you really going to ask him?" Jane asked. "You better be ready to talk for the two of you."

"He's quiet, but at least he has some brains."

Lisa walked quickly to economics class, wondering how Zack would react to her invitation to go to the chamber of commerce luncheon. She knew that he was shy, but she thought of him as intelligent and fairly handsome. Lisa had first noticed Zack when he nervously gave a speech in class about the need for business opportunities for women and minorities. His hands had shaken and drawn aimless circles in the air; he had stared at the back wall. However, after a timid start, conviction had strengthened his voice. Lisa wondered where Zack had been hiding for the previous three years of high school.

After economics, Lisa walked beside Zack to their English class. She never felt nervous with anyone. Some people even found her to be too blunt.

"Zack, I have to go to a chamber of commerce luncheon to give a short speech about Catholic high schools. I can invite another student to go. I don't know how the food will be, but I'd like you to go with me. What do you say?"

Stunned, Zack wondered if Lisa was kidding. "Well, sure. Great." He looked at her happily.

"I'll drive. Friday. Meet me in the school office at 11:45." Lisa stopped walking and turned back to look at Zack. "Glad you're going."

Zack's situation is not unique; many of us exist on the fringe and wish we were somebody else at least part of the time. Fortunately, many people like Lisa exist, too. They are people who give us a richer sense of who we are because they recognize elements in our personality that we might not appreciate enough.

Awareness of the Unique You

To be fully alive as a human being implies being aware of and appreciative of the person we are. Your dog Rover, on the other hand, is not aware of himself as a Manchester terrier. Rover just eats, sleeps, looks at you eagerly for a friendly rub behind the ears, and behaves the way instinct dictates. Essentially, he does not have any awareness of himself as a dog. Only humans are aware of themselves as unique, conscious beings. We do not simply respond to circumstances through instinct—at least most of the time.

Our **sense of identity**, then, is our sense of who we are—the marvelous combination of personality traits, abilities, strengths, weaknesses, interests, and values that is uniquely ours. Our identity is always in the process of formation and remains vaguely mysterious. In other words, we cannot be summed up as a simple list of traits; we cannot be pinned down that easily, for our uniqueness is ultimately a mystery. **6**

Built on Past Experience

Your sense of identity is not developed in a vacuum. It is composed of millions of bits of information that you gather about yourself from events, relationships with people, work, reading, and so on. Everything that happens contributes to your sense of identity. In turn, your future is built on the foundation of this sense of who you are.

Receiving affirmation from other people, particularly from those who are significant to you, is im-

portant for achieving a strong sense of identity. If you think that you are an intelligent person but other people treat you as if you are dull-witted, you will live with a certain degree of insecurity about your intelligence. During much of your life, people have been affirming or challenging your identity, such as in the following instance:

Dan plays the trumpet well, so his music teachers encourage him to apply for a university music scholarship. Competence in music becomes an affirmed part of his identity.

On the other hand, every time Dan tries to fix his car, he either strips the threads off bolts, puts wires

6
Write fifteen sentences that begin with "I am . . ." Then pick the two sentences that best describe you, and check mark any statement that surprises you. Finally, write a summary of what you have learned about yourself from this.

Student art: "Find the Next Piece," pencil drawing by Sara Bednarz, Trinity High School, Garfield Heights, Ohio

back incorrectly, or in some way makes matters much worse. After he botches a job, the mechanic that Dan takes his car to snickers and mumbles something about, "some people have it and some people don't." Dan concludes that mechanical ability is not a part of his identity. **7**

A Strong Center

A clear and realistic sense of identity enables us to go forward with life choices about a career, relationships, and so on. Self-understanding is a center of strength that helps us to cope with conflicting demands and values, significant losses, and tough choices. Conversely, faulty perceptions about ourselves may inhibit our development. An accurate sense of identity enables us to live with **self-esteem**—an understanding of our own worth and an attitude of cherishing ourselves, even when others may put us down or devalue us. **8**

One caution: Before considering ways of gaining a stronger sense of who you are, realize that your identity is never final. Each accomplishment, every argument, and most events—the whole stream of life—continually shape us. Our identity is like a grain of sand that lodges in an oyster. Over many years layer upon layer of pearly substance builds up around the grain, until it becomes a pearl. At each stage of development the pearl has value, but it becomes more precious as it grows.

Knowing Yourself

Knowing yourself involves honestly addressing these questions:
- What am I feeling?
- What do I want?
- What are people telling me?
- What are my talents?
- What is out of my control? within my limited control?

What Are You Feeling?

Feelings or emotions are essential facets of who we are; they need to be acknowledged. Too frequently people are told to ignore how they feel: "Don't feel that way!" Think about how ridiculous that command is. We cannot help what we feel; we just feel. Emotions are reactions, not intentions. Strong feelings do not go away; they just bubble underneath the surface of our self-control, sometimes becoming a volcano that explodes. It helps to acknowledge them before that happens.

Knowing ourselves requires us to ask in a given situation, How do I feel right now? Feelings can function either as friends or as dictators. It is best

7
Picture some of your past successes, recapturing the full scene: who was there, what happened, how you felt. Successes help us to form our sense of identity. Write about one success and why you felt good about it.

8
Imagine that you are looking in the mirror before going to school in the morning. Write a list of the mental comments you make.
- Are they positive or negative?
- What are the sources of this mental feedback?

to treat them as friends, or they will become dicta-tors. This is illustrated in the following instance:

- *The dictator.* Sandra has the habit of making Tina look stupid in class. Tina is furious but cannot find a way to express that anger. If she says something to retaliate, Sandra's friends may come down hard on her or ridicule her. Tina is more than a little trou-bled, but she tries to tell herself that she is not an-gry anymore. Nevertheless, whenever Sandra's name comes up in conversation, Tina says some-thing rather nasty, putting Sandra in a bad light. Tina finds herself tied in knots by her anger. Clearly her anger is operating as a dictator here, although not consciously. A feeling is dictating Tina's behav-ior, making her less than free.
- *The friend.* Suppose that in this situation, instead of denying her reactions, Tina treats her anger as an intimate friend who is letting her know just how hurt and humiliated she feels. Now she must de-cide what to do. Tina may opt to talk privately with Sandra about how the cutting comments in class affect her. Or she may choose to say nothing to Sandra. Then Tina might release her anger physi-cally, by jogging, for example. Either way, Tina de-cides not to let the embarrassing remarks affect her self-image. In this situation, anger is Tina's friend, a teacher who gives her insight into herself.

By treating our feelings as friends and refusing to let them be dictators, we can learn a great deal about ourselves. **9**

What Do You Want?

Closely related to knowing our feelings is know-ing our **wants** or desires. We cannot decide what to do with our life unless we know what we want. We are barraged by other people telling us what they want us to want—in TV commercials, songs, billboards, fashion magazines, and even in conver-sations with our family and our friends. As a con-sequence, knowing what we want is difficult. The tendency is to falsify our desires, to pretend that we want something in order to please someone im-portant to us or to conform to some social norm.

Some people wake up at age forty realizing that they have never done anything that they wanted to do. In *That Hideous Strength,* by British novelist C. S. Lewis, the character Mark comes to such a ter-rible realization:

He looked back on his life not with shame, but with a kind of disgust at its dreariness. . . . When had he ever done what he wanted? Mixed with the people whom he liked? Or even eaten and drunk what took his fancy? . . .

. . . He was aware, without even having to think of it, that it was he himself—nothing else in the whole universe— that had chosen the dust and broken bot-tles, the heap of old tin cans, the dry and choking places. (Pages 287–288)

What we want forms our identity and shapes our life. Jesus recognized this fact when he said to his disciples, "'For where your treasure is, there your heart will be also'" (Luke 12:34). **10**

Student art: "Sarah at the Pal-ace," watercolor by Amy Wester-man, Holy Cross High School, Louisville, Kentucky

9
What feeling is hardest for you to express? Why? What feeling is easiest for you to express? Why? Write a personal goal about how you would like to handle your feelings.

10
Write "I want to" fifteen times in a column, skipping a line after each phrase. Then complete the statements, noting longings that will help you be fully alive. For example, "I want to learn how to cross-country ski."

What Are People Telling You?

Every conversation with another person, even the "Hello! How are you?" type, tells you something about yourself. "Hello! How are you?" is, at least, a recognition by the other person that you exist. If the other person says, "Hello, Pat!" you know that you are acknowledged in an individual way. If the same person stops, looks attentively at you, and then says, "Hello, Pat! How are you?" you sense that you are significant in that person's eyes.

Your relationships provide millions of pieces of data about yourself, some of them affirmative and some of them negative. All these pieces contribute to your sense of who you are. However, this information should not be accepted without examination. In other words, we do not necessarily gain an accurate sense of ourselves merely by picking up other people's perceptions of us and living as they expect us to. If a student has been marked by others as a wild troublemaker because of a couple of instances of poor judgment, that student can either choose to accept that evaluation and continue to act that way, or decide not to live out the negative image people have. Freedom and uniqueness

Student photo: **Untitled, black-and-white photo by Lisa Olivieri, Northwest Catholic High School, West Hartford, Connecticut**

require that we listen to what other people tell us about ourselves and then decide within ourselves whether we accept those evaluations. **11**

What Are Your Talents?

A **talent** is an ability or an aptitude that has value; it is often thought of as a gift, in the sense that a person seems to be born with it. A violinist does not choose to have perfect pitch; she or he is born with it. A great gymnast is born with a certain kind of body. The discipline and practice needed to create a master violinist or a great gymnast have to be combined with the genetic gifts of musical aptitude or a certain body structure.

Talents are not just physical or intellectual. Aspects of personality can also be unique gifts. Some people are excellent listeners. Other people are witty or always seem to take the initiative. Unfortunately, people commonly forget about the gifts of personality. School letters are given to athletes and band members, but few awards are given to recognize the talent of being a good friend, listening with understanding, or acting with kindness.

Before talents can be developed, they first must be acknowledged. Saint Paul urged the Corinthians to recognize their individual talents as gifts from God:

Now there are varieties of gifts, but the same Spirit; and there are varieties of services, but the same Lord. . . . All these are activated by one and the same Spirit, who allots to each one individually just as the Spirit chooses. (1 Corinthians 12:4,11)

Each of us is gifted in some way. To be full persons we need to take some time to reflect on exactly what our gifts are. **12**

What Is Out of Your Control?
Within Your Control?

To the extent that talents are inherited, they represent an area that is out of our control. However, what we do with our talents is within our limited control. In coming to a sense of identity, we would do well to sort out which factors that make us unique may be out of our control and which are more within our control. The factors that are out of our control include such variables as these:

Cosmic. Our birth was a unique event over which we exercised no power. Likewise, someday we will die. We are influenced by occurrences out of our control, such as earthquakes and hurricanes, gentle rains and clean, new-fallen snow.

Genetic. Genes have a strong influence on who a person is. Certainly we are a unique combination of our parents' genes, but a combination nonetheless. This may affect our appearance, our health, our aptitudes and talents, even to some degree our personality traits. Few forwards on basketball teams are the offspring of short, stocky parents.

11
List five comments that other people typically make about you. Next to each comment, describe how you feel about the remark. Do you accept or reject their opinion?

12
Inventory your talents and skills. Write "I can" fifteen times in a column, skipping a line after each phrase. Then complete the statements. For example, "I can relax with most people and become their friend."

Cultural. We have no control over the culture into which we were born and raised—as a member of a particular family, living in a certain country and region, and as part of a particular religious, ethnic, and economic setting. These cultural factors have much to do with our identity.

Circumstantial. Finally, we are shaped to a degree by circumstances—major historical events, accidents, chance meetings—occurrences that seem to be pure luck or pure misfortune. You probably know or have heard about someone who became paralyzed by an accident; that one event has had a profound effect on that person's life and identity.

In summary, our identity is influenced by cosmic, genetic, cultural, and circumstantial factors over which we have no control. However, *we do have some control over our response* to these factors. Our identity is in our hands to the degree that we understand where we have come from and can react consciously to that background.

The Apostle **Saint Peter**, as portrayed in the Christian Testament, serves as a good example of someone who shaped his identity rather than letting it be totally the product of his background. He was a Jewish fisherman, married, and probably illiterate. Peter lived in a land under Roman dictatorship. His work was hard. Some days his catch was good, and other days his nets were empty.

One day, along came a stranger, Jesus, who invited Peter to follow him (Matthew 4:18–20). Peter was not a likely candidate to be the first Apostle or the "rock" upon which Jesus would build his church. Nevertheless, Peter overcame the parts of his background that would have kept him a fisherman and used the facets of his being that allowed him to be brave, impulsive, and resolute. Rather than letting genetics, culture, and circumstances largely determine the life we lead, we can grow, like Peter, by using the traits we have in the circumstances in which we find ourselves. In Peter's case, and in ours, it is a matter of moving with the grace God offers us.

For Review

- What is a sense of identity?
- What is self-esteem?
- Explain why our feelings need to be acknowledged.
- What is a talent?
- What factors are out of our control in making us who we are? What is in our control?

Autonomy: The Ability to Shape Your Own Life

A strong sense of identity generally produces **autonomy**, a healthy ability to shape our own life and actions. In turn, acting responsibly and shaping our own affairs brings about a more secure sense of identity. Therefore, a strong sense of identity and autonomy reinforce each other.

Making Choices with Consequences

Making choices that have consequences—with the realization that you will have to live with those consequences, both positive and negative—is the stuff of autonomy. Robert Frost expressed such choices symbolically in his poem "The Road Not Taken":

Two roads diverged in a yellow wood,
And sorry I could not travel both
And be one traveler, long I stood
And looked down one as far as I could
To where it bent in the undergrowth;

Then took the other, as just as fair,
And having perhaps the better claim,
Because it was grassy and wanted wear;
Though as for that the passing there
Had worn them really about the same,

And both that morning equally lay
In leaves no step had trodden black.
Oh, I kept the first for another day!
Yet knowing how way leads on to way,
I doubted if I should ever come back.

I shall be telling this with a sigh
Somewhere ages and ages hence:
Two roads diverged in a wood, and I—
I took the one less traveled by,
And that has made all the difference.

When we exercise autonomy, we go ahead and make a choice, knowing that we cannot necessarily take it back, nor can we have it both ways. We might feel terribly pressured to make a choice that everyone else approves of. We may want to watch others to see what they do and imitate them. But if we are autonomous, we make the choice according to our best understanding of things, and let the approval or disapproval of others fall where it may.

Not relying on the approval of other people does not mean that an autonomous person is insensitive to the needs, wishes, or opinions of other people; a

Student art: "Facing the Future," linocut by Joanna D'Gerolamo, St. Agnes Academy, Memphis, Tennessee

mature person naturally takes others into account in decision making. In this sense, autonomy is different from **independence**, a state of relying on ourselves, not on others, to fulfill our needs or to give insight. The autonomous person is able to rely on his or her own judgment and competencies to make decisions and meet his or her needs, but that person is also able to rely on others and to have a sense of give-and-take with them. Autonomy includes **interdependence**, that delicate and healthy blend of independence and dependence. **13**

Gaining Independence from Family

At this stage in your life, you are probably gaining increased independence from your family, an important part of eventually becoming autonomous. Perhaps you are already on the journey of learning to function capably on your own. Here are some examples of young adults who are trying to gain independence, with varying degrees of success:

- Jeffrey, a high school student, commits himself to earning a significant part of his college tuition during the summer months. "It's important to me to rely on my own earning ability."
- Becky's mother threw her out of the house because Becky disapproved of her mother's live-in boyfriend and was always arguing with him. Now Becky lives with a friend, works after school, and struggles to finish her senior year. She is determined to go to college at least part-time. But it is a hard life, and Becky realizes she misses her mom and being a regular kid at home.
- After graduating from technical school, Rob could not get a job that paid well, so he went back home

to live with his folks. Now Rob avoids his parents, staying in his room and rarely talking with them. "It feels like I'm in high school again."
- Cheryl is so delighted about having no curfew in her first year of college that she stays out every night until two or three in the morning. She is exhausted most of the day and skips many morning classes. Finally, Cheryl admits, "This is crazy. My days and nights are reversed. I've got to get my schedule back to normal, or I won't be able to stay in school."

Becoming financially self-reliant, coping with hurtful family relationships, having the freedom to learn from our mistakes, and struggling with frustrations to our independence—all of these are part of the journey to gain independence from family. **14**

13
Think about a recent situation in which you were too dependent on other people (for example, parents or friends). Write about that situation.

14
Write about recent situations in which you (a) acted independently, resulting in personal growth, and (b) acted independently, with negative results.

False Autonomy

A couple of forms of false autonomy exist, behaviors that offer the illusion of independence from family.

Groupthink. Sometimes people in the transitional period into young adulthood make a sharp break from their parents or family by taking on the practices and views of a different group of people. For example, persons who join cults or gangs often do so to assert their independence from the values and lifestyles of their parents or family, but in fact they may be trading one form of dependency for another. Even a fraternity or sorority can function this way. Dependent people feel the need for a group to give them a sense of belonging and identity. In too many of these organizations, senseless initiations or dehumanizing practices are the prices a person pays to assume the identity of the group.

"Jailbreak" pregnancy or marriage. Another false form of autonomy is the "jailbreak" pregnancy or marriage. A young woman may be under the illusion that having a baby will cut her free from her family. Then she can have someone who needs *her;* she imagines she will have a life of her own with her baby. Thus she takes on the tremendous task of parenting without the necessary maturity and life skills to make it work. Similarly, both young men and young women may see a teenage marriage as their way to escape their family of origin, especially if life with their family has been very difficult.

Learning Interdependence

Genuinely autonomous people are neither lone warriors facing the world nor cold machines that operate unfeelingly. They are interdependent, capable of give-and-take, trusting both themselves and others. Here are some of the lessons of interdependence we can discover:

- learning to be strong enough to be sensitive to the needs of other people
- growing into a firm identity that allows us to consider other points of view and to change
- becoming aware of our own resources—talents, skills, knowledge, and feelings—so that we can be confident, not threatened, when involved in conflict
- recognizing that we sometimes need help and that our own identity will not be compromised by accepting aid from others when we need it

To be interdependent means to function well on our own while realizing our need for others and their need for us. Interdependence also implies that others help us to learn working knowledge and skills—from repairing flat tires and using computers to entertaining guests and listening well. We rely on others to teach us hundreds of practical life skills, and we teach others as well. This interdependent lifestyle builds our sense of identity. **15**

Paul's Balance

Saint Paul, the Jewish leader who became Christianity's apostle to the Gentiles, is a useful example of the balance between independence and dependence, which is essential to autonomy. In his second letter to the Christians at Corinth, Paul told them about some of his trials:

Five times I have received from the Jews the forty lashes minus one. Three times I was beaten with rods. Once I received a stoning. Three times I was shipwrecked; for a night and a day I was adrift at sea; on frequent journeys, in danger. . . . And, besides other things, I am under daily pressure because of my anxiety for all the churches. Who is weak, and I am not weak? Who is made to stumble, and I am not indignant? (2 Corinthians 11:24–29)

No doubt, Paul was tough, yet he was in touch with the feelings of the Christians.

Paul's faith in God made him strong. His recognition of his own weaknesses made him sympathetic: "So, I will boast all the more gladly of my weaknesses, so that the power of Christ may dwell in me" (2 Corinthians 12:9). Paul needed God's help and boasted about it. His letters to the Christian communities are filled with requests for help.

Like Paul, we can be interdependent. In fact, living in this way is part of growth.

Different for Every Relationship

While we are considering the delicate balance between independence and dependence, we need to recognize that we can never be completely interdependent with all people in all situations. No one is. We may feel more give-and-take with a close friend than with our younger brothers and sisters, who might take more than they give. Our relationships differ one from another, so our experiences of interdependence will vary according to who we are relating to. It helps to be aware of the dynamics at work so that we may grow toward relating interdependently wherever possible.

15
Write about a way you have been successfully interdependent, that is, involved in a give-and-take relationship.

Being Responsible with Freedom

Autonomy implies freedom from coercion or constraint. Such freedom is essential to our own life and development. However, we do not live alone; we live in a society of people who have rights and needs, who are all free. The freedom of all people requires that we respect and respond to the needs and rights of others.

Christian freedom means that we can see the big picture beyond our own narrow interests, and are able to respond to the needs of real situations and real people. Freedom includes responsibility. If we are confined to the prisons of our own whims and wishes, we are not free. Freedom means that we grow and express ourselves within the context of others' needs as well as our own. When freedom becomes unlimited choice without regard to others, it is no longer freedom but license.

For instance, a person racing a car down a city street at fifty miles per hour because she or he wants to see how fast the car can go is not acting freely. She or he is simply a prisoner to compulsion and whim. The driver is not taking into account the real situation, which might include other cars or a child who wanders into the path of the speeding car.

On the other hand, if the driver is speeding to the hospital because his or her grandfather has had a stroke while riding in the car, the driver might be choosing the most responsible free action. Considering the whole situation—life hanging in the balance, little traffic, and few pedestrians on the street—to drive slowly might be irresponsible. In other words, acting freely means that we consider the entire situation and respond accordingly for the good of all.

For Christians, freedom is seen in the context of freedom from sin and freedom to love. In one of his Epistles, Saint Peter sharply rebuked people who lead others into error and perversity: "They promise [others] freedom, but they themselves are slaves of corruption; for people are slaves to whatever masters them" (2 Peter 2:19). Sin—selfishness, injustice, abuse of others, and so on—can dominate our life. The promise of Jesus' Resurrection is that sin can be overcome and that people can be free to love. **16**

For Review

- What is autonomy? How are autonomy and a strong sense of identity related?
- What is interdependence? How is autonomy not the same thing as independence?
- Describe two forms of false autonomy.
- What is the difference between freedom and license?

16
Write a goal for your growth in autonomy. For example, develop your judgment about study time so you do not wait until the last minute to do assignments. Then list the concrete steps that will help you to reach your goal.

Personal Power: Flowing from Identity and Autonomy

Growing in a sense of identity and in autonomy produces a welcome result—**personal power**, the ability to influence our own life and the people and events around us.

The Need for Power, the Joy of Power

Being powerful—that is, bringing about change in the world around us—is not something that Christians should shy away from. We are meant to be powerful people who also empower others. Consider some examples of what happens when people are powerless:

- Because they received no response to their repeated cries, many babies in a severely overcrowded orphanage in Peru stopped crying; they gave up on expressing their needs. Although the babies were being fed regularly, some of them died because they could no longer communicate their physical distress. The inability to influence the world around them in this most basic way became fatal.

- People who are abused as children experience a terrifying form of powerlessness. When they become adults, some are more apt than other people to abuse their own children, out of a distorted need to assert their own power.

We need power. The deprivation of power, as demonstrated in the previous examples, can lead to violence and tragedy. People need to know that their own actions and voice can make a difference in the world.

To go from hesitancy and a feeling of having no impact to a sense of being filled with strength can be a joyful experience. Mary, Jesus' mother, and the Apostles felt this joy when they recognized that the power of the Holy Spirit had come into them at **Pentecost**. This power erased their fears: "And suddenly from heaven there came a sound like the rush of a violent wind. . . . All of them were filled with the Holy Spirit and began to speak in other languages, as the Spirit gave them ability" (Acts of the Apostles 2:2–4).

The joy of Mary and the Apostles at Pentecost was not unlike the joy that we know when we realize our own power to reach out and make a difference in the world around us. This power has a positive effect on our sense of identity and autonomy. From a Christian point of view, people must be able to help shape their own lives and influence events—that is, they must have power—if they are to become fully alive persons.

A Positive, Not a Negative, Difference

The word *power* often carries negative connotations. We may think of power as destructive or evil rather than constructive. Think of the contexts in which the word is used: "a powerful lobby," which imposes its interests on the public good; "a powerful dictator," who dominates an entire nation with his or her own will; "powerful multinational corporations," which can exploit cheap labor in poor countries; "a power-hungry corporate climber," who seeks to amass control while stepping over others.

Those are all examples of **negative power,** or power used badly. This is a limited notion of power. Power can be positive if it is used to influence

one's own life and the lives of others in growth-producing, healthy ways. Two positive kinds of power are nurturing power and shared power.

Nurturing Power

Power used to foster another person's well-being is **nurturing power.** Parents exercise this kind of power for their children by feeding them, changing their diapers, and later teaching them how to ride a bicycle. The power to nurture comes from a genuine concern for those who have little power of their own—children, sick people, and poor people.

Shared Power

When our personal power is used to complement or increase other people's power, we have **shared power.** This kind of power can be seen in Jesus, who passed on his mission to the Apostles, sharing with them his power to build the Kingdom. God's grace is evident when power is shared.

Listen to the excitement conveyed by this young man in talking about a meeting during which power was shared:

- It was a different kind of meeting. First of all, we were working on something we all believed in—raising money to help Katie's family with medical bills when she got so sick. We all jumped in with suggestions. When it came to actually deciding which projects we should do, everyone spoke up

and also listened; no one insisted on having it their way. By the end, we settled on two projects, and everyone took a piece of the responsibility. These people are great to work with.

Shared power is evident in many friendships. For instance:

- Susan encourages Tuan to try out for the school play and even listens to him practice because she knows that he would be excellent in it. Susan does this despite knowing that if Tuan gets the part, he may be too busy to spend much time with her. She wants to see him use his potential because Tuan has supported Susan on things that were important to her.

Sometimes shared power means speaking out or taking a stand so that others have a chance to better themselves—to use their own power. Consider the example of **Nelson Mandela,** the black South African leader who went from being a prisoner of the racist apartheid regime to, in 1994, being the first president elected freely by South Africans of all races. He used his power not only to speak out for his own race but also to build bridges of trust with the white government so that whites could release their grip of control over the majority black population. In the process, all South Africans gained power, in the sense of making a positive difference in the world. God's grace was surely at work in this transformation. **17**

For Review

- What is personal power?
- Describe two kinds of positive power.

17
Complete these two sentences with as many examples as you can think of for each:
- I used my power to nurture others when . . .

- I shared my power with others when . . .
Then review your lists. How would you evaluate your sense of your own power?

Stepping Out in Faith

Giving shape to our life is a great adventure full of risks, growth, pain, and joy. We are creating a lifestyle, a way of living in the world. The way ahead may seem hazardous at times. Yet we are not alone in stepping out on this journey. Jesus is with us, ready to hold us up when the going gets tough. We are a bit like Saint Peter, who, in Matthew's Gospel story (14:23–33), sets off to walk across the water, confident that he will reach Jesus. But when the wind comes up and the sea gets choppy, Peter loses his nerve and begins to sink—only to be saved from drowning by Jesus. Let us step out in faith like Peter:

Spirit of Jesus, give us courage to make this journey
 into the future that holds so much promise
 but also so much anxiety.
Help us grow into a strong sense of who we are
 as unique persons gifted and loved by God,
 meant to make a difference in the world.
When we get scared in the times ahead,
 don't let us lose heart.
Hold us up when we lose our nerve,
 and fill us with a passion to live life fully. Amen.

2
Growth for Life:
Learning and Creating

Our Need to Grow

Socrates, the great philosopher and teacher of ancient Greece, urged his students to live consciously and reflectively. Claiming, "The unexamined life is not worth living," he inspired his followers to wrestle with the meaning of their life.

It is hard to argue with the wisdom of Socrates. But we can also affirm the reverse of his little maxim: The unlived life is not worth examining!

Think about people you know who truly *live* life to the full. Most likely they are persons who are constantly growing, not content to get stuck in a rut. (Did you know that the only difference between a rut and a grave is the depth?) They seek out new experiences, challenging themselves to grow beyond the familiar. They soak up what they learn from life and use their learning to create something of value.

Deep down we all have the longing to grow beyond where we have been, to learn and to create. We need only watch children to see how natural this longing is. In the first few years of their life, children readily absorb their culture's language, an enormous accomplishment. They are curious about the whys and hows of everything. They love to paint and draw, to sing, to play out imaginary scenes, to build a tall castle of blocks or a cozy cave of blankets under a table. The desire to learn and the desire to create come naturally to us, as gifts from God.

However, somewhere along the line, around early adolescence, children become self-conscious and unsure about themselves. They lose their spontaneous tendency to explore and imagine. More and more, they voice the flat statement, "I'm bored." Perhaps that is not such a bad thing, for it can be at least a sign that they recognize life could be so much more than it presently is, even if they do not know what to do about it. **1**

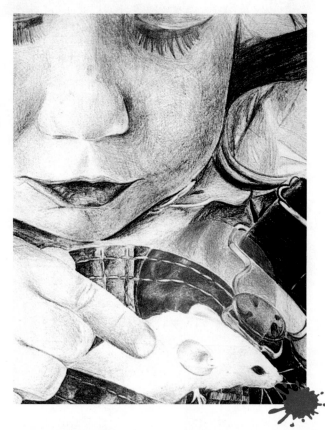

Climbing Out of the Rut

Consider the story of Dee, who comes to such a recognition of her need to grow beyond the rut she has gotten into in her first year of college:

Dee sat on the bar stool, glaring at Rosie, Larry, and Brian, who were drunkenly trying to play pool. "It's a good thing the felt is already torn up," she muttered to herself angrily as Larry jammed his pool cue into the tabletop, making the cue ball hop wildly. Dee's companions laughed outrageously.

"Hey, Dee. Come on and play some pool!" Larry yelled through the smoke and clamor that surrounded the patrons of Kelly's Bar. "And bring me another beer."

This command further infuriated Dee. "That jerk. He can get his own beer," she fumed to herself. Her eyes stung from the smoke. "This is great. I can just imagine how smelly my sweater's going to be if we ever get out of here."

Dee felt like kicking herself for agreeing to spend yet another Friday night in a bar watching drunk acquaintances play pool. All she wanted to do was go somewhere to relax after a hard week of classes. She would have enjoyed sitting someplace comfortable, instead of on a wooden bar stool, and simply talking—getting to know Rosie, Larry, and Brian better. She wondered if such a thing as a sober social life existed around the university.

Dee's mind drifted to thoughts of what the next day at brunch in the student union would be like. Of course the main topic of conversation would be how awful everyone feels from drinking so much. Dee groaned inwardly, "I suppose I'll have to speak in whispers at brunch because, as usual, the people at my table will all have hangovers."

Dee was distracted momentarily from her daydream when Larry lurched into her as he ordered another beer. "How come you didn't get me a beer?" he charged. But as soon as the sweating bottle was in Larry's hands, he forgot to wait for Dee's answer and stumbled back to the pool table.

1
List two or three times recently when you felt bored. Then answer these questions in writing:
• Why were you bored?
• Did you figure out what to do about your boredom? If so, what?

Student art: "Denim and Fur," color pencil by Allison Hawkins, Notre Dame Academy, Toledo, Ohio

Now, looking at her watch, Dee wondered how much longer she would have to wait before arguing with Larry about not letting him drive home. "This is a terrible way to have fun and relax," Dee grumbled to the face that stared back at her from the mirror across the bar.

Dee's kind of dilemma is certainly not unusual. Many of us find ourselves following the same old recreational routines even though we know they do not refresh us. Perhaps Larry, Brian, and Rosie also will wonder the next day why they got so drunk on Friday night. **2**

Dee's discontent has a positive side. It serves as an invitation to grow, to reach the **potential** that

life offers her—the promise that is within her because of who she is. Before long, if she finds others who also want to grow, she will probably climb out of the rut, learning new things about life and being creative with her potential.

Saying Yes to Our Unique Potential

We are wonderfully gifted with a whole gamut of ways to learn and to create. However, to use these gifts we first need to acknowledge our almost limitless **capacity to develop ourselves.**

An Abandoned Gold Mine?

John Gardner, an internationally known educator and psychologist, made this observation about the tendency to ignore our potential:

It is a sad but unarguable fact that most human beings go through their lives only partially aware of the full range of their abilities. As a boy in California I spent a good deal of time in the Mother Lode country [the location of a principal ore deposit], and like every boy of my age I listened raptly to the tales told by the old-time prospectors in that area, some of them veterans of the Klondike gold rush. Every one of them had at least one good campfire story of a lost gold mine. The details varied: the original discoverer had died in a mine, or had gone crazy, or had been killed in a shooting scrape, or had just walked off thinking the mine worthless. But the central theme was constant: riches left untapped. I have come to believe that those tales offer a paradigm [model] of education as most of us experience it. The mine is worked for a little while and then abandoned. (*Self-Renewal,* pages 10–11)

2
Does the story about Dee seem realistic to you? Do you ever feel like Dee? If so, describe in writing a situation you have been in that parallels her situation.

Developing ourselves, as Gardner suggests, begins with an acknowledgment that we are full of potential. Some students, because of poor performance in school, give up on themselves as learners and creators. They believe that they have no potential to grow, thus abandoning their gold mine. **3**

Needed: The Right Setting, Room to Fly

Ironically, though, some people who do not believe in themselves in a school setting may be wizards in other settings. Perhaps the high school environment simply does not give them enough room to take off and fly. A person may finally progress once he or she identifies a passionately loved interest, whether that is in college, technical school, or a nonacademic setting. Consider this conversation from the ten-year reunion of a high school class of 1986:

"How about that? Maureen Fitzgerald as a TV news anchor! Remember how she'd sit in the back of our history class and never say a word to anyone? Who would've thought she'd be talking to a whole city on TV every night?"

"Yeah, it's amazing. She said she took a journalism class, and something clicked for her. She got on the newspaper staff at the U, and she's never been the same since. But listen to this about Jerry. Remember he flunked business math? Now he's a millionaire! Owns his own company!" **4**

Other examples of such surprises are people like **Saint Thomas Aquinas**, the most influential Catholic theologian, and **Albert Einstein**, the great physicist. Aquinas, who would later write huge volumes about all aspects of theology, was dubbed the Dumb Ox as a schoolboy. Einstein barely graduated from a university because he had a hard time passing the life science classes. Each of us, like these brilliant people, has a unique, perhaps not always straight, path to learning and creativity. We need to affirm that fact and not needlessly compare ourselves to other people.

Becoming a "New Self"

In the Christian perspective, human beings are called to develop the full range of their potential,

3

Write your reflections on what Gardner says about potential as it relates to you personally. Do you have potential that is untapped?

4

Pretend that you are at your ten-year high school class reunion. Write an imaginary conversation that some classmates could have about you.

including their intelligence and talents. In his letter to the community of Christians at Ephesus, Saint Paul affirmed the importance of developing the gifts that God gave us:

I . . . beg you to lead a life worthy of the calling to which you have been called, with all humility and gentleness, with patience, bearing with one another in love. . . .

But each of us was given grace according to the measure of Christ's gift. . . .

The gifts he gave were that some would be apostles, some prophets, some evangelists, some pastors and teachers, to equip the saints for the work of ministry, for building up the body of Christ. . . .

Be renewed in the spirit of your minds, and . . . clothe yourselves with the new self, created according to the likeness of God in true righteousness and holiness. (Ephesians 4:1–12,23–24)

In Paul's vision, our gifts were given for a purpose—the building of a loving and faithful community. Developing our potential, in his view, meant that *we become a new self.* Learning and creating are intended to transform us into fully alive disciples of Jesus, building fully alive communities that enable people to grow even more.

For Review

- Explain the meaning of Gardner's analogy of the abandoned gold mine.
- According to Saint Paul, what is the purpose of our gifts, and why should we develop our potential?

Growth by Learning: A Lifelong Quest

You already have learned a tremendous amount in school, and college or technical school offers more to learn. However, a great bulk of **learning**—or growth in knowledge, insight, and skills—is done outside of formal education, in the school of life. You have been a pupil in *that* school since the day you were born, and you will remain enrolled until the day you die.

Formal schooling is crucial to our development as an individual and as a competent, contributing member of the community. But every new situation, no matter where it happens, can be an opportunity to learn.

In the School of Life

The following examples illustrate people who are growing in knowledge, insight, and skills in the school of life—at times with pain or with joy, through mistakes and through small victories:

- Now that he lives away from home, Ted has his own checking account, but he has never bothered to balance his checkbook. One day four checks bounce, costing him one hundred dollars in penalties and plenty of embarrassment. Ted learns very quickly how to balance his checkbook.
- Carmen was laid off when the factory she worked for closed down. She has two children to support. After a period of shock and then restlessness, she decides to open a small carpentry business, doing interior remodeling, garages, and room additions.

Carmen has always had a knack for carpentry, but she has no business experience. So she soaks up every bit of information she can about advertising, obtaining loans for equipment, buying supplies, billing and accounting, and eventually managing workers. Over time, Carmen becomes successful at her business.

- Since their baby was born three years ago, Hien and Trung have become experts in childbirth, breast-feeding, nutrition, childhood illnesses, stress management, infant and child development, discipline for young children, safe and enriching toys, day-care options, and fun ways to pass rainy days.

- Len's parents have discovered that he has a severe drug addiction. The treatment program that they find for him involves the whole family in counseling, which enables Len, his parents, and his brother to see what kinds of family situations have been affecting Len negatively. Now they are trying to relate to one another in new, healthier ways.

- After high school, Chandra takes a job at a nursing home as an aide. Part of her responsibility is to join the elderly residents at their weekly sing-along. There she discovers how music can speak to the hearts of older people, especially the most impaired, and how it helps them to communicate feelings that would otherwise go unexpressed. She is so fascinated by this that she decides to go on to college and major in music therapy.

The people in these examples are letting life be their teacher. Because they are open to their experience—whether it be a minor crisis (bounced checks), a marvelous joy (the birth and growth of a

baby), a major sorrow (a family member's drug addiction), or a happy discovery (an insight into a possible career)—they are growing in knowledge, insight, and skills. **5**

Taking the Risk

Those who can draw meaning and growth even out of seemingly devastating events, rather than retreat from life in fear, are the deepest learners.

5
Write a one-page description of a lesson you have learned in the school of life.

Choose Life and Freedom

Author Molly Dee Rundle expressed this quality of openness to experience that leads to fullness in living:

Sometimes we are prisoners in prisons of our own design. We've carefully built our walls; we've made our prison safe and comfortable, and then we have chosen to lock ourselves inside. And we do not call it a prison at all, we call it our home or work or responsibility. We are very careful to post guards so that nothing threatens the security of our prison. Some of us live and die there and suppose that we have been happy and that living was good.

But sometimes, something or someone happens to us and the walls are shattered, and we lie helpless and exposed . . . in view are new horizons, new ideas, new experiences. When this happens many of us quickly gather the stones and rebuild our prison and retreat inside, but some few look around and crawl out of the rubble and gaze into the distance and wonder what "stuff" the world is made of. They venture out to taste and smell and feel. These people never build prisons again. They are willing to risk the hurt and possible failure of living and loving and dying with no guarantee of safety. They live with only the promise that there is fullness in living. They take the risk and choose life.

To be a lifelong learner is to choose freedom over the prison of security and sameness. **6**

No Clinging to Safety

Jesus certainly could have chosen the security of living safely over the freedom of doing what he knew he was called to do as God's Son, the Messiah. He was called to create a new way of living and invite others to that way. He challenged the Pharisees, healed sick and possessed persons, forgave sinners, and instructed his disciples. For living out his convictions he was executed. Yet Jesus knew that he had made the choice to live fully—not to retreat behind fear and a shallow life. Knowing that his convictions would probably soon lead to his own death, Jesus proclaimed a profound truth:

Those who want to save their life will lose it, and those who lose their life for my sake will find it. For

6
Agree or disagree with this statement and explain why in a paragraph: *People today tend to be too focused on their own security.*

what will it profit them if they gain the whole world but forfeit their life? Or what will they give in return for their life? (Matthew 16:25–26)

Another way of expressing this truth is this:

Those who
cling to the safety of self-interest,
refuse to grow through tough times,
try to control their own narrow life,
and despair of creating a better world
will forfeit a meaningful and happy life.

But those who
let go of their own self-interest and love others,
learn and grow through hard times,
open up to all that life has to teach them,
and try to create a better world
will find life, and therefore death,
to be full of wonder and richness.

The truth that we find life by apparently losing it is the paradox Christians know as the **paschal mystery:** we go through death to life, as Jesus went through death on a cross to Resurrection.

Jesus challenges us to give ourselves to life, to learn and grow through all that happens to us. Whatever ways we use to learn, formal or informal, the growth of learning frees us for a fuller life.

What Learning Does for Us

The moment we gave our first cry at birth, we learned our first lesson. We felt hands touching us, a body warming us. As we experienced hunger, we cried. Instinctively we nursed. That satisfied our hunger. We struggled to focus our eyes on our parents. Although we did not have any words for the people and things that we saw, tasted, touched, heard, and smelled, we were learning.

By our nature we are learners. From birth on, learning is life-giving; it enables us not only to survive but also to have a full life. Here are some reminders of what learning does for us:

Learning offers choices. Acting out of ignorance is like walking into a pitch-black room expecting to put together a thousand-piece jigsaw puzzle. Learning is the light that allows us to see the pieces. We may still have a hard time doing the puzzle, and perhaps we will decide not to complete it. But without light, we cannot even see to make the choice. Learning helps us to understand clearly and thus gives us the chance to choose among options in life.

Learning overcomes fear. Walking in the dark can be fearsome. We might crack our shin on the sharp corner of an end table or stub our toe on a chair leg. Living in the darkness of ignorance can be threatening, too. For example, ignorance of other cultures can lead to fear of people from those cultures, especially if they do not look, dress, speak, or act like us. By dispelling ignorance about what causes us to be fearful, learning opens the way for enriching experiences.

Learning gives competence. Gaining competence in a variety of life areas is an important developmental task for young adults. Competence is the ability to engage effectively in specific behaviors that help us accomplish our important goals. Competence includes a working knowledge and the skills needed to accomplish our goals—from being a great softball player to being a good friend, from leading a meeting to toilet training a child. A full life will require some combination of intellectual, physical or manual, and social competencies. These competencies are the products of learning—whether in formal educational programs or in the school of life. **7**

Learning helps us cope with change. Change seems to be one of life's few constants. If we are to cope with the challenges of such changes, lifelong learning is essential. At various points in life, we probably will need to know how to do the following:

• refocus relationships
• gain new job skills
• become accustomed to different work environments
• respond to new requirements of family members

Learning enables us to cope with these types of adjustments.

Learning: Our Own Task

No one else can learn for us. Here are seven guidelines for taking responsibility for your own learning:

1. *Form habits of learning.* Listen and read carefully, develop self-discipline, and foster a curiosity about the whys and hows of things.
2. *Set goals.* Decide on a purpose for your life, whether it is a career goal or simply a skill that you want to have, and relate your learning to that purpose.

Student art: Untitled, black ink drawing by Rosemary Meyers, John W. Hallahan High School, Philadelphia, Pennsylvania

7
Write an inventory of forty of your intellectual, physical, and social competencies: for example, using a computer graphics program, driving a car, helping people feel at ease. Then record your reflections on these questions:

• Could you add even more capabilities to this list?
• What does this list tell you about your ability to learn?
• Which of these competencies will be most important to you throughout life?

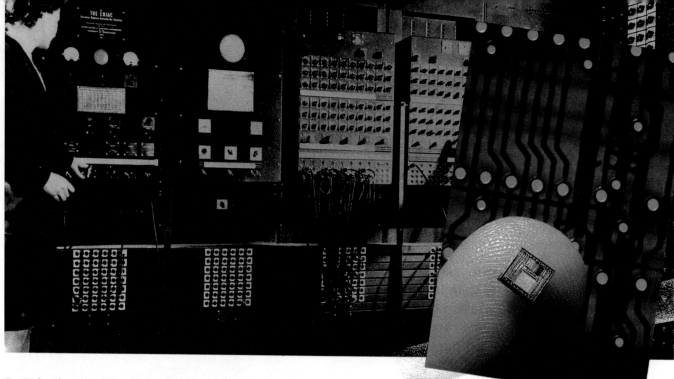

3. *Take the initiative.* Take the opportunities available for learning, whether through new experiences, formal education (evening and Saturday college classes or job-training programs), or resources in the community (club and church workshops, museums, libraries).

4. *Be open.* Be receptive to the people and events around you. Just as important, do not be afraid to look inward at your own world of emotions, fears, fantasies, virtues, and vices.

5. *Be flexible.* Be ready, if necessary, to change your way of thinking, to tolerate the ambiguity of venturing from the secure known to the insecure unknown. Remember, if scientists years ago had remained content with the cathode-ray tube, today we probably would not have the microchip or any of its related computer inventions.

6. *Do not simply settle for what is expected.* Learn the things that you want to learn, even if they don't conform to what everyone else expects. Learning is for you, not to please everyone else.

7. *Have courage.* Learning may lead you into interests that people close to you do not share, and that can be lonely. Learning may cause you to ask questions that make others uncomfortable because you see the gap between what is and what could be. Be willing to go where learning leads you. **8**

For Review

- What is learning?
- Give an example from this chapter of learning in the school of life.
- What is the meaning of the paschal mystery? How does it relate to learning?
- What does learning do for us?
- List seven guidelines for taking responsibility for our own learning.

Photos: Flexible thinking has enabled the evolution of computers from the 1946 bulky "Eniac," the first general-purpose electronic calculator, to today's computer chip that sits on a fingertip.

8
Which of the guidelines for taking responsibility for your own learning do you need to work on the most? Explain briefly in writing.

Growth Through Creating: A Gift of Our Own Making

The Creation story in the Bible states that human beings are created "in the image of God" (Genesis 1:27). Take this a step further: If God is a creator and we are made in God's image, then by our very nature we, like God, are meant to be creative. A simple definition of **creativity** is the drive to bring something new into being.

Indeed we have a longing in us to bring about something wonderful that was not there before. Our sexuality urges us to reproduce, to bring about new life. The history of technology gives evidence of the human tendency to invent new products and approaches, to "build a better mouse trap." Even the earliest traces of prehistoric human beings show that they were creative and artistic, expressing themselves by painting on the walls of their caves. On a simple level, many of us have tried to write our signature in unique, new ways—for the fun of it. The creative impulse accounts not only for great paintings, sculptures, inventions, and discoveries but also for the great lives people have lived. Creative people—**Mary, Jesus, Buddha, Hildegard of Bingen, Benjamin Franklin, Marie Curie**—bring about new visions and possibilities for humanity.

The Creative Impulse

Many of us might not think of ourselves as creative, but we all have that little spark in us somewhere that wants to bring something new into being. Finding a new unity in things is exciting, whether you are composing a song for a rock band, writing an insightful paper for a class, or dreaming up a new game to use with the young kids at the recreation center where you are a summer counselor. The ability to create is a skill that transfers into personal satisfaction, interesting employment, and a sense of contribution to the world. **9**

"Wonders with Nothing"

The award-winning science fiction and fantasy writer Ursula K. Le Guin said that "the open soul can do wonders with nothing." One of the stereotypes about creative people is that an innovator, artist, or great leader must be highly educated, well traveled, and widely experienced. Many of the creative geniuses of the twentieth century were just the opposite. Among the Nobel Prize winners for literature, **John Steinbeck, William Faulkner,** and **Ernest Hemingway** never finished college. **Emily Dickinson,** the very influential American poet,

9
Describe in writing a moment or occasion when you acted under the creative impulse. What was the outcome?

hardly ever left her house after she was twenty years old. Nelson Mandela, the first black president of South Africa (see page 26), spent most of his adult life, twenty-seven years, isolated from the world in prison. **Anne Frank** was only thirteen when she wrote reflections in her diary about life as a Jew in hiding from the Nazis, thoughts that would later move people all over the world. These creative persons had open souls and minds. They were learners because they were sensitive to every experience and saw all of life as their school.

Creative people seek to know as much about life as possible. They have inquisitive minds that are never totally satisfied with what they already know, so they ask a lot of questions. Creativity begins with openness to external reality and to a person's own feelings, ideas, intuitions, or images. Creative people also develop appropriate skills necessary to their field. For instance, a would-be sculptor may envision beautiful statues in her or his mind, but if she or he cannot weld, cast bronze, mold plastic, or use a chisel, she or he will never be a sculptor.

Creative Young People

Creativity is hardly confined to older people, nor is it limited to artists, inventors, or religious geniuses. Creativity is about putting intelligence and passionate interest to work to bring about something that was not there before. It may consist of figuring out a novel way to make people happy, or organizing a group for a cause. On the next page are a couple of examples of young people making a creative difference with their lives.

Student art: "Life," ink drawing by Alison Becker, Pope John XXIII High School, Sparta, New Jersey

Justin Lebo of Paterson, New Jersey, started racing bikes when he was ten. He would buy "junkers" and fix them up. He loved fixing them up more than using them; it was a real passion for him. After a couple of weeks he had two bikes collecting dust. He recalled a nearby home for boys and talked his mother into driving him over there so that he could give the repaired but unused bikes to the kids. The boys were overjoyed, but Justin realized that two bikes were not enough; the kids might fight over their use. So he decided to assemble bikes for all twenty-one residents. He hit all the garage sales and thrift shops. A neighbor heard about what Justin was trying to do and wrote a letter to the local newspaper asking for help. Soon offers of old, broken-down bikes flooded in. By Christmas, Justin had assembled twenty-one bikes for the boys at the home. By the time he was fourteen, he had fixed and given away around two hundred bikes. Justin says, "Once I overheard a kid who got one of my bikes say, 'A bike is like a book; it opens up a whole new world.' That's how I feel, too. It made me happy to know that kid felt that way. That's why I do it." (Based on Hoose, *It's Our World, Too!* pages 49–55)

*   *   *

At age fifteen, Joel Rubin of Cape Elizabeth, Maine, was fed up with the slaughter of dolphins—intelligent, gentle mammals of the sea—by the giant tuna canning companies. Their method of catching tuna with drift nets was relatively simple and cheap, but it needlessly trapped dolphins in with the tuna. The dolphins quickly died from a lack of oxygen. After months of wondering what to do about it, Joel struck on a novel, effective idea: he talked his schoolmates into writing hundreds of personal postcards to the homes of three key executives of the H. J. Heinz Company, owner of Star-Kist. He figured that by sending an avalanche of postcards to their home addresses, the mail would have more impact because it would be seen by the executives' families, too. Before the campaign got started, Joel wrote to the president of Heinz asking him to cease buying tuna caught in drift nets. When the executive failed to reply, the postcards started going out. Soon the Heinz president wrote to Joel complaining about all those protest cards sent to his home. Not long afterward, the Heinz Company gave in. Soon other big tuna companies stopped buying tuna from fisheries that used drift nets. "What happened is amazing," Joel says. "It just goes to show that if you really try, and plan, you can make a difference." (Based on Hoose, *It's Our World, Too!* pages 94–100)

These young people and many others like them show that human creativity is abundant if we just figure out a way to tap into it. Their creativity not only makes them more alive but brings life to a world so badly in need of it. **10**

Some How-to's of Creativity

Steps in Creating

Certain steps can be observed in most creative enterprises. These steps do not necessarily occur in the order they are listed below, and they may be repeated at different points in the process. With that in mind, this outline of steps gives us a way to sort out what happens in the usually untidy (but productive) process of creating:

1. *Preparation to innovate or create,* during which a person gains the factual knowledge and skills needed to deal with the problem or idea
2. *Concentrated work* on the problem or idea (As inventor Thomas Edison said, "Genius is 1 percent inspiration and 99 percent perspiration.")

10
List two problems or issues that bother you. Focus on one of them and bring some creative energy to it like Justin Lebo and Joel Rubin did. Outline a response to the issue.

3. *Rest and retreat* from the problem or idea—a time to clear the mind and emotions, which usually ends up as a period for incubating new strategies

4. *An "aha" experience,* during which sudden new insight is gained, accompanied by exhilaration

5. *Trying out* the insight or approach that is the result of the previous steps to see how it works, appears, or sounds

Whether the effort is by a teenager struggling to write a rock song for a band or a great classical composer writing a concerto, the creative process essentially requires openness, preparation, leisure, insight, and work. The process of creating leads to an expansion of our soul, to energy, to new visions of life.

Tips to Foster Creativity

Here are some practical ways to encourage your creativity:

Give your intuition and imagination room to function. Many of us distrust our intuition and imagination, but creative thinking is not possible without them. To give intuition and imagination room means to use leisure time that is not crowded with things to do. Creativity grows in the quiet, unhurried space of a walk in the woods, a quiet sit in a rocking chair, or some other uncluttered moment. **11**

Have a creative space. Most creative people set aside a definite time and space in which they are most productive. Some writers have their creative peak early in the morning. Many authors have a special chair or desk at which they discover their best ideas.

Interact with innovative people. Stimulating companions can give a charge to your work. People who get enthusiastic about their ideas will usually get you excited, too.

Ask questions. If you can gather enough courage to make inquiries, especially of other creative people, you can learn a lot that might be useful for your own projects. Practice open-ended questions that cause people to talk more—questions like, "What do you think of . . ." rather than "Did you like . . ."

Break out of ruts. Eating two slices of toast with peanut butter and jelly for breakfast every morning or listening to the same type of music all the time are examples of the simple ruts we can fall into. All we accomplish by walking in a rut is making the rut deeper and deeper. We can foster creativity by eating something different in the morning or by listening to jazz or blues or classical music. **12**

11
Imagine that you have three days of free time but little money to spend. Outline in detail how you will use this time. Be creative.

Student art: "Frozen," watercolor by Amy Westerman, Holy Cross High School, Louisville, Kentucky

12
List ten changes you would like to make that would bring new life in small ways: for example, read more than just the headline each day or learn how to cook one thing each week. Start each sentence with "I'd like to . . ."

Set and keep deadlines for yourself. A deadline helps push you along to get things done. Creative people make things happen. Talking about a project is not creativity; doing it is. Without deadlines, our energies tend to drain away too easily.

Focus your attention and dig deeply. To be a creator you have to know more about your particular project than the average person. Justin Lebo's knowledge of bikes made his creative giving possible. You have to develop a keen relish for learning in your special area of interest. Innovators focus their attention and are constantly picking up new information and insights. Many creative people have whole files of notes and ideas that they have collected about their interests.

See problems and conflicts as opportunities for creativity. Too many times we tend to view problems and conflicts as things to be avoided. Many creative people are actually spurred to action by questions and adversity.

Above All, a Compelling Attitude of Caring

Beyond any steps, techniques, or tips for creativity lies an essential attitude of caring. *Christian Century* quotes a mother who wrote to her daughter in college about the immense sense of caring that is the mark of creativity. Recalling her daughter's devastation when basketball legend Michael Jordan announced his retirement from the NBA in 1993, the mother reflected in her letter:

You know I'm not much of a fan, but I do have a theory about what made Jordan so compelling to watch. I don't think it was just the glitter of his style, though, of course, even I could see that he did incredible things. I think it was the fact that he didn't just rely on all that natural talent. There was a perfectionist quality to him, the attitude of a craftsman. And I think that is what you were responding to in him—especially as you became an increasingly knowledgeable fan. He communicated the sense that he cared about how the game was played—and wanted it done right.

People like that are always compelling, and I think they see something very important about life. I'm less and less drawn to well-rounded people, more and more attracted to those who do something—almost anything—with care. And it doesn't much matter what it is that so commands our energy and attention. It may be basketball. It may be writing. It may be raising some children. It may be managing an office. To engage our powers as best we can in some task—that should be the goal. . . .

Find something you care about and devote yourself to it with a whole heart. **13**

Time for Renewal: Essential to Creativity

The chance to grow by being creative depends on a good many circumstances. Among them, an essential one is having **leisure**, time that is not filled up with work and other duties. Leisure has the power to re-create us, to give us fresh energy and form us anew. The word *recreation* contains such a meaning. Without periods of renewal, we lose the capacity to be creative; we are too depleted to generate new ideas, to bring forth beauty through art, or to pour energy into something we care deeply about. We need empty times in life in order to regain the passion and enthusiasm that fuel the creative process.

13
What is one thing you care about so much that it could mobilize your energy and attention?

The Power of Emptiness

An ancient saying by the Chinese sage Lao-tzu recognizes this creative potential of "emptiness," of time unstructured by demands and obligations:

We put thirty spokes to make a wheel:
But it is on the hole in the center that the use of the cart hinges.

We make a vessel from a lump of clay;
But it is the empty space within the vessel that makes it useful.

We make doors and windows for a room;
But it is the empty spaces that make the room livable.

Thus, while existence has advantages,
It is the emptiness that makes it useful.

Leisure is like emptiness. Just as the space in a vessel is essential for the vessel to be useful, so is leisure necessary for us if we are to grow. We need empty times to open our head and heart to listen, to think, to breathe freely, and to be in touch with ourselves. **14**

Empty, but Not Necessarily Inactive

Periods of leisure can be empty of demands and obligations but also very active. For example, four friends who spend ten days together on a canoe trip may keep quite active. They paddle their way across lakes, carry canoes and packs overland, collect wood for fires, cook, set up tents, and spend a lot of time swatting mosquitoes. With all this "work," camping is still considered to be leisure because the element of duty is missing, the sense of having to. The pine forest sunrises and lakeshore sunsets make the effort more than worthwhile.

A Sabbath for God and for Us

In the Book of Genesis, we are told that even God rested after working for six days to create the world:

[God] rested on the seventh day from all the work that he had done. So God blessed the seventh day and hallowed it, because on it God rested from all the work that he had done in creation. (2:2–3)

The wisdom of this passage from the Creation story is that if God took a rest, we certainly can, too. In other words, it is a godlike practice to contemplate the wonders of creation, to rest in and appreciate the life that has been given to us by God. This is the meaning behind the Jewish and Christian practice of keeping the **Sabbath** as a day free from the usual obligations of work and meeting deadlines (for Jews the Sabbath is Saturday; for Christians, Sunday). With our contemporary society's urgent agenda of keeping business going and expecting constant productivity, the true practice of the Sabbath has all but disappeared from our culture. Yet creativity depends on allowing ourselves the time for renewal that is our right as human beings. We need the Sabbath. **15**

Jesus understood his own need for leisure that would bring him refreshment and new strength for

---

14
Brainstorm a list of objects that require emptiness to be useful. Then write your reflections on this question: *What experiences of emptiness—times when you have been free of demands and tasks—* *have had great value to your development as a worker, a student, or simply a human being?*

15
React to this statement in writing: *I personally could benefit from a real Sabbath every week.*

his mission. The Gospels cite many instances when Jesus, either alone or with his disciples, withdrew to pray and meditate. He is also pictured enjoying companionship at many banquets, even making wine for the guests at a wedding feast. Jesus knew the importance of leisure.

The Value of "Wasted" Time

Making a welcome space for leisure in our life is not a luxury but a necessity if we are to fulfill our potential as creative beings. Renowned psychologist Rollo May summed up the re-creating potential of leisure in his words about "wasted" time:

We can use [leisure] for random thinking, reverie, or for simply wandering around a new city for a time. Yes, the time may be wasted. But who is to say that this "wasted" time may not bring us our most important ideas or new experiences, new visions, that are invaluable? The "letting be" and "letting happen" may turn out to be the most significant thing one can do. (*Freedom and Destiny,* page 177)

For Review

- What is creativity?
- Besides the work of artists, what are some other ways that creativity is expressed?
- Give an example from this chapter of a young person's creativity.
- List five steps in creating.
- Give eight tips to foster creativity.
- What is leisure? How does it relate to creativity?
- Why do we need the Sabbath?

Not Burying Our Talents

Do you remember the parable Jesus once told about the talents (Matthew 25:14–30)? In it, a man gives each of his three servants a different number of talents, or weights of silver. Two of them go off and work to invest and increase their talents, but the servant who was given only one talent fearfully hides his, afraid that he will lose it. When the master finds out, he is very upset with the one who buried his talent and thus wasted it. Let's ask that we can grow as Jesus' story urges us to grow:

Jesus, we know you weren't talking
    about multiplying our money,
But about growing through the gifts
    we've been given—
  talents (the kind *we* know, not the silver kind),
  opportunities, time, relationships,
  all our life events, even hardship and tragedy.
These are our "silver pieces" that you urge us not to
    hold tightly,
  lest we end up one day as safe but small people.
Let us be free with these gifts, investing them in life,
  learning the lessons of a lifetime,
  and creating what has never been before.
Then may we grow someday
  into the great soul that we were meant to be.
Amen.

3

Work:

The Power to Create a New World

Work: It's Essential

Work is sustained effort that has a purpose. That purpose might be to produce a car, design a lamp, cook in a Chinese restaurant, or teach English to high school students. In its broadest sense, work includes all unpaid but purposeful effort (a parent caring for a child, a son doing the family dishes, a woman organizing a neighborhood crime watch, a teenager studying). However, in this chapter we will be discussing work in the sense of a person's usual means of earning a living.

People generally spend forty to fifty years of life working at various jobs and pursuing one or more careers. That represents about one hundred thousand hours of employed work. This work is significant for us not only because it occupies so much of our lifetime but also because it plays such a major role in shaping us—our identity, our significant relationships, and our sense of meaning in life. Work gives expression to our power and creativity, enabling us to provide for ourselves and our families, and to build, influence, and contribute to the world. And, as psychologist Rollo May reminds us, "Power is essential for all living things" (*Power and Innocence,* page 19).

When There Is No Work

When people are deprived of work, they experience powerlessness and loss of meaning. **Forced unemployment** is destructive not simply because of the financial loss it entails, which is hard enough to bear, but because it delivers such a blow to one's sense of self, one's effectiveness, one's reason for being.

In *The Grapes of Wrath,* a novel about the Great Depression, John Steinbeck describes the devastation connected with lack of work. Driven off their land by a bank's foreclosure on their loan, the Joads join thousands of other families in similar circumstances on the roads to California. They bring with them dreams of work and the better life that will come with it. Instead, in California the hoards of hopeful migrants find they have been fooled with lies. Landowners have lured them out there with promises of work, because they want the hungry, unemployed people to compete for jobs, thus keeping wages low. Homeless, scared, penniless, and starving, the migrants realize the awful truth:

And gradually the greatest terror of all came along.

They ain't gonna be no kinda work for three months.

In the barns, the people sat huddled together; and the terror came over them, and their faces were gray with terror. The children cried with hunger, and there was no food.

Then the sickness came, pneumonia, and measles that went to the eyes and to the mastoids.

And the rain fell steadily, and the water flowed over the highways, for the culverts could not carry the water.

Then from the tents, from the crowded barns, groups of sodden men went out, their clothes slopping rags, their shoes muddy pulp. They splashed out through the water, to the towns, to the country stores, to the relief offices, to beg for food, to cringe and beg for food, to beg for relief, to try to steal, to lie. And under the begging, and under the cringing, a hopeless anger began to smolder. (Pages 554–555)

Steinbeck, writing back in the 1930s, understood the dynamics of unemployment, a cycle that we can still see today. Lack of work leads to a sense of

powerlessness and frustration, which promotes deep, hopeless anger. Today we can see this anger erupting as violence and desperate, self-defeating behaviors in neighborhoods where unemployment is high.

A Place in the World

Many working people would probably agree with the following comments from Barbara, a woman in

Photo: **A mother and her children face the grim realities of poverty during the Great Depression of the 1930s.**

her thirties who has been in sales and market research. Her words convey the significance that work can have in human life:

"To be occupied is essential. One should find joy in one's occupation. . . . Work has a [negative] sound. It shouldn't. I can't tell you how strongly I feel about work. . . .

"Work has a dignity you can count upon. . . . There's quite a wonderful rhythm you can find yourself involved in in the process of any kind of work. It can be waxing a floor or washing dishes. . . .

"Everyone needs to feel they have a place in the world. It would be unbearable not to. I don't like to feel [useless]. One needs to be needed. . . . Everyone must have an occupation.

"Love doesn't suffice. It doesn't fill up enough hours. . . . I don't think [we] can maintain [our] balance or sanity in idleness. Human beings must work to create some coherence." (*Working,* pages 422–424)

Purpose is what gives life coherence. Work has a purpose, so, in the words of Barbara, it "has a dignity you can count upon." Work generally enables people to "feel they have a place in the world" because they are needed to accomplish the purpose of their work. **1**

For Review

- What is work, and why is it so important to us?
- Describe the dynamics that are often a part of unemployment.

Why Work?

We long for work that has dignity, even if we do not necessarily express ourselves in those terms. Finding a role with dignity in the world of work is one of the key developmental tasks for young adults.

Many people your age hold part-time jobs, so work may already be an issue for you. If you go on to college after graduating from high school, a specific career choice may still be some years away. If you choose to study a job specialty in technical school or plan to get a job directly after high school, work issues are more immediate. Regardless of which path you will be taking next year, time spent now on thinking about the role of work in your life is time well spent.

Our motives for working are as varied as any other aspect of our personality.

To Earn Money

Most of us work to earn money so that we can meet our basic needs. Income is not a bad motive for work; it is a reality. Even when money is our primary motive, work can be fulfilling for other reasons as well. This is evident in the comments of Delores, a waitress:

"I became a waitress because I needed money fast and you don't get it in an office. My husband and I broke up and he left me with debts and three children. My baby was six months. [I needed] the fast buck, your tips. . . .

"I have to be a waitress. How else can I learn about people? How else does the world come to me? . . .

1
Reflect on this question in writing: *If I were finished with my schooling and could not find work for a long time, how would I react?*

Everyone wants to eat, everyone has hunger. And I serve them. . . .

"People imagine a waitress couldn't possibly think or have any kind of aspiration other than to serve food. When somebody says to me, 'You're great, how come you're *just* a waitress?' *Just* a waitress. I'd say, 'Why, don't you think you deserve to be served by me?' It's implying that he's not worthy, not that I'm not worthy. It makes me irate. I don't feel lowly at all. I myself feel sure. I don't want to change the job. I love it." (*Working*, pages 294–295)

Delores needs to make money, but she enjoys her work and sees it as a role that has dignity. Her job has meaning for her.

To Fulfill Ambitions

Many people see work as a way to fulfill their ambitions.

- Janine wants to work as an engineer in the space program because she has always been fascinated by the challenge of space. She finally has the chance to do so after engineering school, and she finds the work exciting and energizing.
- Kenyatta has desired since childhood to be just like his third-grade teacher, who turned his frustrated life around when she discovered his learning disability and helped him through it. He begins to fulfill this ambition in his first year of classroom teaching.
- Monica has longed to be a trainer of sea mammals (like seals, dolphins, and porpoises) since she visited the zoo as a child and was charmed by the gentle, friendly creatures. Now, with advanced education in marine animal behavior, she takes a job at an aquarium.
- Kevin has spent all his waking hours outside of school fixing up old, beat-up cars that he then sells. He would rather fix cars than do anything else in life. After high school, he takes a course in auto mechanics at the technical college, works for a garage, and eventually opens up his own repair shop. **2**

To Develop a Sense of Identity

Work is one way that we clarify who we are. Work gives us an arena within which to answer these questions:

2
Do you have an ambition that you have always wanted to fulfill? If so, write about that ambition and how you might fulfill it through work.

- What specific talents or skills do I have or could I develop?
- What characteristics do I possess that are particularly appreciated or admired by other people?
- How will I react in a given situation?

A job can give us the opportunity to discover strengths within ourselves that we did not even know were there. For instance:

A month ago, Wanda began her job as a medical clerk in a busy, understaffed emergency room of a major metropolitan hospital. She has been observing the reactions of other emergency-room staff members when patients or families approach them to get information, complain about a long wait, and so on. Some of the employees resent these "intrusions" and want to "put the complainers in their place." Other staff members stay calm and are helpful. Wanda herself has developed a real knack for soothing patients and family members when they are upset, by taking a genuine interest in them and their concerns. It is a part of herself that she had never realized before this job. **3**

To Do What One Loves to Do

People whose jobs entail doing what they love to do tend to work with a special enthusiasm. They bring to their tasks a joy and a commitment not found in individuals who feel constrained to work by circumstances and would choose some other work if they could. People who enjoy their jobs are renewed by their work. Someone once said, "Happiness is being paid to do what you would do anyway."

Jeff, a senior at a Catholic high school in Milwaukee, gives this advice to people his age:

Follow your bliss! If you're fascinated by something, consider it a gift from God. If you have an interest or a talent, thank God by following it. You can't go wrong doing what you love. **4**

To Build a Better World

The desire to build conditions for a better life for the earth and its inhabitants is another motivation for working.

- A veterinarian who helps farmers keep their animals healthy clearly does something good for society.
- A chemist who researches new, low-pollution fuels for cars performs an important service to the planet and to all life.
- A friendly and efficient nurse's aide in a nursing home meets the physical and emotional needs of patients.

3
Interview two people who have had a minimum of five years of full-time work experience. Ask them these two questions:
- What have you learned about yourself through your work?
- What have you learned about the workplace and what it means to be a worker?

4
Think of someone you know who loves her or his work, who finds it a joy to go to work. Describe the person in writing.

People in such positions frequently are very conscious that their work is contributing to a better world, and they find that awareness motivating.

In the above examples, it is easy to see the connection between the work and the building of a better world. However, service professions are not the only jobs that build the earth. All jobs performed with dedication can contribute to a better world (provided, of course, that the results of the work are not detrimental to life).

- Workers on an aircraft assembly line build the earth by doing their work carefully. If rivets are installed sloppily, the lives of future passengers could be endangered.
- Accountants who are honest and competent ensure that the government receives the taxes it needs to function, and they help their employers to run efficient businesses that employ people and provide goods and services.

Assembly-line workers and accountants who do their jobs well may not think of their work as contributing to a better world, but it can, even without their knowing it!

To Answer a Call

Some people see their work as more than a job. They see it as a **vocation**, or calling. You might be familiar with the term *vocation* as meaning a **Christian vocation**—a call by God to live in either the married, the single, the religious, or the ordained state of life. But in a broader sense, vocation can mean any calling to a work that seems important for a person to do.

People with a sense of vocation feel that some need in the world is calling to their depths for a response, and that this work is very specially theirs to do. These people may be in the helping professions—occupational therapists, nurses, social workers, teachers, or youth ministers—or they may be writers, park naturalists, or restorers of old buildings. What is important is the passionate conviction that these people have that they are *meant* to do this work.

Pat, the administrator of a school for dropouts, described his sense of calling, which came after a long period of drifting in which he felt no purpose in his life:

Student art: **Untitled, acrylic and tempera on paper, by Rocio Alcaraz, Alverno High School, Sierra Madre, California**

"[I] drifted. . . . [Then] suddenly I had the urge. At one time, I'd have said I had the calling. I started teaching. . . .

". . . My work is everything to me. . . . I'd rather die for my work life than for my personal life. I guess you can't really separate them. . . .

"I run into people who say how much they admire what I do. It's embarrassing. I don't make any judgments about my work, whether it's great or worthless. It's just what I do best. It's the only job I want to do. . . . This is my life." (*Working,* pages 489, 491, 493)

Pat found it hard to neatly define how or why he received his calling, but his sense of vocation was real and compelling. Many people long for that kind of purpose in their work.

One of the dozens of working people interviewed by Studs Terkel observed, "'I think most of us are looking for a calling, not a job. Most of us . . . have jobs that are too small for our spirit. Jobs are not big enough for people'" (*Working,* page xxiv).

We may debate whether that comment is accurate, but it is probably true that the human heart yearns for more than a paycheck from a job. Although we may work because of financial necessity, what keeps us happy and productive in a job is more complicated than money. Job satisfaction has to do with meaning and meaning may be harder to come by than money. **5**

For Review

- List and briefly explain the six motives for working discussed in this section.

A Christian Vision of Work

The Dignity of Work

In simplest terms, work has **dignity** and value when it meets some aspect of human need, when its purpose is to contribute to the common good,

Student art: "I Plant America's Fields," lino-cut by Cissy Paig, St. Agnes Academy, Memphis, Tennessee

5
Agree or disagree with each of the following statements and explain why in writing:
- **It is human nature for people to do as little work as they can get away with.**
- **People work primarily for money; recognition and satisfaction are much less important.**

and when a worker is treated with respect. As **Pope John Paul II** said, "The basis for determining the value of human work is not primarily the kind of work done, but the fact that the one who is doing it is a person" (*On Human Work,* number 6).

Work as Participation in God's Creation

The Christian tradition has long been concerned with the meaning and dignity of work. Work was one of the first topics of the Bible. The Creation account given in Genesis describes God's commanding the newly formed humans:

"Be fruitful and multiply, and fill the earth and subdue it; and have dominion over the fish of the sea and over the birds of the air and over every living thing that moves upon the earth. . . . I have given you every plant yielding seed . . . and every tree with seed in its fruit; you shall have them for food. . . ." And it was so. God saw everything that he had made, and indeed, it was very good. (1:28–31)

Later, after sin had entered the human scene, being fruitful and taking on the role of caretakers of the earth became more difficult. Humankind had to work harder to survive. God said, "'By the sweat of your face / you shall eat bread'" (Genesis 3:19). We are still charged with the same task by God, but the writers of Genesis explained that we work hard because of the disharmony in creation caused by sin. Yet creation itself is very good.

If we believe that all creation is God's work, building the earth becomes a form of participating in the process of creation, a **coworking with God.** By working for the good of humankind and nature, of which we are a part, we become involved in the process of creation.

- Swimming instructors participate with God in creation when they teach children to swim. The instructors not only impart a survival skill but also help the children to enjoy water, one of God's wonders. God created the water, and the instructors help kids to appreciate it.

Art: "Creation of the Animals," by Jan Brueghel, a sixteenth-century Flemish painter

- Workers at a factory that produces insulated windows and doors join in the process of creation by helping people to live in warmer homes while conserving heating fuel, a precious resource of the earth.
- Researchers at a company that specializes in telephone and computer communications systems join with God in bringing the people of the earth together, by developing the tools to put diverse peoples, organizations, cultures, and interests in touch. **6**

Jesus the Worker

Jesus was a model for working. As a young man he probably became quite used to hard work. After all, he was raised in the household of a carpenter. If Jesus lived like other boys and young men of his era, he learned his father's trade. He probably practiced it until he began his public ministry.

When Jesus' work became preaching the Good News, healing, and counseling his followers, his work probably seemed even harder to him. In three short years he journeyed by foot throughout his country. Crowds gathered to hear him. Jesus not only gave spiritual nourishment to the people but in several instances also fed their physical hunger. He summarized the motivation for his lifework when he said, "'I must proclaim the good news of the kingdom of God to the other cities also; for I was sent for this purpose'" (Luke 4:43). Jesus, a man of action, felt the urgent demands of his lifework because he was *sent* by God to do that work.

Neither Jesus nor the Apostles lived in luxury. For example, wherever Saint Paul was preaching, he usually sought work as a tentmaker in order to feed himself. He did not want to be a burden on anyone. Paul was convinced that by working, Christians build the Kingdom of God.

The Church's Affirmation of Work

The dignity of work has been a part of the Christian tradition from Saint Paul to Pope John Paul II. In his letter ***On Human Work,*** John Paul II taught that through work, people become more human. He added that work has dignity because through it, we are participating with God in creation. Affirming the value of human work, John Paul II referred to the Vatican II document ***On the Church in the Modern World.*** In that document, the world's bishops proclaimed that it is the responsibility of Christians to build up, not to shun or neglect, the world.

In the Christian worldview, work has the potential to contribute to the building up of the world and to the welfare of humanity. In other words, work can be profoundly meaningful.

6
If you have a job right now, can your work be understood as a part of God's creative process? Explain your answer in a paragraph.

Student art: "The World—It's in Your Hands," watercolor, ink, and pencil by Rose A. Honnert, Oldenberg Academy, Oldenberg, Indiana

Work and Meaning

Almost any kind of work can have meaning and be a powerful expression of our creativity. We give meaning to our work, not the other way around. This brief story makes the point. Three men were breaking up rocks.

"What are you doing?" a passerby asks.

"Making little rocks out of big ones," says the first worker.

"Earning a living," answers the second.

"Building a cathedral," says the third. (Donnelly, *Spiritual Fitness,* page 83)

It is not too hard to imagine which of the three workers felt best about what he was doing and found a sense of dignity in making little rocks out of big ones. The way we approach and view the work we do plays a key role in whether we feel our work has meaning. **7**

Work can have meaning for us in two ways: by the type of work we do and by the way we work.

The Type of Work

Most jobs can be meaningful, fostering the good of people and of the earth, even if the work does not involve direct service to people in need. We need not be doctors, nurses, social workers, or teachers to have meaningful work.

Jobs That Help

Think about work that is not the direct service type but that *does* help. For example, a contractor who builds solid, decent houses fosters the well-being of the people who will live in those houses. A medical lab technician who is careful about doing tests accurately serves the patients who depend on the results. An engineer designing a can opener to work more easily is contributing to the good of its future buyers.

Jobs That Hurt

Unfortunately some jobs are destructive by their very nature—for instance, jobs that do not respect

7
If you have ever had a job, consider how your attitude toward the job affected how you did the work. Write a one-page reflection.

the dignity of all human life. The manufacture of cigarettes can contribute to the deaths of thousands of smokers by heart disease, lung disease, and cancer. Drug companies that send dangerous or untested drugs to poor countries cause potentially grave harm to people there. Manufacturers of chemical, nuclear, and biological weapons put people and the planet in great jeopardy. Many jobs are in a gray area, however—not clearly destructive in themselves but not clearly helpful either, and possibly harmful. **8**

Jobs That Degrade Workers

When a particular kind of work requires that women and men become simply replaceable parts in a large operation, when they are treated as machines and begin acting like machines, work can get stripped of its dignity and meaning. One worker talked about his job in this way:

"You come in each day: you're timed on this job. . . . All right; today's output: 240. And that's your number; and you think of the 240 until you've done it; and you're number-minded; and when you go home the boredom is there with you." (*Work and Play,* page 176)

Even if a person has a positive attitude, this kind of work dulls the spirit. Soon a split widens between work and the rest of life. For eight hours a day the person feels that he or she is not living.

The Way We Work

Three dimensions of how we work affect the meaning of our work: an emphasis on quality, care for people who are customers or clients, and concern for coworkers.

Emphasis on Quality

A concern for **quality** is a commitment to excellence in every aspect of the work. Besides enhancing pride and dignity in the workers, it obviously yields superior products and services. An emphasis on quality simply makes good business sense. Before the 1970s, U.S. businesses led all other nations in the quality of their products. Then many U.S.

8
List two types of jobs that you consider fundamentally destructive and two types that you consider to be in a gray area. For each one, write a brief explanation of why you think as you do.

Student art: "Machine: Men at Work," ink block print by Allison Hawkins, Notre Dame Academy, Toledo, Ohio

businesses became sloppy about the quality of the autos they made, the televisions, the radios, and so on. Soon U.S. manufacturers were laying off hundreds of thousands of workers because consumers were buying higher quality products made abroad. Fortunately, this trend is reversing, as many U.S. businesses have turned their attention back to quality and excellence.

Here is a more immediate example of the meaningfulness of quality work. An auto mechanic who performs a wheel alignment competently and carefully takes pride in the work and senses his or her dignity through the work. But the emphasis on quality also helps the customer. A careless alignment can cause problems for the car owner—tires may wear unevenly, steering may become difficult, and ultimately an accident could result. Doing quality work satisfies the worker and the customer. It is Christlike, and it just makes sense to do the very best we can. **9**

Care for Customers and Clients

Work will be more meaningful if we keep in mind that all work influences, for good or for ill, the people who are our customers or clients. A busy judge, Mary Elizabeth Toomey Dunne, seeks to remember that truth in her daily duties:

My job as an administrative law judge is to determine whether people who have claimed an injury at work have been treated fairly under the law, and—if not—to provide an opportunity to remedy the situation. . . . I am assigned an average of 69 cases a day, which means that I have five minutes for each person to come before me and receive the justice that the system provides. . . .

There are so many people coming through my courtroom that it is easy to simply label them as a number on the calendar. Rather than allowing this to happen, I try to write down birthdays, anniversaries, or other information that can personalize the hearing.

On the back of my nameplate on my desk is taped the prayer of St. Teresa of Ávila:

Let nothing bother you
Let nothing dismay you
Everything passes
Patience gains all
God alone is enough

This prayer reminds me throughout the day that it is only with God's support that I can fulfill my call to be Christ-like in all that I do. (*Of Human Hands,* pages 77, 79)

9

Give an example in writing of how a worker's attention to quality made an impression on you. Describe details of that worker's concern for quality.

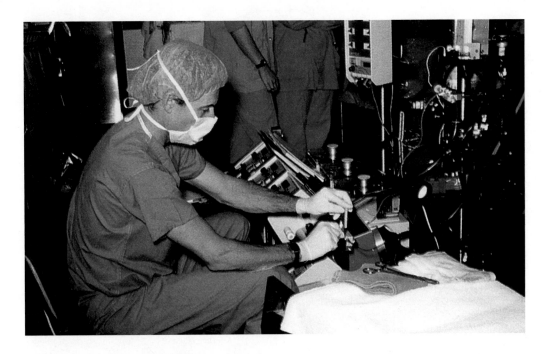

Concern for Coworkers

The principle of treating our neighbors as we ourselves wish to be treated applies in the workplace. We cannot be intimate friends with everyone at work, but we can be courteous and helpful. We can be cooperative—pitching in and taking responsibility, not blaming other workers for problems that belong to everyone, and not trying to make ourselves look good at the expense of others.

We can also show concern for other workers by doing our tasks right, making sure that we do whatever we can so that other workers can carry on with ease where we have left off. If an airline representative writes up a plane ticket correctly, the customer is well served; but in addition, other representatives or flight attendants will not have to handle an irate passenger whose flight arrangements have been mishandled. **10**

We will find no scarcity of ways to put meaning into our work. The challenge is to discover the work that truly is our own, that expresses who we are as unique individuals and who we want to become.

For Review

- According to John Paul II, what is the basis for determining the value of a particular work?
- How does work involve us with God in the process of creation?
- Give two examples each of "jobs that help" and "jobs that hurt."
- What are three dimensions of how we work that affect the meaning of our work?

10
For a job you are familiar with, write a list of guidelines for workers on how they should treat one another.

Toward a Life's Work

Making an informed decision about what work to choose can save us the tremendous pain of being in the wrong job. Many times people must take a job simply to make a living, and people rarely find a job in their youth that they stick with until retirement. In fact, most workers change not only jobs but also careers several times. So high school students should prepare themselves to find work and a career that fits them at their present stage in life, with the understanding that they will probably change jobs and even careers several times throughout their lifetime. **11**

Choosing a Career

The following suggestions about career selection can be helpful when considering future work:

Assessing Yourself

The best way to begin thinking about possible careers is to assess your interests, personality, and skills to see how these aspects of yourself might relate to future work.

Interests. Each day you are involved in a wide variety of activities. Over the last seventeen or eighteen years you have done some things that you liked and other things that you found disagreeable. Try to describe what you like to do. Consider jobs you have had, extracurricular activities, hobbies, courses in school, and so on. **12**

Personality. One way to think about your personality is to consider whether you prefer working

with things, people, or data. If you like to work with things, maybe you should consider truck driving, engineering, diesel mechanics, or computer programming. If you prefer working with people, you might gravitate toward teaching, sales, ministry, or public relations. If you like data, you might consider accounting, proofreading, or statistical analysis. All the occupations listed here are worthwhile, but their appeal to you depends on your personality. You may have a personality that gravitates toward two of the three. In that case, look for work that combines those two areas. For instance, suppose you are inclined to work with both people and data. A career in information science, which

---

11
What do you think each of the important people in your life (family, friends, significant teachers) expects or hopes for you in terms of a career? Write down how you react to each of those expectations.

12
List ten things you like to do that *might* indicate work that would be meaningful for you—reach back even to earlier years of your life.

Student art: "Me (In Thought)," charcoal by Shawn M. Beirne, Holy Cross High School, Louisville, Kentucky

involves helping people find the data they need in libraries, computer networks, and other research resources, might be just the field for you. **13**

Skills. You must consider the skills that you have or ones that you can develop. After all, some people like playing basketball, are absorbed by it, and dream of making a career of it, but they may lack the skill to play professionally. You need to be realistic about what you can do or have the capacity to learn if you are going to successfully choose a life's work.

Looking Beyond Stereotypes

You must choose a career that you want rather than one that society considers appropriate for you.

- Both women and men can become respected judges.
- Nursing is not strictly women's work.
- College teaching is no longer the sole preserve of men.
- Computers do not know the sex of the graphic designer using them.
- Children respond marvelously to male as well as female day-care workers.
- Today women are opening small businesses by the thousands.

The lesson here is to be open to all possibilities when considering your options for a career. Be as free as you desire to be in your search.

Considering Work Environments

Certain work environments suit each of us best. Some of us work best alone; others hate to be alone. Working outdoors has an appeal for some; for others, having an artificial houseplant in an air-conditioned office is as close as they want to come to nature. Some people enjoy an on-the-road job; others see travel requirements as very disrupting to life. The work environment is an important consideration.

Looking at Clusters of Work

Some examples of clusters of work are agriculture, health care, social services, the arts, home economics, marketing, and public relations. Each of these clusters includes many occupations. It is best to look at whole clusters before becoming focused on a specialty.

For instance, the cluster of health care includes such occupations as physical therapist, dietician,

13
Write your reflections on the following questions:
- Do you prefer to work with data, people, or things?
- How does your preference show itself?

A KWIK HISTORY OF WORK

13,000 BCE

2,500 BCE

nurse, rehabilitation counselor, dental hygienist, doctor, radiologist, medical lab technician, speech therapist, occupational therapist, and respiratory therapist. Each of these occupations also has its own specialties.

Contacting People in Your Fields of Interest

Once you have narrowed your focus to a few occupations, interview people working in those fields and, if possible, spend some time observing them at work. Too frequently students are convinced that they want to pursue a certain line of work because the pay seems good or because the field has many openings. Once they have interviewed and observed people in those careers, they either will be more convinced that the field is for them or they will realize that it's not. Either way, the students will be able to make a realistic assessment about the career. **14**

Trying Out Careers

You can get firsthand experience in a given field. Find work now in jobs related to your interests.

Whether you are considering a liberal arts area, engineering, electronics, or cosmetology, if you can find summer, holiday, or part-time employment in that field, you will learn many valuable lessons.

Many colleges offer internships and co-op programs for students. For example, a marketing student may gain useful skills by taking a semester away from campus to work as an intern in a marketing firm. The student receives credit toward the marketing major as well as invaluable work experience.

Volunteering

Many volunteer opportunities offer people a way of serving others while exploring possible careers. Chances to volunteer exist for high school and college students, as well as for college graduates. Lots of people with satisfying jobs have discovered their life's work by volunteering. For example: A physics major, having joined the Peace Corps and taught in a village school in Africa, returned to the United States and became a teacher. A Lasallian volunteer who worked in a settlement house in a poor urban

14
Interview someone who does the type of work that you would like to do. Make up your own questions in addition to these:
- How did you get into this line of work?
- What do you like most about your job ? least?
- What purposes, goals, and values does this work serve?
- Would you encourage someone to go into this work? Why?

neighborhood went to Columbia University to prepare himself to manage nonprofit relief organizations. A high school senior who worked every Saturday with children with disabilities decided to study physical therapy. **15**

Developing Skills for Work

You need to develop two different kinds of skills to be an effective, contributing, and satisfied worker: career-content skills and transferable life skills.

Career-Content Skills

As a high school senior, naturally you may be thinking in specific terms about the skills you will need to make a living and to use your potential in satisfying, contributing ways. You are probably focusing on **career-content skills,** that is, those skills that belong to a specific job: auto repair, computer programming, dentistry, nursing, sales, personnel management, electrical engineering, forestry management, and so on. Such skills are learned in technical or vocational schools, colleges and universities, and on-the-job training.

Transferable Life Skills

Skills we carry with us from one job to another or from one situation to another are **transferable life skills**—such things as organizing time, carefully observing, cooperating in a group, manipulating objects with dexterity, analyzing, persuading, listening, making decisions, and creating. Transferable skills help us to manage our life productively. We may develop them in the process of formal schooling or in the context of other experiences.

Crucial in a changing world. In a world that witnesses a technological revolution at least every decade, the crucial nature of transferable life skills becomes apparent: *People who have acquired many transferable skills are in the best position to adapt to a changing world.* They bring a wealth of applicable skills with them wherever they go; they can flex with the changing opportunities for employment.

The significance and broad applicability of transferable life skills does not discount the importance of career-content skills. Pursuing a particular field of interest and developing a certain expertise in that field are highly advisable. However, consider

15
Investigate volunteer opportunities in your community. Write down how any one of these opportunities might help you explore a career.

this: Every career-content skill can be broken down into its component parts, which are transferable life skills. So by developing transferable skills (in the context of school, volunteer activities, a hobby, or a job), you are actually creating the building blocks of career-content skills. **16**

Even from a fast-food job. Take a part-time job as an example. A high school student who has an after-school job in a fast-food restaurant is developing these skills:

- memory (recalling orders and how much lettuce to put on a double burger)
- listening (paying attention to instructions and requests)
- time management and organization (figuring out how to accomplish all the tasks that need to be done during a rush period)
- customer relations (serving customers pleasantly even when customers are grumpy or the worker is not feeling pleasant)
- teamwork (pitching in to get the work done rather than sticking only to individually assigned tasks)
- manual dexterity (quickly and efficiently assembling twenty-five burgers on demand)

That student's transferable skills of memory, listening, time management and organization, customer relations, teamwork, and manual dexterity are likewise the building blocks for a host of extremely diverse career-content areas.

We need to look at the experiences ahead of us as chances to develop transferable life skills—not only for their usefulness in a future career but also for their value in enabling us to become competent, well-rounded, fully alive persons.

For Review

- List six suggestions that can help a person to select a career.
- What is the difference between career-content skills and transferable life skills? Which are most crucial in a changing world?

16
Which transferable life skills do you already have to some degree? List them, and next to each, write situations where you might need that skill:
organizing
reading critically
writing clearly
speaking articulately
making decisions
creating
listening
remembering
eye-hand coordinating
evaluating
empathizing
praising
playing
manipulating physical objects
cooperating
analyzing
persuading
leading
negotiating

More Than a Living

We need to work not only to support ourselves and our families but also to have purpose, to realize our potential, to accomplish things, and to contribute something of value with our life. Unfortunately the pressure on young people today to find jobs that earn a living is enormous. At a time when good jobs for recent graduates are scarce, these same job seekers are often burdened with huge financial obligations. Work can become simply a way to make a living rather than a way to devote ourselves to something we love and something worth doing well. It is important to not let the pressure to earn money overwhelm us, so that we get to experience the joy of work. **17**

Let's ask the Holy Spirit for guidance in leading us to good work:

Spirit of God, guide us as we try to figure out
   what to do with our life.
We are pressed with anxieties:
   Will we be able to find a job?
   Will the job pay enough?
Help us to see the big picture.
Help us to long not just for a job but for *good*
   work—the work that *we* most need to do,
   and the work that the *world* most needs us to do.
Amen.

17
Do some dreaming. Project yourself forward ten years. What sort of work would you like to be doing? How about in twenty years? What would be your optimal lifetime achievement as a worker? Write your reflections.

4

Money
and Possessions:

Happiness Is Not for Sale

Putting Money in Its Place

In North America, no aspect of life seems to cause as much stir as money and possessions. Think of TV shows that have gained popularity by depending on the public's fascination with wealth: game shows, programs about the lifestyles of rich celebrities, and most soap operas. Giant indoor shopping malls have become entertainment centers, where the main event is spending money. Scandals involving huge sums of money wrack government and business. Marriages end because of differences over money and possessions.

Deciding what role money and possessions will play in our life has a huge impact on the lifestyle we create for ourselves. Such decisions tell very powerfully who we are and what we value.

Consider this discussion among a group of high school seniors who have a variety of attitudes toward money and the things it can buy:

"Holly, lend me a pen for a minute?"

"Okay, if I can find one in this mess." Holly began sorting through her purse, looking for a pen. She emptied some of the junk out on the table to make the hunt easier.

Brad stared at all the odds and ends that emerged from Holly's purse and suddenly snatched up one of them. "Good grief, you actually buy lottery tickets. That's dumb."

Grabbing the ticket out of his hand, Holly stuffed it back in her purse. "You'll think it's dumb when I win the four-million-dollar jackpot next week in the Powerball drawing!"

Denny's eyes glazed over. "What I could do with four mill! I'd start with a Grand Am. I could get all the clothes I need. Then I could travel anywhere I want, just live off the jackpot the rest of my life."

Brad jumped on Denny's fantasy: "You've got enough now to wear different clothes every day. I'd put the money in stocks and bonds. Let it grow. Then follow the investments."

Holly smirked. "How boring, but typical of you, Brad. You'd probably still bum money from us. Besides, I quote, 'Buying lottery tickets. That's dumb.'"

"Okay, then what would *you* do with it?"

"I've got seven younger brothers and sisters. I'd set up a scholarship fund for them. Then I'd buy us a new house so everyone could have their own room. I'd get some new clothes, too, and go to the U instead of Metro State. How about you, Tawanda?"

"Did you see that show about what happened to people who won the lottery big? Everybody started sucking up to them. They all suddenly had zillions of friends with their hands out. All these creeps started coming around with these deals for them. I don't mess with that stuff. I like my life just fine. Somebody once told me, 'Tawanda, if you have money, you don't need friends. Think about it.' It got me thinking that if you have money, sometimes you don't know who your real friends are. So just leave me out of that nonsense. One person may win four million dollars, but thousands of others just waste their money on those stupid tickets, money they should be using for groceries and bills. Lotteries are a big rip-off."

"Well, *somebody's* going to win it, and I hope it's me," countered Holly, a bit embarrassed.

"Tawanda, you always put stuff down!" Denny turned to Holly: "When's the last day to buy tickets? Maybe I'll get a new Lexus coupe instead." **1**

Some people, like Denny, dream about having lots of money so they can buy anything they want, do whatever they want, go wherever they want. Others, like Brad, equate money with security; they hold on to it tightly, fret about it, follow it, manage it. Still others, like Holly, see money as the way to solve problems and make everyone happy. Finally, people like Tawanda put money in its proper place—behind other values such as friendship and responsibility.

We live in a money economy; money and purchasing are an inevitable part of our life. But we do not have to become possessed by money or the things it can buy. We can put money and possessions in their proper place.

Enough Versus Excess

We need an accurate **sense of perspective**—a healthy, objective distance—about money and possessions. We have to sort out what is enough from

1
State your position on this proposition: *Playing the lottery is dumb.*

Student art: Untitled, paint, ink, and watercolor by Gabriella Perez-Martinez, Alverno High School, Sierra Madre, California

what is excessive. Without such a perspective, we could begin to expect more of material things than they can possibly deliver. We might expect them to satisfy our deepest yearnings—in short, to make us happy—when in fact they can never do that.

In order to survive and lead dignified lives, human beings need money and the things money can buy. Food, shelter, clothing, and medical care are obvious **survival needs.** But to live beyond the level of sheer survival, money is also needed for **"thrival needs"**—education, transportation, entertainment, provision for the future (contributions to social security, retirement plans), and so on. These are all necessary for a decent life, and they all require money.

Not recognizing the realistic need for money is foolish. Most of us can see the wisdom in the familiar saying, "You can't live on love." Practicality and a sense of responsibility for our life require that somewhere along the way to adulthood, we begin to provide for our own needs, to support ourselves.

So money and possessions in themselves are not bad; they are necessary to carry on our life. However, to live happily and freely, and to avoid becoming a slave to money and material things, we need a sense of balance and proportion about these goods. We depend on money to live a dignified life, but what constitutes such a life can be interpreted in varying ways. Even the basic survival needs of food, shelter, clothing, and medical care can be defined in radically different ways. To a Peruvian peasant or an Indonesian factory worker, for instance, North America's suburban version of an adequate shelter would be considered a mansion. And in the chapter opening story, adequate clothing might mean very different things to Denny and to Tawanda. **2**

2
Think about someone you know who seems to have a healthy perspective on money and possessions. Write about how that person shows this perspective.

Extra Goodies

Of course, **discretionary income**—income over and above what will cover necessities—can add benefits to one's life. A person with extra money has options and choices that others may not have—to buy a better car, to travel more widely, to go to an expensive private college, to invest money and make more money. That person can also purchase things that give a feeling of well-being and pleasure—beautiful and fashionable clothes, a terrific CD system, a boat, or fancy ski equipment. In addition, money can furnish a person with power and influence, the ability to get things done and move the system around: "Money talks."

Choices, **pleasure**, and **power** are the usual motivators for having more than enough money to take care of necessities. Like money, these "extra goodies" are not bad in themselves, but they need to be treated with a healthy distance. Immersion in purchased things and experiences can dull us to the many creative ways that we can enjoy life and accomplish things without spending a lot of money. We need to be cautious about constantly turning to purchases to create happiness in our life, for the kind of happiness that money can buy fades very quickly. These purchased goods offer the illusion of "buying the good life," but they cannot deliver the lasting happiness they seem to promise. **3**

For Review

- What is meant by an accurate sense of perspective about money and possessions?
- What needs are included in the basic requirements for living a decent, dignified life?
- What usually motivates people to have more money than is needed for the basics? Why should we be cautious about these motivators?

3
Recall a time when money or possessions made you happy. Then recall a time when all the money and possessions in the world could not guarantee happiness for you or someone else. Summarize your reflections in writing.

The Pitfalls of Possessing

Several illusions about having money and possessions deserve careful scrutiny:
- confusing wants with needs
- confusing social image with self-worth
- confusing spending with freedom

Confusing Wants with Needs

A high school senior, Jimmy Carrasquillo, told his story in a 1992 issue of *Newsweek,* about how he mistook his wants for his **needs** and assumed that he had to work long hours at an after-school job in order to meet his "needs."

Because Jimmy was always asking his mother for money, she suggested that he get a job. So, despite taking a challenging schedule of courses, playing several sports, and participating in other extracurricular activities, Jimmy began working twenty-five hours a week at Montgomery Ward.

I was burning out, falling asleep at school, not able to concentrate. . . .

My third-period history teacher was really concerned. She was cool. . . . I'd fall asleep in her class. She'd scream, "Wake up!" and slam her hand on my desk. I'd open my eyes for about two minutes, pay attention and go back to sleep. . . . She said, "Why? Why all this?"

I told her it was for the things I need, when actually it was for the things that I wanted. Needing and wanting are different. Needing something is like your only shoes have holes in them. But when a new pair of sneakers came out and I liked them, I'd get them. My parents didn't feel it was right. . . . Within two years I had bought 30 pairs. . . .

My priorities were screwed up. . . . One week in the winter I had to work extra days, so I missed a basketball game and two practices. . . .

. . . If I hadn't been so greedy, I could have been at practice. But I kept working. . . .

Slowly, I've come to deal with managing money a lot better. . . . This year I decided not to work at all during football season. I have a lot more time to spend with other players. . . . I'm more confident and more involved in the classes. . . . I look at all the sneakers in school and think, "I could have those," but I don't need them. Last year I thought that being mature meant doing everything. But I'm learning that part of growing up is limiting yourself, knowing how to decide what's important, and what isn't.

Fortunately, Jimmy learned the difference between his needs and his wants. Until he got to that point, however, he was overtaken by **greed**, an insatiable desire to acquire more and more. **4**

Greed: It Cannot Be Satisfied

Greedy people do not usually think of themselves as greedy. Rather, they imagine that the things they want really are needs. They actually feel needy and deprived until they get what they want. They believe that if they can just acquire the desired objects, they will be satisfied. But it is the nature of greed to never be satisfied. Some critics of North American society claim that greed drives much of our economy, because, to a large extent, the economy's growth relies on people's restlessness and dissatisfaction with what they have.

Alan Durning, of the Worldwatch Institute, offers this commentary on the relationship between material consumption and happiness:

Since 1950, American consumption has soared. Per capita [per person], energy use climbed 60 percent, car travel more than doubled, plastics use multiplied 20-fold, and air travel jumped 25-fold. We are wealthy beyond the wildest dreams of our ancestors.

But all this abundance—while taking a terrible toll on the environment—has not made people terribly happy. In the United States, repeated opinion polls of people's sense of well-being conducted by the University of Chicago's National Opinion Research Center show that Americans are no more satisfied with their lot now than they were in 1957. Despite phenomenal growth in consumption, the list of wants has grown faster still.

A Cry for "Soul Food"

Greed, the relentless hunger for more (money, possessions, food, power, pleasure, and so on), is really a symptom of a much deeper hunger that is only masked by acquiring more and more possessions. Greed signals that the person's **"soul needs"** are not being satisfied; the greedy person longs for **"soul food"**—nourishment for a starving spirit. Not recognizing that deeper need within himself or herself, yet feeling constantly needy, the person turns to material ways to fill the void. Because material possessions can never fill a void in the soul, the sense of emptiness only grows as the individual desperately tries to fill the gaping hole by acquiring more. Thus greed grows, perpetuating itself.

4
List five things that you feel you need and would buy if you had the money. Then write all the reasons you can think of for why you need each item.

It is easy to be fooled into thinking that the things we crave are actually things we need. Here are some questions we can use to evaluate our awareness in this area:

- Do I equate money or possessions with happiness?
- Do I harbor the belief that if I only had a certain amount of money or certain things, I would be happy?
- Do I turn to buying things when I feel restless or unsatisfied? **5**

Confusing Social Image with Self-worth

Another illusion that needs examination is the confusion of one's **social image** with one's **self-worth**. Buying things that will make one look good to others can become a substitute for having a genuine sense of self-worth. Purchases driven by status consciousness that have become run-of-the-mill for some middle-class teenagers include one-hundred-dollar Gucci watches, six-hundred-dollar car stereos, eight-day vacations to Cancun, Mexico, and even personal beepers (not for making drug deals but for communicating with friends!). A 1992 *Newsweek* article put it this way:

Blame it on peer pressure: when you go out with friends, "you don't want to say, 'I can't do that, I don't have the money,'" explains Kirsten . . . a senior at Manchester West High.

In recent years, too, high school proms have become occasions for extravagant consumption, with young people spending enormous sums of money to keep up with the social expectations.

As much as we like to deny it, we often judge our self-worth and other people tend to judge our worth by what status items we have. Even though we want to be seen as valuable in ourselves, most of us have not yet learned to see beyond appearances—even our own appearances.

Equating our social image, based on status criteria, with our self-worth can eat away at our integrity. We enter a vicious cycle: Buying makes me feel important. When I plunk down money for a high-status purchase, my ego feels a boost. If spending fifty dollars feels good, spending one hundred dollars will make me feel even better. If having a three-year-old car feels good, having a brand new

5
Do you feel pressure to have more money? If you do, is the pressure to have money for things you *want* or for things you *need?* If you don't feel such pressure, why do think you don't? Write about your reflections.

car will make me feel even better. The trouble here is obvious: If we equate self-worth with socially approved consumer items, we will always feel less than adequate. There will always be something bigger, brighter, and newer to buy. Our perception of our own value will depend on exterior things, not on the belief that we are essentially good and worthwhile, created in God's image and loved by God as we are. **6**

Here are some helpful questions to gauge how much we equate self-worth with social image:

- Have I ever told myself, even subconsciously, things like, "I'd really be attractive or popular or a hit if I had . . ."?
- Do I judge other people's value on what they have or how much they spend?
- Do I get a rush when I buy an item that I know will make me the envy of my friends?

Confusing Spending with Freedom

Our society, which puts **freedom of choice** at such a premium, fosters the illusion that spending or purchasing is a way of expressing our freedom. Certainly, purchasing things can be a form of free choice. However, that is the most limited understanding of freedom: freedom as the ability to select from a number of options.

If we consider the deeper meaning of freedom—as the ability to ponder, reflect, question, decide, and act responsibly—we might come to the conclusion that rather than enhancing freedom, a focus on spending erodes it.

Compulsive Spending

Erosion of freedom is particularly true for people whose spending is out of control. These people are **compulsive spenders**, buyers, or shoppers, and they represent the extreme end of materialism, an addiction to spending. Their "rush" is found in the spending itself, rather than in the enjoyment of the item purchased. Here is testimony from Mike Mallowe, a self-confessed "shopaholic," in an article from *U.S. Catholic:*

Some people drink.
  I shop.
  Too often, I buy.
  Do I have a problem? You betcha. . . .
  No one should ever trust me with money. I'm still a long way from taking the cure. I'll find a place to spend it faster than most people can count it. Drop me down in any city, any country, and I will find a bargain—something that I just can't pass up; something that I refuse to live without; something that the little voice inside me tells me will make it all feel better once I tell the clerk to wrap it.

6
What consumer items are most socially approved or expected among your peers? Write an inner dialog between you and one of these items, beginning, "If I didn't have you, I would . . ." or, "Because I don't have you, I . . ."

Compulsive spenders cannot resist the impulse to buy. Alluring items seem to command, "Buy me, buy me!" This compulsion is the opposite of freedom, yet shopaholics may be able to convince themselves that when they buy something, they are never freer. **7**

Here are some self-evaluative questions recommended in a 1991 *USA Today* publication, by a psychiatrist who treats people addicted to spending:

- Do you shop to relieve feelings of disappointment, boredom, loneliness, sadness, or low self-esteem?
- Does your shopping cause conflict in the family or inner guilt?
- Do you frequently buy unneeded items impulsively, and are you unable to leave a store to think about a purchase?
- Do you engage in "revenge spending," buying expensive items in defiance of someone? **8**

The Credit Card Trap

One of the greatest encouragements to spending is **buying on credit.** Plastic "instant money" credit cards give the illusion of increasing the buyer's freedom because she or he can purchase items without actually having the money to buy them. Consumer spending increases by nearly one quarter when credit cards are used instead of cash. Many people cannot resist the impulse to purchase something on the spot, especially when they can delay paying for it. Add to this the phenomena of TV shopping channels, extended TV "infomercials," and all the usual techniques of advertising, and we have the ingredients for a frenzy of spending in this society. As a result, an enormous number of people carry huge debts on which they are paying terribly high interest.

According to many psychologists, one mark of a mature, free person is the ability to live with **delayed gratification**—to wait for pleasure if necessary. Mature individuals are not trapped by the childish attitude, "I want what I want when I want it." Yet the fact that consumer debt is skyrocketing in our society because of credit purchases seems to indicate that **immediate gratification**, not delayed gratification, is typical of our culture. It is not hard to figure out which type of gratification represents the exercise of true freedom. **9**

Gambling

In recent decades, **legalized gambling** in the form of lotteries, casinos, and race track betting has mushroomed in the United States. Of course these forms of gambling bring in lots of revenue to governments that sponsor or regulate them, as well as huge profits to casino owners. Not surprisingly, along with the increased revenue comes a huge jump in gambling addictions. Now governments are discussing the need to dedicate considerable portions of their gambling revenues to set up treatment programs for these latest victims of addiction.

In the back of every problem gambler's mind is a voice that says that the big win is just one deal away and that the money will take care of everything. A 1993 *Newsweek* story of Karen H., an addicted gambler, illustrates this point:

As a child in California, she boasted she was the best card shuffler in second grade. As an adolescent, she flipped baseball cards for pennies with the guys. By high school she was shooting dice. As a newlywed, she organized friendly poker games. On and on the frenzy went until cards, football pools and backgammon nudged aside even her husband and kids. "I can remember one day when my son, who was 11 or 12

7
In writing, tell the story of one of your own impulse purchases, a time when you could not resist the "buy me, buy me!" message.

8
Take the shopaholic quiz; jot down your answers to those questions and this one: *Could I ever be a shopaholic?*

9
Bring an advertisement to class pasted on a sheet of paper. On the same sheet, explain how the advertisement seeks to create a false sense of need in the reader.

at the time, had a dentist's appointment and I told him to wait on the corner for me after school," says Karen, [now] the international executive secretary of Gamblers Anonymous. "I was off playing cards, and he was standing there three hours later."

Problem gamblers become addicted to the rush of gambling itself. Living on the edge propels them. What starts with the desire to make money and have some fun may lead eventually to catastrophic debt, irresponsibility to loved ones, and even criminal behavior. Gambling addicts lose control over their own life.

Estimates are that of the eight million compulsive gamblers in the United States, about one million are teenagers. Most teens start with sports betting, cards, and lotteries. Soon they are trapped like Greg, described in a 1991 issue of *Time:*

He began placing weekly $200 bets with bookies during his sophomore year in college. "Pretty soon it got to the point that I owed $5,000," he says. "The bookies threatened me. One said he would cut off my mother's legs if I didn't pay." Still Greg continued to gamble. Now 23, he was recently fired from his job after his employer caught him embezzling. **10**

Here are some questions to check our attitudes toward gambling:

- Am I ever tempted to gamble so I can "get rich quick"?
- If I gamble, do I feel a rush while gambling, and do I want to repeat that feeling?
- Has gambling ever damaged my relationships with friends or family?

The pitfalls surrounding money and possessions can trap us so effectively that we fool ourselves into

thinking that they make us free. In a society that promotes these illusions, the teachings of Christianity offer a stark countercultural perspective.

For Review

- To what does Jimmy Carrasquillo attribute his confusion of his wants with his needs?
- What is greed? How does it perpetuate itself?
- Describe the vicious cycle created by equating our social image with our self-worth.
- How are compulsive spenders not free?
- How does buying on credit contribute to the loss of true freedom?
- Describe the typical thinking and motivation of problem gamblers.

10
Interview someone you know who gambles. Ask the person about his or her reasons for gambling, feelings while gambling, and effects of gambling on his or her life and relationships. Prepare a short report on the interview.

Student art: Untitled, India ink, dip pen, and color pencil by Fernando Ramirez, Marist High School, Chicago, Illinois

The Christian Approach: Unmasking the Illusions

From the previous discussion of the pitfalls of possessions, it is no wonder that the Christian Testament offers so many warnings about the dangers of pursuing riches. The Christian vision aims to unmask the illusions about wealth and possessions that easily trap us. It invites us to live freely, with our eyes wide open.

Be Wary of Riches

Saint Paul, writing to his friend Timothy, talked about the personal hazards of living a life devoted to the accumulation of wealth. He might have been addressing this advice today to any of the people described earlier in this chapter:

Of course, there is great gain in godliness combined with contentment; for we brought nothing into the world, so that we can take nothing out of it; but if we have food and clothing, we will be content with these. But those who want to be rich fall into temptation and are trapped by many senseless and harmful desires that plunge people into ruin and destruction. For the love of money is a root of all kinds of evil, and in their eagerness to be rich some have wandered away from the faith and pierced themselves with many pains. (1 Timothy 6:6–10)

Saint James used colorful and tough language to warn those who grew rich at the expense of their workers that their rewards would not last forever:

Come now, you rich people, weep and wail for the miseries that are coming to you. Your riches have rotted, and your clothes are moth-eaten. Your gold and silver have rusted, and their rust will be evidence against you, and it will eat your flesh like fire. You have laid up treasure for the last days. Listen! The wages of the laborers who mowed your fields, which you kept back by fraud, cry out, and the cries of the harvesters have reached the ears of the Lord of hosts. (James 5:1–4)

The Christian Testament conveys a deep distrust of a preoccupation with money and possessions. Although riches in themselves are not evil, they can easily get in the way of what is important and valuable in life. Wealth can fool us into thinking that we have control of life and give us the illusion of ultimate security and freedom, when, in reality, true security and freedom have their source in God. In addition, riches often are gained at the expense of poor people. **11**

Freedom from Slavery

The Christian message is that we should be free of slavery to material things. Jesus understood the trap of money: "'No one can serve two masters; for a slave will either hate the one and love the other, or be devoted to the one and despise the other. You cannot serve God and wealth'" (Matthew 6:24).

The U.S. Catholic bishops, drawing their inspiration from Jesus, recognize how enslaving the pursuit of wealth can be. In their pastoral letter *Economic Justice for All: Catholic Social Teaching and the U.S. Economy,* they call Christians to a different kind of freedom than the freedom to buy: "Americans are challenged today as never before to develop the inner freedom to resist the temptation constantly to seek more" (number 75).

11
List five factual instances in which the love of money was the root of evil. Then list five other instances in which money itself (as opposed to the *love* of money) was used to contribute to the common good.

A KWIK HISTORY OF FAVORITE POSSESSIONS

The Christian Scriptures and the Tradition of the church ask us to be wise enough to resist the slavery that masquerades as freedom.

A New Attitude Toward Ownership

In the biblical vision, everything on earth belongs first and foremost to its Creator. The earth and all that it contains are God's, and in the words of the early church father **Saint Cyprian**, "Whatever belongs to God belongs to all." In his letter *On Human Work*, Pope John Paul II echoed Saint Cyprian when he wrote, "The right to private property is subordinated to the right to common use, to the fact that goods are meant for everyone" (number 14). This notion of ownership—that the goods of the earth really belong to all of us—has profound implications:

- The **right to private property** is not an absolute right; what we own is lent to us by God so that we may tend it for the good of all. We are not free to use our possessions in ways that hurt other people or the earth. **12**
- The accumulation of wealth and resources by a minority of the world's population betrays the gift of creation.

Given this biblical vision that the goods of the earth are for everyone's use, the Christian attitude toward ownership of money and possessions is characterized by sharing, simplicity, and equality.

Sharing

The early Christian communities practiced a life of **sharing** quite literally. The Acts of the Apostles records, "All who believed were together and had all things in common; they would sell their possessions and goods and distribute the proceeds to all, as any had need" (2:44–45). As a consequence of this policy, Acts later states, "There was not a needy person among them" (4:34).

A Fair Balance

Jesus taught that sharing is an obligation for his followers, so Christians might ask, How much giving is proper? Saint Paul gave Christians a guideline to follow in a message to the community of Corinth—a rich, powerful city where the church prospered. He was writing to the Corinthians to ask for donations to the community in Jerusalem, which was literally on the verge of starvation due to a famine. After complimenting the Corinthians for their previous acts of generosity, Paul wrote:

I do not mean that there should be relief for others and pressure on you, but it is a question of a fair bal-

12
Do you agree that we have no absolute right to private property? Compose a short argument for or against the statement.

ance between your present abundance and their need, so that their abundance may be for your need, in order that there may be a fair balance. As it is written,

"The one who had much did not have too much, and the one who had little did not have too little." (2 Corinthians 8:13–15)

Fair balance—these two words were the key to Paul's advice.

Later in the same letter, Paul added another piece of advice for the Corinthians:

Each of you must give as you have made up your mind, not reluctantly or under compulsion, for God loves a cheerful giver. (9:7)

Just as love cannot be forced out of someone, neither can true sharing of resources be forced; it is, after all, an aspect of loving. If we give, we should do so freely and cheerfully. **13**

Neighbors in Need

In just about any direction that we look, people are in need. The U.S. Catholic bishops describe some of these neighbors in their pastoral letter on the economy:

Homeless people roam city streets in tattered clothing and sleep in doorways or on subway grates at night.

Many of these are former mental patients released from state hospitals. Thousands stand in line at soup kitchens because they have no other way of feeding themselves. Millions of children are so poorly nourished that their physical and mental development are seriously harmed. (*Economic Justice for All,* number 172)

Most of us could give examples from our own communities of people in need of economic help.

Jesus called his followers to share with their neighbors so that everyone would have enough to live, not simply to survive but to live in dignity.

Simplicity

Another characteristic of the Christian attitude toward ownership is **simplicity.** A simple life does not imply poverty or starvation; it does not mean that we go about in rags. Simplicity means that we live close enough to the limits of our resources that we can rely on God's love for us.

Neither Too Much nor Too Little

One of the best descriptions of simplicity comes from the Book of Proverbs:

Give me neither poverty nor riches;
feed me with the food that I need,

13
Recall a time when you shared something you owned with someone else. Why did you share? How did it feel? Record your reflections on the benefits of cheerful giving.

or I shall be full, and deny you,
  and say, "Who is the LORD?"
or I shall be poor, and steal,
  and profane the name of my God.

(30:8–9)

Too many rich people tend to act as if God were not in charge of the universe, puffing themselves up with the feeling of security that comes with money. On the other hand, having too little can drive people to desperate acts. Having just enough money is satisfying and does not push people to any extreme.

Live Simply, Live Free

Simple living is having enough but not too much, being generous and warmhearted, and enjoying the goodness of people instead of fretting about acquiring more possessions. But simple living is not simple to do. Considerable thought is required to sort out what is necessary, what is luxury, and what is just plain silly. Additionally, simplicity demands that we have enough strength of personality to act generously and deliberately instead of being dragged along by our every whim or by every advertisement.

If you want to experiment to see if you are free from your possessions, try this: Do an inventory of the objects in your room. Pick one of your possessions—something you do not need, but a favorite thing, not an item ready to fall apart. Put the possession away under lock and key. Do not get rid of it, just keep it away from yourself.

Then spend one week, a couple of weeks, or however long it takes to learn to live without this possession. Remind yourself frequently that you are the same good person without this unnecessary thing. If you run into a patch of anxiety, ask yourself: Do I want to be free, or do I want to be enslaved by owning lots of stuff?

If the freedom is worth it, detach yourself from another unnecessary possession. Provided that you don't rush out and buy other stuff, you can set yourself free in this way, one possession at a time.

In the midst of this liberation you might ponder how you could use the time, space, energy, or money that you have saved by not having this possession. For what good purpose, for yourself or others, could it be used? **14**

Equality

Another characteristic of the Christian attitude toward ownership is the notion of the fundamental

Student art: **Untitled, color pen drawing by Audrey Marcello, Our Lady of Mercy High School, Rochester, New York**

14
If you decided to simplify your life how would you do it? Try to outline a simplicity of life plan:
- **What would you give away?**
- **What would you keep?**
- **What ways could you have fun without spending money?**

equality of all persons in God's sight. Certainly no discrimination based on class distinctions should exist among Christians; wealthy persons should not be treated any better than poor persons. In Saint James's letter to the Christian community, he wrote:

Do you with your acts of favoritism really believe in our glorious Lord Jesus Christ? For if a person with gold rings and in fine clothes comes into your assembly, and if a poor person in dirty clothes also comes in, and if you take notice of the one wearing the fine clothes and say, "Have a seat here, please," while to the one who is poor you say, "Stand there," or, "Sit at my feet," have you not made distinctions among yourselves, and become judges with evil thoughts? . . .

You do well if you really fulfill the royal law according to the scripture, "You shall love your neighbor as yourself." But if you show partiality, you commit sin and are convicted by the law as transgressors. (James 2:1–9) **15**

Once again, the central principle for Christians—loving our neighbors as we love ourselves—gives us guidance on how to live our life.

Four Guidelines

These four guidelines summarize the Christian teaching on how to handle money and possessions:

1. *Celebrate the Creator's gift.* The earth is God's. We are simply guardians and helpers in tending creation. God has given us the earth to provide for our needs. All life is a gift to be celebrated and cherished—not to be possessed and hoarded as if we will own it forever.

2. *Remain free.* We need not be taken in by advertisements that tell us that happiness consists of owning a certain car or having the ultimate sound system. We do not have to be possessed by possessions. Instead, we need to love ourselves enough to know that we are valuable and lovable just as we are.

3. *Share generously and cheerfully.* Sharing our money and possessions with others is one way of living joyfully, without the burden of excessive wealth. God promises great blessings to those who give to help their neighbors, especially those who give from their scarcity, not just their abundance.

4. *Live simply.* To live simply means to consume only what we need. It means that we may have more to share with other people and that we are not shackled by owning a lot of possessions

---

15
Using a modern-day scenario and wording, write a situation like the one James described in his letter.

Student photo: Untitled, color photo by Kim Lambert, St. Agnes Academy, Memphis, Tennessee

We give but little when we give of our possessions. It's when we give of our selves that we truly give.

that have to be protected. In the words of **Saint Elizabeth Ann Seton**, "Live simply, so that others may simply live."

For Review

• Summarize the perspective on money and possessions given by Saints Paul and James in their Epistles.

• Explain this statement: The right to private property is not an absolute right.

• List four guidelines that summarize Christian teaching on how to handle money and possessions.

Where Your Treasure Is . . .

We are economic beings, needing financial and material resources to survive. But we need to put our economic needs into a healthy perspective, one that recognizes their value and importance but does not make them the be-all and end-all of existence. We need to see our economic decisions as having the potential to contribute to the creation of a loving community, where everyone's needs are met simply because they are human beings who have dignity.

Student art: "True Giving," mixed media, by Emily Hillard, Notre Dame Academy, Toledo, Ohio

Our decisions about money and possessions tell very powerfully who we are and what we value. In the Sermon on the Mount, Jesus spoke of the decisions that form our heart and soul:

"Do not store up for yourselves treasures on earth, where moth and rust consume and where thieves break in and steal; but store up for yourselves treasures in heaven, where neither moth nor rust consumes and where thieves do not break in and steal. For where your treasure is, there your heart will be also." (Matthew 6:19–21) **16**

In our quest to live fully and freely, we need to ask ourselves where *our* real treasure is and let go of the rest.

God, enter our heart and mind.
We are making important decisions;
please help us
to make good ones.

God, you were not popular or athletic.
You did not have a nice car or wardrobe.
Help us look at this example
and realize that the heart and soul make one great!
Amen.

(Terra Ryan
Thomas More Prep–Marian, Hays, Kansas)

16
Write a one-page reflection on this question: *Where is your treasure?*

5

Suffering and Healing:
Toward Full Humanity

The Many Faces of Loss and Suffering

Suffering. The word has a chilling sound to it; it is something we would rather avoid enduring or even thinking about. But try as we might to avoid it, we will suffer; it is inevitable.

Necessary Losses

Being human by its nature entails certain losses that occur all through life, not just when someone dies. Think about some of the inevitable losses you have already experienced, each of which caused you a certain degree of pain and suffering:

- You left your mother's womb—a warm and secure place—to face a cold, jarring world.
- You lost the coziness and familiarity of being at home with your family when you went off to day care or nursery school.
- You left behind a world of constant play and freedom when you took on the responsibility of being a student.
- Perhaps you left your friends behind when you changed to another school or moved. Or maybe you simply grew away from certain friends (or they grew away from you), and you no longer hung around with them.
- You shed your childhood ways and your much-loved toys as you moved into adolescence. You became less carefree and also perhaps not as close to your family.
- Facing graduation, you are about to experience other losses—the constant companionship and satisfactions of high school and perhaps the security of living at home. You may be about to leave the town you have known and move into a whole new world.

You can probably project ahead decades and see hundreds of such losses coming up in the ordinary events of your life. Even in times of joy, such as if you become the parent of a baby, you realize that you will be losing something—your freedom to do what you want when you want or perhaps the comfort of sleeping all night.

Reflect for a moment on each of these losses, both the ones you have experienced and the ones you may see ahead in life. You will no doubt recognize that although each loss contains its own sorrow and hardship, losses are crucial for you to move into fuller life as a human being. Life is filled with such **necessary losses**, and without them we cannot grow. This reality is somewhat like the prairie seed that springs forth into new, lush grasses only after being burned in a fire or trampled by herding animals: We human beings can reach our full humanity only through the suffering and loss that we are constantly trying to avoid!

Other forms of suffering, however, seem less necessary to us, but they happen in the normal course of everyone's life: for example, being rejected, falling and breaking a bone, losing a long computer assignment that took hours to produce, being disappointed in not making a team. Sometimes young people hear others dismiss their suffering with comments like, "These are the best years of your life," or "Well, I wish I was your age again, let me tell you." This says to young people that their real pain is not taken seriously, that it should not even be discussed. But suffering needs to be talked over and attended to; we need to learn skills for coping with our losses. **1**

1
Summarize in a paragraph how you have been taught to deal with pain, suffering, and fear. What kinds of comments do you typically hear from family members when you are suffering?

When Suffering Seems Senseless

What is hardest to cope with are the sufferings that seem totally senseless. For instance:
- A mother and father grieve over the death of their baby, who just slipped away one night in her sleep, a victim of sudden infant death syndrome.
- A teenager has a long bout with depression that seems unexplained by events in her life.
- A friend watches in horror as his longtime buddy from the neighborhood gets dragged into a tough gang, heavy drug use, and a spiral of violence.

Dan Nguyen Tran, a student at Brockton (Massachusetts) High School, describes the agony that accompanied a great, seemingly pointless tragedy in his family:

I would like to take this time to tell you about my sister Suzy and how she has brought my family around in circles and nearly choked us to death. Suzy is a one of a kind person, let alone a sister. She is the porcelain effigy of innocence and life. She is the kind of girl who makes you want to live and to be happy just for being alive. Suzy is a top of the line student, honor rolled so long she's dizzy with genius. The only problem is that she is a social hermit, so quiet and unobtrusive. She is so lonely, and so alone, and I think that's why she did what she did. She wanted to go to college at UPenn and become a business tyrant when she grew up. But she couldn't because of what she did. Because of where she went so far she couldn't ever come back, ever. She flew up so high in the sky, and hung there so motionless and still. Hanging there like a half filled balloon that had reached the end of its journey to the top of the sky. When Suzy killed herself she blackened my soul dirty and shot me square in my childhood. . . .

At the funeral, people mourned. There were a lot of people from Suzy's classes there, but they were all acquaintances and not friends which is what she really needed. . . . It was a miracle my family hung through the ordeal still standing. . . . We depended on each other to keep us in line and not to circle fast in the past and fall.

. . . We didn't talk about it really until almost a year afterwards when summer came. During the whole year, it felt as though she was just at college since we had expected her absence for that. But when summer came, the confetti illusion blew up into grief and pain. Scattered emotions and sorrows strewn around us and falling and pulling us so low. . . . My parents who had grown apart, began to realign their emotions and we all worked together to refine the grief.

I have been trying to get on with my life since then. (*Words by Kids,* page 17) **2**

2
Tell a story in writing of your own personal suffering or of the suffering of someone close to you.

In times of immense loss such as a death, especially a tragic death, people may offer hollow condolences like, "God never sends more than you can deal with," or "It's just God's way of testing you," or "God must have wanted it this way." Such comments do God and those who suffer a great disservice by effectively telling them to cut off their grieving, not to question, and to accept quietly what has happened. In addition, they suggest an image of a rather coldhearted God who wills our pain.

A Feeling of Disintegration

It is hard to see what fuller humanity can possibly emerge from suffering, such as that endured by Dan Nguyen Tran's family. A theologian's description of **suffering** helps explain how destructive it can feel to a person and why it seems that nothing good can come from it:

Suffering involves a person's perception of the threat of disintegration—loss of integration. It is the distress accompanying events that threaten one's intactness, one's togetherness, . . . [one's] own coherence as a self. (Nelson, *Body Theology*, page 125)

When we suffer a great tragedy or sorrow, we feel that everything (including ourselves) is coming apart. Another personal account illustrates the sense of disintegration that suffering can bring. In this account, a seventeen-year-old young woman describes her brother's reaction to their parents' divorce.

"For six months after the divorce, my little brother was in his own little world. He didn't want any con-

tact with anyone in the family. He moped around the house like a sad little puppy dog. Whenever I looked at him, he just glared at me with hatred in his eyes. Whenever my mom asked him to do his chores, he just yelled at her and punched her with a tight fist until her arm was all red. He banged his head against his wall until he had a big lump on his head. At night, he didn't want anyone around because he felt like no one wanted him around. He was afraid for a week and a half because he had the idea of being hurt again. He felt like a big tight knot, because of all the

Student art: **Untitled, acrylic painting by Trinidad Peña, St. Peter's High School, New Brunswick, New Jersey**

anger he was experiencing. When my dad had finished packing and was on his way out the door, my brother clung to his leg and screamed bloody murder for half of an hour until his face was red as a beet. Two hours later he sat in a corner with his face as white as a sheet because he feared that he would never see my father for the rest of his life." (*Take Time to Play Checkers,* page 74)

From the outside, we may have enough perspective to know that given time, this little boy will probably be okay, that he will see his father again, and that they will even have wonderful times together again. But from the inside, the boy *perceives* that his very self is being destroyed and falling into pieces. **3**

Suffering hurts; it is full of pain, sorrow, and anguish. It feels like a terrible assault on the way things should be—united, whole, and integrated. With our world and ourselves feeling shattered, we cannot help but ask, "Why? Why is this happening? Why do people have to suffer? Why do *I* have to suffer?"

For Review

- Give two examples of necessary losses involved in growing up.
- Why does great suffering feel so destructive to a person?

3
Write a paragraph describing a time when you were suffering, but other people did not perceive the situation as you did. How did you feel?

The Big Question: Why?

Before we can consider the question *why*, which has come up again and again in the history of humankind, we will first take a look at two sources of suffering.

Two Sources of Suffering

From the Cycles and Processes of Nature

"For everything there is a season, and a time for every matter under heaven" (Ecclesiastes 3:1). **Natural causes** take their toll on all living creatures, bringing suffering great and small. Lightning, earthquakes, tidal waves, hurricanes, fires, and floods all cause suffering. A blizzard traps cross-country skiers in its icy grip and kills them. A drought parches farm and grazing land, burning up corn and soybeans and starving livestock. Lesser varieties of suffering can be due to natural causes too: A vacation is spoiled by bad weather. A fall off a bike keeps a school's star basketball player on crutches all through basketball season.

We also experience the sufferings inherent in our own personal life "seasons." In the spring and summer of our life, most of us grow strong and full physically (although even in these seasons we can become ill suddenly and die). In the fall and winter of our life, we begin to suffer from weakened muscles, lessened stamina, and declining health. No matter how well we take care of ourselves, the natural cycle of human life leads inexorably to death.

From Human Choice

The other source of suffering resides in the human heart—the source of **moral choice.** Immense suffering, for individuals and for whole groups or societies, can be caused by people's apathy, hardness of heart, greed, and decisions to harm or neglect others. The pages of the daily newspaper are filled with instances of suffering that result from human choice: domestic violence, child abuse, rape, murder, drive-by shootings, drug trafficking, genocide, job losses from factory closings, pollution, and so on. Quieter sufferings that do not make the newspapers are likewise results of moral choices: the hurt of being excluded because of race

Photo: A tornado in Saragosa, Texas, brings wreckage to buildings and also to people's lives. Tornado damage is an example of suffering due to natural causes.

or background, the loss of a person's good reputation by others' gossip and slander, the failing of a course because a person did not study.

Some sufferings result from a mix of both natural causes and human choices. For instance, cancer is caused by natural processes, many of which are beyond human control or choice. But in many cases, human choices also influence the development of cancer. Human beings choose to pollute the environment with carcinogens (cancer-causing agents), thus putting whole populations at risk. Human beings choose to smoke and expose their family members to their secondhand smoke. Another example is a car accident: some choice may be involved (whether to speed or drive in bad weather or drive while intoxicated), but natural causes also play a part (the force of the wind, the slickness of the road). **4**

Whether the suffering results from natural causes or human choices, we are often brought to the question of *why*.

"Why Does God Allow This?"

For believers in God, the big question becomes, "Why does God allow suffering?" They wonder, if God is all-good and all-powerful, why does God let innocent babies die of AIDS, or of beatings at the hands of abusive parents, or of cancer? If God loves us, why doesn't God stop teenagers from committing suicide?

In the Hebrew Scriptures, our ancient Jewish ancestors asked similar questions of God:

Why, O LORD, do you stand far off?
  Why do you hide yourself in times of trouble?

(Psalm 10:1)

Why do you look on the treacherous,
  and are silent when the wicked swallow
  those more righteous than they?

(Habakkuk 1:13)

Protesting questions such as these echo through the Bible. **5**

In the twentieth century, God's seeming neglect of the suffering of innocent people received its most excruciating challenge during the **Shoah,** or Holocaust, when Hitler and the Nazis systematically murdered millions of people. **Elie Wiesel**, now a noted writer and Nobel Peace Prize winner, was a teenager when the Nazis loaded him, his family, and the Jews of his small Romanian town into cattle cars headed to concentration camps and eventual death. Starved, beaten, witness to the deaths of family and friends, Wiesel survived, but the terror of the camps raised the most desperate of questions.

In his account of his teen years in various concentration camps, Wiesel tells of how the Nazis ordered the hanging execution of three prisoners—two men and a boy. The guards ordered the other prisoners to watch the hangings and then parade past the bodies. Wiesel remembers:

At a sign from the head of the camp, the three chairs tipped over.

Total silence throughout the camp. On the horizon, the sun was setting.

"Bare your heads!" yelled the head of the camp. His voice was raucous. We were weeping.

"Cover your heads!"

Then the march past began. The two adults were no longer alive. Their tongues hung swollen, blue-tinged. But the third rope was still moving; being so light, the child was still alive. . . .

4
List three actual recent instances of suffering, one resulting from moral choice, one due to natural causes, and one due to a mix of both.

5
Write a lament for the suffering you see in the world. Put it on poster board and illustrate the suffering with pictures.

For more than half an hour he stayed there, struggling between life and death, dying in slow agony under our eyes. . . .

Behind me, I heard [a] man asking:

"Where is God now?"

And I heard a voice within me answer him:

"Where is He? Here He is—He is hanging here on this gallows. . . ."

That night the soup tasted of corpses. . . .

"What are You, my God," I thought angrily, "compared to this afflicted crowd, proclaiming to You their faith, their anger, their revolt? What does Your greatness mean, Lord of the universe, in the face of all this weakness, this decomposition, and this decay? Why do You still trouble their sick minds, their crippled bodies?" (*Night,* pages 61–63)

The questions raised by the *Shoah* about why God would allow such a tremendous evil are some of the most difficult to struggle with.

"What Did I Do to Deserve This?"

The kind of suffering most of us have to deal with is on a much lesser scale than what Wiesel endured in the camps. However, our pain is still real, and it makes us question why it happens to us.

In our search for answers, we might begin to wonder what we did wrong that caused our suffering. This question often puts us on a torturous search for our fault. In the case of other people's suffering, we may wonder what they did to deserve such a fate.

The **Book of Job** in the Bible contains a well-known story about the mystery of why people suffer. In the beginning of the story, Job is an exemplary, successful man who has led a blameless life. He seems blessed with every good thing. As the story goes on, one by one Job loses everything that is important to him—his children; his thriving business of sheep, camels, oxen, donkeys, and servants; his health—everything except his life, miserable as it is. Three friends try to console him by examining why he deserves such a fate. They believe that if he can only figure out what he did wrong, he can understand why he is in such trouble, repent, and maybe come out of his misery. Job steadfastly maintains his innocence, insisting he has done nothing to deserve his awful fate. But his friends are not convinced.

The end of the story is a bit of a puzzle, and we will get to that later. But part of the ending is that God scolds Job's friends for blaming Job for his own suffering. God is clear that Job did not bring on his misery by doing something wrong. **6**

6

Have you ever asked, "Why is this happening to me?" Think of a time and write about it in a short narrative. Did you ever figure out why it happened to you?

"Does God Want Me to Suffer?"

A commonly held notion is that God tests us with suffering. This attitude is reflected in the comment of nine-year-old Lance, who told a newspaper reporter in Minneapolis, "'People die because it is a test for relatives and friends on how they overcome their sadness. The way they overcome their sadness judges if they go to heaven or not'" (*Take Time to Play Checkers,* page 217). The "test" explanation of suffering is cold comfort for someone who is grieving, and it makes God out to be mean.

The God of the Bible, though, does not will our suffering. In fact, in story after story in the Hebrew Scriptures, God urges the Israelites to *end* suffering. God blesses Abraham to form a community. God moves Moses to lead the Israelites out of slavery in Egypt. God inspires commandments that give shape and order to the Israelite community, to bring harmony among them. God wills that among the Israelites the widows and orphans be fed and treated with special care. Prophets are chosen to warn the people away from their evil deeds, deeds that in themselves lead to suffering. The prophet Isaiah depicts God saying:

Can a woman forget her nursing child,
  or show no compassion for the child of her
    womb?
Even these may forget,
  yet I will not forget you.

(Isaiah 49:15)

This motherly God would hardly send suffering just to test us.

The Bible tells us that the Israelites often called out to God in their anguish and suffering, sometimes even blaming God for all that had befallen them. But they realized deep down that God was their support, loving and providing for them. Consider Psalm 22. It begins with the Psalmist crying:

My God, my God, why have you forsaken me?
  Why are you so far from helping me, from the
    words of my groaning?

(Verse 1)

But after pouring out such sentiments, the Psalmist goes on to call on God and then to praise God for saving him:

But you, O LORD, do not be far away!
  O my help, come quickly to my aid!

(Verse 19)

From the horns of the wild oxen you have rescued
    me.
I will tell of your name to my brothers and sisters;
  in the midst of the congregation I will praise
    you:
You who fear the LORD, praise him!

(Verses 21–23)

The writers of the Psalms could be upset with God, but they always came back to acknowledge that God loved them and traveled with them.

In short, God does not will people to suffer. In some cases people suffer because of their own unwise choices, or because of others' sinful choices that affected them badly. But that does not mean that God *wanted* them to suffer. 7

Student art (on facing page): "The Inmate," graphite drawing by Amy Brookshire, St. Agnes Academy, Memphis, Tennessee

7
Why do people tend to identify God as the source of suffering? Have you ever heard people blame God? Write what they said. 7

A Loving God Who Does Not Control

To get an insight into God's role in human suffering, perhaps we need to shake up some of our understandings of God. *Is* God all-powerful in the sense of *controlling* everything that happens? It is hard to reconcile a controlling but good God with the reality that injustice and senseless suffering happen. Does God control every event? Here is the answer of a Jewish rabbi, Harold Kushner, who addresses suffering that comes through moral choices, as well as suffering that happens from natural causes:

Not Controlling Moral Choices

Why, then, do bad things happen to good people? One reason is that our being human leaves us free to hurt each other, and God can't stop us without taking away the freedom that makes us human. . . . God can only look down in pity and compassion at how little we have learned over the ages about how human beings should behave. (*When Bad Things Happen to Good People,* page 81)

Not Intervening in Laws of Nature

Laws of nature do not make exceptions for nice people. . . . God does not reach down to interrupt the workings of the laws of nature to protect the righteous from harm. . . .

And really, how could we live in this world if [God] did? . . . Would this be a better world, if certain people were immune to laws of nature because God favored them, while the rest of us had to fend for ourselves?

. . . I don't believe that an earthquake that kills thousands of innocent victims without reason is an act of God. It is an act of nature. Nature is morally blind, without values. It churns along, following its own laws, not caring who or what gets in the way. . . . God stands for justice, for fairness, for compassion. For me, the earthquake is not an "act of God." The act of God is the courage of people to rebuild their lives after the earthquake, and the rush of others to help them. (Pages 58–60) **8**

Finally, a Mystery

We may be able to take God out of the picture as far as willing or causing our suffering. But the question remains, Why do we suffer?

An "Answer" for Job

The biblical story of Job, which we looked at earlier, ends with a rather ambiguous, some would say unsatisfactory, answer to this question. The notion that Job deserved his suffering or that God was punishing him is soundly dismissed. However (in chapters 38 to 41 of Job), God really provides no "answer" as such but only tells Job not to question the majesty of God! In other words, the message of the story is that life is governed by a divine mystery that is too great for human beings to grasp. Suffering can't be "figured out"; it just *is*. This "answer" is more likely to help us live more patiently with tragedy than to understand it. (Incidentally, even the author of Job, who was trying to honor the mystery of suffering, could not stand to let the story end without reversing Job's fortunes and making everything come out right!)

Not Why, but What Next?

Thea Bowman, a Franciscan sister, was a well-known lecturer, singer, teacher, and preacher. Even

8
Write a response to this proposition: *It would be unjust for God to intervene in the cycles of nature.*

struggling human beings to reach out to one another, to help one another, to love one another, to be blessed and strengthened and humanized in the process. Perhaps it's an incentive to see Christ in our world and to view the work of Christ and to feel the suffering of Christ.

"I know that suffering gives us new perspective and helps us to clarify our real value. I know that suffering has helped me to clarify my relationships. . . . Perhaps suffering stops us in our tracks and forces us to confront what is real within ourselves and in our environment."

As Sister Thea understood in the midst of her own dying process, the significant question about suffering is not really *why* it happens but *what we do with it* once it does happen. Suffering ultimately cannot be explained. But if we face it constructively and allow it to transform us into a more loving person, it can be the source of our redemption. **9**

For Review

- Describe two sources of suffering. Give an example of suffering from each kind of source and from a mix of both.
- Briefly explain what the Bible says about *(a)* whether suffering is always the result of something we did wrong, and *(b)* whether God wants us to suffer.
- How does Rabbi Kushner answer the question, Why do bad things happen to good people?
- What is God's answer to Job about why we suffer?
- What is the more significant question about suffering, according to Sister Thea?

as she lived with terminal cancer, Thea inspired thousands of people with her spirit of joy and her way of communicating the beauty and power of African American spirituality. Not long before she died, an interviewer for *U.S. Catholic* asked her why she thought people suffer. Sister Thea replied:

"I don't know. Why is there war? Why is there hunger? Why is there pain? Perhaps it's an incentive for

9
Do you think people are satisfied with the notion that why we suffer is a mystery? Cite an example to illustrate your reaction.

Photo: Sr. Thea Bowman, FSPA

Jesus: The Redemptive Power of Suffering

The Christian approach to suffering has at its center the paschal mystery—the mystery of Jesus' passing over through his life, Passion, death, and Resurrection. Christians believe that through this mystery we are **redeemed**—saved from sin and the power of evil, and destined for glory forever.

The Compassion of Jesus

Jesus did not want to see people suffer. During his whole ministry, he tried to alleviate suffering. Jesus, quoting the prophet Isaiah, told people that God had sent him

> "'to bring good news to the poor,
> . . . to proclaim release to the captives
> and recovery of sight to the blind,
> to let the oppressed go free.'"
>
> (Luke 4:18)

People's suffering stirred Jesus to compassion and action. At the synagogue on the Sabbath, when he noticed a man with a withered hand, Jesus' critics watched to jump on him if he cured on the Sabbath, which their legalistic customs forbade. Defying their narrow views, Jesus looked at them "with anger; he was grieved at their hardness of heart" (Mark 3:5). Jesus then restored the man's hand to health, showing that charity comes before any other consideration.

Jesus so identified with suffering people that he made caring for them the prerequisite for having eternal life. As he taught in the story of the last judgment, eternal life would be reserved for those who fed the hungry, clothed the naked, visited prisoners, and gave drink to the thirsty (Matthew 25:31–46). He told his disciples that they should "'proclaim the good news, "The kingdom of heaven has come near." Cure the sick, raise the dead, cleanse the lepers, cast out demons'" (Matthew 10:7–8).

One with Us, Even in Death

Jesus, both human and divine, suffered with all of humanity. As fully human, he was not exempt from the suffering that we know—loneliness, fear, rejection, betrayal, pain, and finally, death. Jesus is one with us—Emmanuel, or **God-with-us**—in all things, including suffering and death.

Jesus was put to death because his life and message were a threat to some of the powerful people of his time. He did not seek to die, and he certainly bled, cried out, and writhed in agony while he was tortured on the cross in a horrible, unjust execution. But he freely accepted death with love, not bitterness; he did not try to escape from it, and he forgave his executioners. **10**

New Life Through Death

Death, as we know, did not have the last word with Jesus; three days after his horrible Crucifixion, he was raised from the dead. His death and Resurrection contain a great saving truth: Those who suffer with love experience a new, richer life, even during their time on earth. Those who die with love will know this glorious life forever. "Eternal life" is not only for life after death; we can glimpse it even as we live in this world.

Thus the meaning of suffering for Christians is this: It can be the means of our redemption. Through suffering we can be transformed to full humanity. The issue is not so much *why* we suffer as *how*. For Christians, who unite their suffering with Jesus and believe Jesus is with them through their darkest moments, their suffering can change them into more loving, deeper persons. For them, death loses its sting; it is "'swallowed up in victory'" (1 Corinthians 15:54).

For Review

- Give two examples from Jesus' life and teaching of his compassion for those who suffered.
- With what attitude did Jesus face his own suffering and death?
- What is the meaning of suffering for Christians?

Transforming the Pain

The "risen life" that is the fruit of suffering does not come automatically. In fact, we all know of people who suffer but do not necessarily come out better for it. They become bitter, instead of loving, through suffering and pain. And rather than accepting the suffering that is part of being human, people may try various strategies to avoid it. Most of these—like drugs, alcohol, and irresponsible sex—only lead to increased suffering. Some avoidance mechanisms just change the way suffering is experienced. For example, some people avoid intimate, loving, committed relationships to dodge the possibility of being hurt. So instead of allowing themselves the possibility of being hurt by love, they suffer loneliness, feelings of emptiness, and restlessness. **11**

Accepting Risk

To choose what is life-giving means that we accept the possibilities of pain, allowing them to transform us. If we want joy, we have to be open to pain; if we want love, we must be open to loss, as in these situations:

- No one in Rafael's family had ever graduated from high school, much less gone to college. But Rafael was determined to make it to college. His uncle constantly gave him a hard time about not being part of the family, saying things like, "We aren't good enough for you, eh?" His father would come home from his night security guard job, crash, and hardly speak a word to Rafael. No one could help him with his schoolwork. Despite threats, he avoided the gang in his neighborhood. Rafael plugged

10
Think about a time when you suffered a lot. Write a prayer to Jesus in which you imagine him supporting you through your experience.

11
What are some other ways that people seek to avoid pain, only to suffer instead in different ways? Compose a list of examples.

away, determined to do better, fearing that something would get in the way. He confided to his religion teacher, "I want to do something to make things better for my people."

- Sam never considered himself very attractive, but he liked Liza a lot. Every guy wanted to go out with her because she was funny, smart, and beautiful. She could be intimidating because her tongue became a sharp sword when she was crossed. On the other hand, Sam was just a middling student and somewhat shy. In brief conversations he sensed that she liked him okay. Still wondering if it would work, he finally plucked up his courage and asked Liza out, knowing that he might get shot down, and that would hurt.

- Sarah loved her grandmother. The elderly woman had showered the girl with all the affection she had been denied at home. When Sarah moved in with her grandmother to help her out, her parents had been angry and hinted that it was good riddance. Now Grandma was gasping for life at the hospital. She had broken her hip in a fall; pneumonia had set in. Death seemed imminent. Sarah stood vigil at her grandmother's bedside. In her grief, voices also haunted her, "What's going to happen to me now? Mom and Dad don't really want me back. Maybe I shouldn't have moved in with Grandma. No, that's crazy. She loves me." Tears streamed down Sarah's face as she watched her grandmother struggle for breath.

Being fully alive often demands the risk of pain. Once we accept that pain is the price of human existence, we need to ask ourselves: "Okay, what do I do with my suffering? How can I let it be transformed to something positive?" *We may not have control over some causes of our suffering, but we can make choices about our response to it.*

12
Write a "loss history" of your life: identify all the things you have left behind and note how you reacted to these losses.

Healthy Grieving

Some of our worst pain comes from loss: failure at a project, the breakup of an important relationship, the death of a loved one, an illness or injury, and so on. At such times we are often hit with overwhelming feelings of despair, anger, depression, sadness—all aspects of **grief**, the process of mourning and recovering from a significant loss. **12**

If we deny or ignore our grief, we put ourselves at peril. However, allowing ourselves to grieve well can be a source of new life. Consider this account by J. C., a student at Saint Catherine's High School in Racine, Wisconsin. J. C.'s grief over a friend's death started out very rough, but a breakthrough helped this young person grow through the grief:

When my best friend died, a part of my soul died. I stopped eating, quit doing homework and studying, and destroyed most of my friendships. It's not that I was angry at him for leaving, but that I was angry at myself for not saying "good-bye" or how much he meant to me.

As the months passed slowly, I kept the same attitude. I even attempted suicide. Then [my friend's]

mother invited me to their home. After days of hesitation, I agreed. Later we went to his grave. She put her hand on [the grave] and said, "He's in there," then, placing her hand on my chest, added, "but he's still in there. And he always will be. And if you close out the world when you pray to him with your heart, you can hear him answer." Then we embraced and cried.

Now, today, exactly a year to his death, I still feel him in my heart and pray to him. And you know, if I'm really concentrating, I can actually hear him answer!

We often try to deny our grief, hiding it from other people and even ourselves. We become bitter, like J. C., who even cut off friendships. When we ignore our experience of loss or pain, we deny ourselves the possibility for growth and new life. But we can choose to grieve deeply and well, thereby allowing our suffering to be transformed into life.

Let's consider the process of grieving well.

Acknowledge the Loss

Many of us are taught to just shrug off our losses, whether they involve losing a girlfriend or boyfriend, failing to get a starting position on a team, or seeing a longed-for dream dashed. We may have been given the message that we should just grit our teeth and go on. But until we acknowledge the loss, we cannot grieve it, and it will eat away at us. We might break out in anger too readily or find ourselves pulling away from friends. In other words, unspoken losses can gain power over us. So, to grieve in a healthy way, we say yes to our loss. We stare it in the face. **13**

Express Feelings

Grief needs some expression. Bottled-up grief turns sour and leads to chronic anger, cynicism, or even violence. God created us with emotions. If we

befriend them, listen to them, and express them in appropriate ways, we can come through our grief. J. C. stuffed his anger inside, and it turned on him. When he let it pour out with his friend's mother, his grief was washed clean. One of the important aspects of funerals is that they allow family and friends to ritually face the death and release their emotions. Perhaps it would be wise to have other mini-rituals to help us get through other, lesser kinds of losses. **14**

Take Action to Move On

After we face our loss and release our emotions, we might find that we need to take some action in order to move on with life. This does not necessarily mean that our grieving is over. In some cases a loss will affect us deeply for a long time; we may never really be "over" the death of someone we love. But it is healthy eventually to take steps to allow ourselves to move ahead with the rest of life. For example, J. C. decided to go on with life and make his way back into friendships. If we have been dating someone and split up angrily, discarding her or his picture and other mementos of the relationship can help in the letting go. If we had planned on going to a particular college and then were not admitted, we might be angry and hurt. If we face our loss squarely and release our feelings

---

Student art (on facing page): "Coping with Tragedy," pencil drawing by Ben Mercer, Holy Cross High School, Louisville, Kentucky

13
Cite two examples of losses that you and other people your age tend to try to ignore or shove out of consciousness.

14
List some other ways of appropriately releasing our emotions in grieving.

appropriately, we may have the energy to apply to other colleges. Taking such action will help us resolve our grief and appreciate new possibilities.

Embracing the Goodness

In the midst of suffering we may discover what really matters to us. We may even see the small wonders in life that have always been there, but perhaps were overlooked. We embrace the goodness even in our difficulties.

Beverly Elisabeth Mather, a senior at Hingham High School in Massachusetts, wrote about how her world had turned upside down three years earlier. She was the older of two sisters. Then a baby brother, David, was born prematurely and afterward fought a dangerous meningitis disease. Over a six-month period, he had ten operations. Beverly recalls:

Life before David was worlds apart from the way it is now. . . .

My mother and I settled a year's worth of fighting in one night. We needed to be strong together in order to get through the hard times with David. If we had continued to fight, our home would have fallen apart.

Our new beginning started the night David was born. The changes to my life were perhaps the most immediately obvious as I was thrust into the position of a second mother and all that it involved the moment my mother went into labor. . . .

. . . It was hard enough trying to grow up myself never mind to serve as a guide for [my nine-year-old sister]. In time, however, it became second nature. I remember at one point when David was two, he had an infection. . . . He and my mother did not come home [from the hospital] for two weeks straight. But somehow the house stayed clean, the meals got cooked, and the schoolwork was completed in time. After two years I had grown enough to manage whatever needed to be done. In a word, I became the rock for everyone else to lean on.

But, I'm not a rock. This ordeal has caused me as much pain as it has cost everyone else. . . .

. . . But, there is much more involved than the anxiety. David touches everyone he meets, but no one more than us. He colorizes our world and his smile makes us alive. . . .

David, after all he has been through, holds more hope, laughter, and love than anyone else I know. Having him has taught us what the important things in life really are. I pray that I can hold onto his outlook and that someday, in my own way, I'll say what he once said to me.

"I want to be a doctor when I grow up so I can help all the little babies." (*Words by Kids,* pages 7–8)

Student art: "Remembering My Childhood Swing," acrylic painting by Monica Wilson, Holy Cross High School, Louisville, Kentucky

David's suffering brought out Beverly's strength, love, and compassion. She responded to suffering by choosing life. As a result, she discovered the miracle of David's hope and love, and it gave her a sense of purpose. **15**

Becoming Healers

David's suffering called forth his sister's compassion. If we have suffered with another (which is, in its root, what the word *compassion* means), deep in our heart we feel the invitation to relieve suffering, too. If we let it, suffering can bring out the best in us: compassion, action for peace and justice, and healing. In short, we can choose to be transformed by suffering.

The following accounts tell of two young people who turned suffering into healing action.

To Create Safety for Kids

When he was nine, James Ale saw one of his best friends hit by a speeding Thunderbird while playing in the street. James lived in a neighborhood of trailer homes and cramped condominiums in Davie, Florida. The kids had no safe place to play. Angry and distressed about his friend, James set about getting a park built behind the water plant nearby.

James's father told him that he would have to be very organized and prove that they needed a playground. James started with a phone call to the mayor. Feeling brushed off after the first call, he circulated a petition, outlined on a map exactly where the park could go, typed out a letter to the mayor laying out the reasons for the park, and even made business cards for his new advocacy group, Children of Davie. Then he made an appointment to see the mayor in person.

Because James was prepared and answered her questions well, Mayor Joan Kovac took him seriously. Other city officials did not. Action slowed down. When he was not allowed to appear before the city council, James contacted a Miami newspaper, which published the story of what he was trying to do. This publicity did the trick.

Now a park nestles behind the water plant. People call it James Ale Park. It is the busiest of any park in Davie, Florida. The suffering of a friend led to action for the common good. (Based on Hoose, *It's Our World, Too!* pages 68–74)

To Heal the Scars of War

When the Khmer Rouge guerrillas began their bloody rule over Cambodia, Arn Chorn was eight. His family was taken away, and he was forced to work in rice paddies. At twelve, Arn was given a rifle by the Khmer Rouge and told to kill Vietnamese soldiers who had invaded the country to stop the slaughter. "They wanted the smaller ones to go, children like me. . . . Sometimes I didn't know whether I was shooting at a Vietnamese or a Cambodian. I just shot. . . . I had to shoot or be shot. When I killed people, I didn't

15
In a paragraph, tell of a time when suffering helped you or someone you know discover some small wonder or what is important in life.

want to think about what I had done. I would say, 'No, that could not have been my bullet.'"

Sickened by what he was doing, Arn escaped one night with a hammock and his rifle. For six months he wandered the jungles alone. Eventually he stumbled into a refugee camp. At age fourteen, Arn was sponsored by an American family to come to New Hampshire to live. He knew no English, had not been in school since he was eight, and because of his trauma lived in constant fear.

Arn grew to believe that if he could just tell his story, he could begin healing his own traumatic scars of war. But even more than that, he wanted to inspire Americans to sponsor orphaned Cambodian children. So his American father helped Arn give his first speech at church. Arn said, "My name is Arn Chorn," and then the memory of war swept over him. He began to cry. Steadying himself, he went on. He could see other people crying, too. Somehow, it felt good. When it was over, they formed rows of people to shake his hand. They promised to try to help.

Two years later Arn gave a speech as part of a peace rally at the Church of Saint John the Divine in New York City. He was joined by other teens who had suffered from war. A woman who had worked with Cambodian refugees, Judith Thompson, talked to Arn about organizing a group of young refugees from different nations to speak with other young people about war, peace, and hope. Together they launched Children of War.

The Children of War have spoken in dozens of cities to thousands of other children and teens, many who have grown up in the middle of conflicts—shattered families, discrimination, gangs. When they were able to talk—kid to kid—about the things that were bothering them, some could see themselves not as losers or victims but as courageous survivors who had done the best they could in tough situations, like the Children of War.

Even though he still has nightmares and knows nothing of his family's fate, Arn Chorn has dedicated his life to ending war and violence. Children of War continues its work, too. What arose out of suffering is leading to good. (Based on Hoose, *It's Our World, Too!* pages 102–109)

Both James Ale and Arn Chorn allowed suffering to transform them. Their pain did not simply remain dead and lifeless. It brought forth new life, like the prairie seed that can grow into lush grasses only after it has been burned in a fire or trampled by herding animals. **16**

For Review

- Briefly describe the process of healthy grieving.
- In what ways can a person be transformed by suffering?

16
Has suffering ever led you or someone you know to compassionate action? Tell the story in writing.
.

Choosing to Be Redeemed

We will suffer, and our loved ones will suffer. Suffering cannot be avoided. However, it can be turned to good by our choices. Healthy grieving of our losses can lead us back to life, and suffering can help us seek what is important. It can also move us to take action to help other people heal and to build a world of peace and justice. Then suffering will not be a meaningless waste. Redemption comes from suffering.

Addressing new graduates of a school of professional psychology, businessman Gordon Sherman, the founder of Midas Muffler, gave this piece of wisdom:

There is a teasing irony: we spend our lives evading our own redemption. And this is naturally so because something in us knows that to be fully human we must experience pain and loss. Therefore, we are at ceaseless effort to elude this high cost, whatever the price, until at last it overtakes us. And then in spite of ourselves we do realize our humanity. We are put in worthier possession of our souls. Then we look back and know that even our grief contained our blessing.

How can our grief contain our blessing? One way is to bring our grief and pain to God.

Dear God,
When I see the pain and suffering surrounding me,
I feel trapped,
wanting nothing more than to escape.

Please God,
Give me the strength, every day of my life,
to face my troubles up front
and to help others when they are in need of it.

May you stay with me every day of my life, God.

(Liliana Ramirez,
Saint Augustine Religious Education,
Culver City, California)

6
Sexuality:
Energy for Relating with Others

Understanding Sexuality

Bring up sexuality or sex in a conversation, and you will always be amazed at the array of opinions and attitudes people offer. It is an area about which nearly everyone seems to have something to say. That makes sense, because sexuality is integral to every person's identity, and we are all deeply affected by it. Few people feel neutral about matters of sex and sexuality—it is too close to us!

The following discussion among a group of high school students demonstrates the wide variety of feelings and ideas that teenagers have about sexuality and sex:

Kate: Some people put sex as the most important thing in a relationship. Then that's all the relationship amounts to. I feel a relationship ought to be more than sex. Friendship, that's key to me.

Jake: To a lot of guys, sex is like a novelty. In the locker room after practice, they brag about what studs they are and how they hit up on this girl. First of all, they're full of it. Second, sex should be more than like renting a video, a regular thing.

Shelley: Yeah. Two people in a relationship ought to build equal love and honesty and trust so that they have more going for them than sex. It shouldn't be the be-all and end-all in a good relationship.

Vince: I don't think sex should be all planned out. It should be something spontaneous—not something you're planning for years.

Rhonda: Let's be honest though. Sex is a way of saying you love the other person. If you don't love the guy, sex can't be beautiful or a lot of fun.

Kate: I think a guy must be a creep if he tries to manipulate me by saying stuff like, "Gee, we've been dating for three weeks, don't you think it's time for sex?" Oh wow, three whole weeks. Like you really know this jerk.

Rhonda: Sex without love is really self-centered. You can have love without sex though.

Patrick: Get real. I don't think casual sex is all that big a deal if you're careful.

Vince: That's the point though. Sex ought to be special, and in this day and age it's that "no big deal" attitude that makes people careless about other people. Without care—that's what careless means.

Shelley: Patrick, you have a typical dumb guy attitude. What girls really want is for someone to love them and be responsible to them.

Jake: About the only way that sex can have any meaning is in marriage. Then you know you can trust the other person. They'll be there for you. **1**

For many young people, the major issue around sexuality becomes whether to have sex, and that is certainly a good and highly relevant question to be asking oneself at this age. But having sex is only part of the much greater reality of our sexuality, of being persons who are sexual by nature. The first step in considering this topic, then, is to develop this larger understanding of sexuality and its meaning in the Christian perspective.

The Genesis Vision of Sexuality

We were created as sexual creatures—male and female. Sexuality is integral to who we are; it is at the center of being human, an essential part of being made in God's image. The Creation account in Genesis says:

So God created humankind in his image,
  in the image of God he created them;
  male and female he created them.

(1:27)

We Are Relational, Like God

The way we are as sexual creatures is somehow a reflection of the way God is. Being sexual, we are made by God for relationship, made to love and be loved—*like God.* We are sexual not simply because it is a nice way to keep the human species going (although that is also true) but because we are created like God. The longing for relationship is built into us, just as God longs for relationship with us and with all creation.

In their 1991 document ***Human Sexuality: A Catholic Perspective for Education and Lifelong Learning,*** the U.S. Catholic bishops echo the understanding of sexuality found in Genesis:

Our gender, our sexual identity as male or female persons, is an intimate part of the original and divine plan of creation. . . .

. . . We believe human sexuality is a . . . divine gift, a primal dimension of each person, a mysterious

1
Imagine that you are taking part in this dialog. Write your comments on the topic.

Student art: "Eve," plaster and acrylic paint sculpture by Katie Brackmann, Rose Honnert, and Jenny Wissel, Oldenburg Academy, Oldenburg, Indiana

blend of spirit and body, which shares in God's own creative love and life. (Page 7)

As one high school student remarked: "'Sex was God's idea first. He planned it. According to Genesis 1:31, we were created excellent in every way. That includes our sexual abilities'" (*What I Wish My Parents Knew About My Sexuality,* page 124).

Not Shame, but Joy

Chapter 2 of Genesis also conveys a sense that our sexuality is good and blessed, not something to be ashamed of. After God forms Adam and Eve, the account states: "Therefore a man leaves his father and his mother and clings to his wife, and they become one flesh. And the man and his wife were both naked, and were not ashamed" (2:24–25). Adam and Eve experience their sexuality as integrated into their whole lives. They delight in their affection for each other as a gift from their Creator.

We all know the story of Adam and Eve's **Fall,** after which everything, including the spontaneous joy and attraction of sexuality, becomes overshadowed and distorted by sin. Yet we are called to that original created state of healthy, happy sexuality, and through God's grace we can live in that state.

A Basis for All Our Relating

Here is a description of **sexuality** that is consistent with the holistic, integrated notion conveyed in Genesis:

It is . . . the basis of our connection to all things, the foundation of our power to relate as female or male. . . .

We express our sexuality in all our friendships; in the way we parent, work, and play; in our relationship with God in prayer and worship. Sexuality is . . . an energy that produces a cosmic dance of mutual attraction. . . . Sexuality is that embodied energy which links us to others in communication and communion; it is our ability to affect and to be affected by others. (Fischer, *Reclaiming the Connections,* page 75) **2**

Sexuality urges us to overcome our sense of loneliness and selfishness. It is expressed not only, or even primarily, in genital ways. Most often our sexuality comes through in how we act as friends, workers, parents, students, athletes, singers, leaders, followers—in all facets of life. If we assume that sexuality and having sex are the same, we may come to believe that the only way of expressing our sexual energy is in sexual intercourse. But sexuality is an energy toward relationships of all kinds, an emotional, physical, psychological, and spiritual drive to reach out to others.

The Power of Sexuality

We are not addressing faint emotions or weak energies when we talk about sexuality. For young people whose sexuality is influenced by immense biological and hormonal changes, this deep relational drive transforms, enlivens, and expands their whole being. Curiosity and imagination are stirred, thinking is colored, and the body is transformed. The power of sexuality to make us feel different—new and charged with energy—is part of its potential to help us realize our humanity.

This poem by the Spanish poet Jorge Manrique expresses the powerful roller-coaster effect that sexual longing (what he calls love) can have on us:

Love is a force so strong
it rules all reason.
A force of such power

2
Do you agree with the definition of sexuality given here? Would you add, subtract, or alter anything in the definition? If so, what? Write your responses.

it turns all minds
by its power and desire.

· · · · · · · ·

'Tis pleasure with sorrow
and sorrow with joy.
Pain with sweetness
and might with fear.
Fear with daring
and pleasure with rage.
Glory with passion
and faith with desire.

· · · · · · · ·

A kind of madness
in the changes it makes.
Sometimes shows sadness,
at other times, joy,
as it wishes and pleases.

The strong attraction and energy that are part of our sexuality can throw us into a whirl of emotions. We may become drawn toward another person, but he or she may not be interested in us. Or we may become close initially, but then the other person might back away or fall in love with someone else. We may find someone who is attracted to us and love may grow, but then we decide to wait to consummate that love in marriage. Such intense and not always comfortable experiences can result from the strong life energy that sexuality gives us.

Because it is so powerful, sexuality normally assumes enormous significance in a young person's awareness and sense of identity. Eventually, healthy, maturing people are able to put sexuality into perspective and integrate it into the whole of their life. **3**

Celebrating the Gift

One source of a healthy perspective on sexuality is the Bible. The Hebrew Scriptures and the Christian Testament continually affirm the goodness and life-giving nature of sexuality. In the Hebrew Scriptures in particular, the sexual attraction of lovers is described in beautiful and moving terms. For instance, the Book of Proverbs declares:

Let your fountain be blessed,
   and rejoice in the wife of your youth,
   a lovely deer, a graceful doe.
May her breasts satisfy you at all times;
   may you be intoxicated always by her love.

(5:18–19)

The most famous hymns of love in the Hebrew Scriptures are found in the **Song of Songs**, a collection of wedding feast songs written for a husband and a wife to sing to each other. For example, in one song the wife sings these words:

The voice of my beloved!
   Look, he comes,
leaping upon the mountains,
   bounding over the hills.

3

In your experience, what sexual issues seem to be most important to teenagers in their thoughts and discussions? Share your thoughts in a one-page essay.

My beloved is like a gazelle
   or a young stag.

. . . .

My beloved speaks and says to me:
"Arise, my love, my fair one,
   and come away;
for now the winter is past,
   the rain is over and gone."

. . . .

My beloved is mine and I am his.

(2:8–16)

In his letters, Saint Paul recognized the dignity and greatness of sexuality. Paul felt that the body is to be used for love, not for selfish enjoyment that implies no commitment to the other person:

Do you not know that your body is a **temple of the Holy Spirit** within you, which you have from God, and that you are not your own? For you were bought with a price; therefore glorify God in your body. (1 Corinthians 6:19–20; boldface added)

Through the centuries, the church has continued to recognize the great value of the human body. It has urged Christians always to treat their own and others' physical, sexual being reverently and gratefully, not casually. **4**

For Review

- What are two lessons about sexuality that can be found in Genesis?
- What is the Song of Songs? What is its attitude toward sexuality?
- What did Saint Paul say about how we should treat our body?

Valuing Ourselves as Sexual Persons

As discussed earlier, sexuality is much more than sexual intercourse. It is the force that energizes us to find fulfillment in relating to other people. A healthy expression of that sexuality depends on many factors. One factor is that we value ourselves as sexual persons. That includes having a positive body image and appreciating our masculinity and femininity.

Having a Positive Body Image

Having a **positive body image** means that we feel comfortable with our body and that we love our body enough to take care of it.

Feeling Comfortable in Our Own Skin

To be comfortable and feel at home in our own body is not as easy as it might sound. The media take advantage of our need to feel attractive by equating our attractiveness with their products. Discomfort with ourselves as bodily persons seems to be on the increase in our society. Here are some examples of the tactics used in advertising to make us dissatisfied with our own body:

- TV, magazine, and radio ads scream at us for being too fat, too thin, too short, too tall, pimply, yellow-toothed, dull-haired, or otherwise defective. Something, it seems, is always wrong with us.
- Many health clubs and tanning spas capitalize on people's anxiety about the shape and appearance of their body. Some people assume that

4
Write a paragraph that describes how the affirmation of sexuality in the Hebrew Scriptures and the Christian Testament matches—or does not match—what you have learned in the past about the Catholic view of sexuality.

without weight lifting (or the dangerous shortcut of taking anabolic steroids), they cannot have a physique worth anything.

- Fashion magazines do a thriving business by convincing us that what we are currently wearing will not make us suitably attractive to the other sex. There is even a fashion magazine for big (meaning "fat") and tall men; of course, the magazine's purpose is to sell clothes that hide bigness.

A lot of businesses would close if people were comfortable with their bodies, if they valued themselves more as persons and less as appearances. Tragic evidence of the obsession with bodily perfectionism in North American society is the incidence of cases of eating disorders, particularly among young women. The disorders of **anorexia nervosa** and **bulimia** are characterized by a pathological fear of gaining weight. With anorexia nervosa this fear leads to faulty eating patterns, malnutrition, and excessive weight loss. Persons who have bulimia tend to go on eating binges and then induce vomiting to avoid weight gain. Another related disorder is **hypergymnasia**, the tendency to exercise excessively and dangerously to stay thin.

So it is not easy to feel at home in our own skin, even though our body—plump, thin, weak, or strong—is a marvelous creation given to us by God. Saint Paul told the Ephesians, "We are God's work of art, created in Christ Jesus for the good works which God has already designated to make up our way of life." (Ephesians 2:10, NJB). Notice, Paul did not say that only thin, clear-skinned, fashionable people are God's creations or works of art. No, we are all works of art.

At some point in life we must look at ourselves in the mirror and say something like, "I'm five-four, a short guy, but I am lovable and I can love others," or "I'm six-three, tall for a woman, but I am lovable and I can love others." We need to love ourselves in order to love others. **5**

Caring for Our Body

Accepting and loving ourselves implies that we care for our body—by eating wisely, exercising, and taking precautions to prevent illness and exhaustion. These habits promote good health and an increased life expectancy:

- Eating three healthy meals a day, including breakfast
- Avoiding fats and junk food
- Concentrating on grains and high-fiber foods
- Exercising several times a week
- Getting adequate sleep—seven or eight hours each night

5
List the attributes of the perfect male body and of the perfect female body as they are depicted in magazines and on television. Then write your answer to this question: *How has my perception of the perfect body for my sex influenced my acceptance of my own body?*

Student art: "A Powerful Woman," linocut by Amanda Kuhns, St. Agnes Academy, Memphis, Tennessee

- Not smoking
- Avoiding alcohol, or drinking only in moderation

By keeping our body healthy and fit, we have the energy and stamina to enter life-giving relationships. Fitness and health also enhance mental alertness, so even the capacity for working or studying effectively can be affected by the physical well-being of a person. **6**

Appreciating Masculinity and Femininity

- Women are sensitive but illogical.
- Men are insensitive but logical.

- Women should take primary responsibility for child rearing.
- Men should be the breadwinners.

- Women should stick to the liberal arts.
- Men should be engineers or doctors.

We Are More Than Stereotypes

Until the last three decades, statements like those above stood in public opinion as mostly unquestioned truths about what it means to be male or female. Although fewer people would make these comments today than in earlier years, many people still act out of these prejudices. Valuing ourselves as sexual persons does *not* mean that we lock into such **stereotypes** of masculinity and femininity, but that we are free to be full human beings, released from the confines of stereotypes. **7**

Today, psychologists who take a Jungian perspective—that is, follow the theory of psychologist

Carl G. Jung—believe that within each female lies a masculine dimension and within each male lies a feminine dimension. To become whole, a person must bring this dimension to awareness and allow it to be integrated into her or his personality. This realization is hinted at in the Creation story, when God fashions the woman out of the rib from the "earth creature," so that the earth creature will not have to be alone. Maleness and femaleness, the story seems to say, were originally within the same creature. These dimensions of human beings were meant to be united, not separated.

Sexuality not only energizes us to be unified with other people but also urges us to be whole

6
Which of the seven healthy habits causes you the most difficulty? Write a realistic, simple plan to improve on this practice.

7
List any activities that you regularly engage in or just enjoy that are considered stereotypically more proper for the other sex. Write your reflections on how you feel about doing these activities.

persons, using the full range of our intellectual and emotional capacities. This wholeness is what God intended when we were created.

Impoverished Manhood

Consider the following first-person account, by Wayne Eisenhart, of Marine boot camp. Notice how the stereotyped notion of what manhood is all about restricts the recruits and the drill instructor to very limited, violent images of themselves as men:

"The primary lesson of boot camp, towards which all behavior was shaped, was to seek dominance. . . . All else was non-masculine. . . . Recruits were often stunned by the depths of violence erupting within themselves. Only on these occasions of violent outbursts did the drill instructor cease his endless litany of 'you dirty faggots' and 'Can't hack it little girls?' After a continuous day of harassment, I bit a man on the face during hand-to-hand combat, gashing his eyebrow and cheek. I had lost control. For the first time the drill instructor didn't physically strike me or call me a faggot. He put his arm around me and said that I was a lot more of a man than he had previously imagined. In front of the assembled platoon [he] gleefully reaffirmed my masculinity." (Quoted in *Sexuality and the Sacred,* page 337)

The notion of masculinity described here defines men as in control, competitive, dominating, and even violent. They should be tough, not tender and emotional. Above all, men should not be needy. But rather than enhancing or elevating manhood, this notion impoverishes men who are expected to act this way. Such rigid, limited understandings have allowed, even promoted, violent behavior in men. We can see how this notion probably has encouraged much domestic violence and abuse in our society. (It should be noted that even the Marine Corps has moderated some of its former training of recruits away from this stereotyped notion of the "real man.") **8**

"Ain't I a Woman?"

The female counterpart of the masculine stereotype is that women should be soft, dizzy, and helpless. **Sojourner Truth** refuted this notion of being female with passionate conviction. Truth (1797–1883) was a brilliant orator who toured the United States, preaching for the abolition of slavery. She had been born a slave but escaped. She never learned to read or write, but her words were so inspiring that others recorded them. After the Civil War, Truth supported the issue of women's rights. This passage from one of her speeches is a classic argument against stereotypes about women:

8
Write a paragraph agreeing or disagreeing with this statement: *Men still get basically the same message about manhood that the drill instructor gave the recruits.*

That man over there says that women need to be helped into carriages, and lifted over ditches, and to have the best place everywhere. Nobody ever helps me into carriages, or over mud-puddles, or gives me any best place! And ain't I a woman? Look at me! Look at my arm! I have ploughed and planted, and gathered into barns, and no man could head me! And ain't I a woman? I could work as much and eat as much as a man—when I could get it—and bear the lash as well! And ain't I a woman? I have borne thirteen children, and seen them most all sold off to slavery, and when I cried out with my mother's grief, none but Jesus heard me! And ain't I a woman? . . .

Then that little man in black there [a preacher], he says women can't have as much rights as men, 'cause Christ wasn't a woman! Where did your Christ come from? Where did your Christ come from? From God and a woman! Man had nothing to do with Him.

If the first woman God ever made was strong enough to turn the world upside down all alone, these women together ought to be able to turn it back, and get it right side up again! And now they is asking to do it, the men better let them.

Obliged to you for hearing me, and now old Sojourner ain't got nothing more to say. **9**

The Longing to Be Whole

Stereotypes confine us and eventually warp our personality. For instance, if a woman cannot be assertive and independent, she might deny herself the training or education she needs to establish herself in a career suited to her gifts. If a man needs help in a situation but is so afraid to show his vulnerability and to be dependent that he will not ask for assistance, he contributes to his own suffering. In both cases, stereotyping harms the individuals' capacity to be fully alive persons.

The longing that both men and women have to express their feminine and masculine sides—the longing to be whole—comes through in this poem by Nancy R. Smith, entitled "For Every Woman":

For every woman who is tired of acting weak when she knows she is strong, there is a man who is tired of appearing strong when he feels vulnerable.

For every woman who is tired of acting dumb, there is a man who is burdened with the constant expectation of "knowing everything."

For every woman who is tired of being called "an emotional female," there is a man who is denied the right to weep and to be gentle.

For every woman who is called unfeminine when she competes, there is a man for whom competition is the only way to prove his masculinity.

■ *Art (on facing page):* **Sojourner Truth**

9
In your own words, summarize in writing Sojourner Truth's argument against stereotyping women.

For every woman who is tired of being a sex object, there is a man who must worry about his potency.

For every woman who feels "tied down" by her children, there is a man who is denied the full pleasures of shared parenthood.

For every woman who is denied meaningful employment or equal pay, there is a man who must bear full financial responsibility for another human being.

For every woman who was not taught the intricacies of an automobile, there is a man who was not taught the satisfaction of cooking.

For every woman who takes a step toward her own liberation, there is a man who finds the way to freedom has been made a little easier. **10**

Jesus: The Whole Person

A powerful model of someone who transcended sexual stereotypes and used the full range of his intellect and emotions in loving others is Jesus.

Crying is not stereotypically masculine, but Jesus wept. He cried over the death of his friend Lazarus (John 11:32–36), and when he came in sight of Jerusalem and realized that he would be rejected by the people there, "he wept over it" (Luke 19:41). Likewise, Jesus poured the energy of his sexuality into compassion for weak and sick persons and children, claiming care for them as the priority of his ministry and of the coming Reign of God. Jesus told his followers about a God who is a tender, loving father—"Abba," or "Daddy." Jesus was not concerned that anyone would think him feminine. He knew that love calls for tenderness.

When leadership and strength were required, Jesus could express these stereotypically masculine qualities, not because he needed to prove his masculinity, but because love demanded leadership and strength. He was weathered and toughened by a hard life of wandering from place to place. He knew rejection, but he was strong in his convictions, refusing to cower in intimidation from those who despised him. The sensitive and caring Jesus was also the man who drove the exploitative merchants out of the Temple, and who told off the Pharisees because of their hypocrisy.

In short, Jesus acted as the situation demanded; he was free of the stereotypes that confine most people. As a whole person, Jesus gives us a model of what it means to live a full life as a male or a

10
Choose a stanza from the poem "For Every Woman" that most speaks about your experience of yourself. Write an explanation of why this stanza has meaning for you.

Student art: Untitled, acrylic painting by Emily Burns, St. Peter's High School, New Brunswick, New Jersey

female. As we conclude from the Scriptures, Jesus never married, but he expressed his sexuality by directing its energy and power into his ministry. **11**

For Review

- How do the media discourage us from being comfortable with our body?
- Briefly describe three disorders that give evidence of our society's obsession with bodily perfection.
- List seven habits that can promote a healthy body.
- Describe the notion of masculinity that probably encourages domestic violence and abuse.
- In what sense was Jesus a whole sexual person?

When Sexuality Is Distorted

The power and energy of sexuality need to be channeled and expressed through responsible, loving choices. Sexuality can responsibly be directed into friendships, work, creativity, and learning, as well as into a committed sexual relationship with another person.

But the uncontrolled expression of sexual energy distorts what sexuality is intended for—to bond us to others. This distortion is destructive to society and to the person whose sexuality is uncontrolled. Distorted sexuality can have tragic consequences. Noting this, John Updike, whose well-known novels have dealt with many dimensions of distorted

sexuality, remarks: "'Sex is a great disorderer of society. . . . The old naysayers were right at least in this: sex has consequences, it is not a holiday from the world.'" **12**

Let's examine the consequences of some of the distortions of sexuality that we find in our society.

Rape

An extreme but too common example of distorted sexuality is **rape.** This act is condemned by society not because it is sexual but because it is essentially violent, brutal, and dehumanizing. Though usually done by males against females, rape and sexual assault can also be perpetrated by women against men, and between members of the same sex. In a Gallup Youth Survey released in 1994, 28 percent of teenage girls and 14 percent of teenage boys are aware of sexual assaults on themselves or their friends, with 12 percent of the girls reporting that they have been raped.

Some, if not most, incidences of rape are not even recognized for what they are, because they happen on a date or with an acquaintance. But these assaults are rape as surely as is the incident of a stranger jumping out from the bushes to attack. If a man spends money on a woman, or if they have been on a few dates together, he or she may assume that he has a "right" to her—as if she is his property. If she is forced into sex, this is date rape.

Whether committed by a stranger or an acquaintance, rape is a violent act that robs the victim of her or his rights and dignity as a human being. Rape is about power and domination, not about a sexual relationship. Besides the physical harm and violation of rape, it frequently leaves long-term

---

11
Write a description of a time when you were a "nurturing healer" and a description of a time when you were a "strong and confronting person."

12
Bring to class a newspaper article that illustrates the harm that results from distorted sexuality. Write a brief reflection on how the distortion caused harm.

emotional scars that damage the victim's capacity for trusting, intimate relations. **13**

A highly publicized example of a rape mentality in our society was the news accounts of the crimes of the Spur Posse, in Lakewood, California. Nine of this gang of white, middle- and upper-class high school men were arrested for sexual assault, intimidation, and forcible rape. The gang kept score sheets of how many times they had sex. Young women became targets to earn "points" from. Women were not people, but objects—points. The gang members had sexual intercourse for power, control, and status. Though extreme in this case, this mentality is at work whenever someone tries to dominate or hurt another person through sex.

Lust

Lust is the desire to use another person as a "non-person," as an object for one's own sexual pleasure. When we treat others as objects, deep down we believe that they have no soul, that they are not really human. We feel in our gut that they have no value except as they can be used; they are nonpersons. Treating another person as an object is always a distortion of our humanity.

Lust is sexuality gone sour. Because it is so intense, it may seem like love, but it is not. Frequently an individual preoccupied with lust focuses so exclusively on self-gratification that he or she cannot direct energies into the development of friendships, creative projects, service to others, and so on. An eighteen-year-old young woman provides one easily understood commentary on lust:

"Girls often get pressured into having sex by their boyfriends. Most of them have probably heard the line, 'I have those needs.' Maybe they should relieve those needs by lifting cars instead of harassing their girlfriends." (*Take Time to Play Checkers,* page 142)

Girls as well as boys can experience lust. In a 1991 *Newsweek* article subtitled "affection-starved teenagers are giving new meaning to the term boy crazy," advice columnist Ann Landers mused over the twenty thousand letters she received about an article she had written concerning girls aggressively pursuing sex with boys: "'A good many young girls really are out of control. Their hormones are raging and they have not had adequate supervision.'"

Pornography

Pornography reduces sexuality to a depersonalized, secondhand experience of genital sex. It tries to substitute mental pictures, photographs, or movies for human love. In the process, it cheapens and dehumanizes sex, leaving its users empty and deprived of the real relationships that the sexual drive is meant to lead to.

Pornography is a form of deception, ultimately degrading and misleading. It cannot deliver what it promises—sexual fulfillment. It may seem non-threatening to readers or viewers because it demands nothing in terms of a human relationship, but it does not prepare them to relate to real persons. Some people feel powerless or inadequate with real human beings, so they gravitate toward pornography for sexual stimulation and as a substitute for direct human relationships. Pornography frequently involves acts of violence, especially against women, which humiliate and brutalize persons. **14**

13
What are some "lines" that might be used on a date to coerce or manipulate someone into having sex against their will?

14
Describe in writing what you think is the North American culture's attitude toward pornography. Does it fit the view presented here about pornography?

Selling Through Sex

Another example of distortion is the abuse of sexuality by the electronic and print media in advertising—**selling through sex.** Nicole, age seventeen, remarks: "'[Sex is] even used to sell products. It isn't enough just to advertise a car, but there is almost always a half-dressed woman draped over it'" (*Take Time to Play Checkers,* page 143). The implicit message is that if you—a male, the target of the ad—buy this car, you will have women like the one in the ad draping themselves all over you.

Equating commercial products with sexual appeal degrades us because this equation says, "You as a person are not essentially worthy or appealing to others, but you will be if you have this product." Those who abuse sexuality by using it to sell products are simply trying to manipulate people by taking advantage of the powerful and common desire to feel sexually attractive.

Teenage Pregnancy

The drastic increase in pregnancies among unmarried teenagers, as well as the alarming increase in abortions to terminate them, is evidence of distorted sexuality. Whether a baby is aborted or comes to term and is born, the implications of **teenage pregnancy** for the persons involved and for society as a whole are extremely serious. Most seriously, the teenage mother and father are usually too young and immature to assume the enormous task of bringing up the child.

These pregnancies are not the result of responsible, loving choices about sexuality. Instead they usually result from ill-considered, shortsighted decisions and sometimes even from coercion or selfish manipulation. One midwestern married teenager remarked to a reporter:

"I didn't think this could happen to me—not me! My parents sent me to an exclusive school. I had close friends and lived in Hickory Hills. I can't believe I was so naive. I thought getting pregnant only happened to other girls. I'm a fifteen-year-old, and adulthood came down on me like a ton of bricks. One thing I've learned—anything can happen to anybody. Nobody is exempt from anything."

Another story of teenage pregnancy and its consequences comes from the *New York Times Magazine.* A writer interviewed people at random waiting in bus stations in various parts of the country. One of those he spoke with was Anthony Earlston, seventeen, who was en route to a small town in Arkansas. Earlston told the reporter of having been thrown out of his house at age fourteen because of drug and alcohol use, and of his marriage at sixteen to Jerri Lee. His description of their life as

a couple conveys the difficult, unglamorous reality of being teenage parents:

"We dated for about seven or eight months. We started messing around, and worse came to worst. She got pregnant and a baby popped out. But I love him. He's a year and half old. . . .

"When we found out she was pregnant, we went and talked to our parents. They wanted to kill us. But they signed the marriage license. We've been living on our own ever since. It got off to a rough start. She graduated, but I had to quit school, to get a job and everything. I'm a manager of Pizza Hut. Floor manager. It pays six bucks an hour. She works at Engineering Products. She makes plastic parts for them. She works from 11 till 7 at night. I work from 9 in the morning to 10 at night. We make sure we have days off together, because it screws up a relationship when you ain't got no love life, no nothing. We get along great. We have our fights, but we get over them. . . ."

"Sounds like you're handling things well."

"Sounds like it but . . . not actually. Sometimes I'll be sitting up late at night and I wonder what would happen if I didn't have this baby, what would happen if I wasn't married, what would happen if I was living with my parents. I get scared thinking something's going to happen between all three of us. And we're all going to go our separate ways. One of us is going to take the baby. . . . I'm afraid that's going to happen, and I don't want to see it happen. I mean, I get up every night, worrying about that stuff."

Even when people try as best as they can to cope with the results of their unwise choices, the life circumstances they must deal with can wear them down. Recall Updike's remark, "'Sex has consequences, it is not a holiday from the world.'" **15**

For Review

- Why is rape so harmful?
- What is lust?
- How does pornography deprive its users, rather than offer sexual fulfillment?
- What is the message behind advertising that uses sex to sell products?
- What is a serious consequence of teenage pregnancy?

15
Write responses to the following questions:
- In your opinion, why are there so many teenage pregnancies today?

- What are the effects of teenage pregnancy, or the pregnancy of any unmarried woman, on the unmarried mother, the unmarried father, the baby, their families, and society as a whole?

Chastity: Expressing Our Sexuality with Integrity

The Christian vision holds that the virtue of **chastity** is the healthy, integrated way to express our sexuality. Chastity, however, must not be understood simply or primarily as abstinence from sex. At times in our life chastity may require abstinence, but it is not synonymous with either virginity or abstinence; the virtue of chastity is greater than that. Married people, as well as priests and religious, are called to be chaste. Chastity involves above all the integrity of the person, the keeping of one's sincerity and honesty in body as well as in emotion and word.

Sincerity in Body and Heart

Mary Patricia Barth Fourqurean, who has been a campus minister at several universities, wrote an open letter to students about chastity, later published in the Catholic magazine *America*. In it, she acknowledges that the word *chastity* for many people "implies repression or simply the inability to get a date." **16**

But Fourqurean explains that understood properly, chastity is about living a healthy, vital sexual life:

Positively, chastity increases our own sincerity by assuring us that we will not say more with our bodies than we mean in our hearts. It also increases our confidence in the sincerity of others by assuring us (in deed, not word) that our friend seeks more from us than what is skin-deep. Chastity also creates an opportunity for us not to repress but to redirect our sexual energies. . . . *Negatively*, chastity protects us physically from sexually transmitted diseases . . . and AIDS. . . . It protects us emotionally by assuring us that we will not be used merely for someone else's pleasure or power.

Fourqurean goes on to say that chastity means "passionate love" for ourselves, other people, and God, a threefold love expressed in different ways according to our condition in life:

In marriage, chastity does not mean sexlessness but faithfulness, i.e., a *permanent, genital* commitment to our spouse, out of this three-fold love, that is both exclusive and sensual. In celibacy (including both heterosexual and homosexual celibates), chastity means a *permanent, non-genital* commitment to God and therefore to the world, out of this three-fold love. . . . In singleness, chastity means a *temporary, non-genital commitment* to this three-fold love of God, others and ourselves. Many have found this liberating because they are finally freed from having to play sexual games. I tend to image chastity as a *disciplined* warmth, not as ice.

Why Chastity?

Fourqurean explains what she has observed on the university scene:

In my 11 years in campus ministry, . . . I have seen the secret anguish of many students who have been used or abused, and although the fact of this anguish is reported in student newspapers, its extent is not. The hidden experience of these students matters, for they feel deceived by our culture's promises of instant gratification.

16
Respond to this quote: "*'VIRGIN.' It was worse than having herpes. With herpes my friends would be sympathetic and caring. But 'virgin' drew snickers as I would pass in the hallways*" (*What I Wish My Parents Knew About My Sexuality,* page 30).

As a senior man told Fourqurean, "'I think we desire to be deeply challenged and to go for our deepest desires for intimacy, but we end up "settling" for sex.'"

In the same article, a senior woman made these comments about her experience with chastity:

"I read stuff all the time that claims that virginity is unnatural, abnormal or that it makes you a slave to a false idea. . . .

"And yet I don't feel like I'm clinging to old traditions for the sake of security. It's because when I have sex I don't want to say 'Yeah, I guess there's nothing wrong with it.' I want to say 'YES!' passionately with my whole being. Maybe this sounds idealistic, but that's how I feel. Waiting isn't always fun but that doesn't mean I shouldn't wait." **17**

These students' comments point to the reality that sex outside of a committed, permanent relationship is basically dishonest. Outside of marriage, the total, intimate sharing of our body with another through intercourse does not correspond with a total, intimate sharing of our whole life with the other person. It is in some ways an empty gesture, a lie, fooling us into thinking we have given ourselves profoundly because we have experienced something powerful at the physical level. But it does not allow for the deepest love that we seek and want; instead we "settle" for sex alone without all the depth of relationship that intercourse implies.

Sexual Intercourse: Celebrating a Shared Life

Sexual intercourse can bond two people into "one flesh" (Genesis 2:24), but this phrase signifies much more than physical unification. To say that two people are "one flesh" implies that they also reach a depth of knowledge of each other. In fact, in the Bible, another term used for sexual intercourse is *knowledge*.

Intercourse in the context of a total, committed relationship can lead to profound mutual understanding. This is because the commitment allows the two people to become intimate on many levels, not only on the physical level. Those who commit themselves to each other permanently pledge to share deeply the whole of their lives—emotions, struggles, appreciation of beauty, vision of life, attempts to make a welcoming home, a sense of fun, efforts at work, or sorrow from loss or tragedy.

In itself, sexual intercourse does not magically make married partners whole and fully alive. What does bring them closer to fulfillment is the sharing of their life together. When that sharing on many levels is truly happening, then intercourse expresses their love for each other and deepens it. As an act of trust, joy, and emotional and physical renewal, sexual union celebrates the sharing of life in the most intimate way.

17
In an essay, write your reactions to the comments by the two university students.

Two loving and committed people do not instantly have a "perfect" sexual relationship. However, their long-range commitment to each other can take away much of the pressure and anxiety to perform perfectly as sexual partners. One couple described it this way:

> If sexual intercourse is to become the human experience and act of love it should be, it needs freedom from worry, freedom to take time, freedom not to succeed perfectly and [freedom] to try again, in the context of a lovingly shared life. . . . These freedoms cannot ordinarily exist outside of marriage. (Ryan and Ryan, *Love and Sexuality,* page 77)

Chastity before and during marriage ensures that sexual intercourse has this freedom. **18**

For Review

- What is chastity? How is it expressed for married, celibate, and single people?
- What is sexual intercourse meant to express and celebrate?

Created to Be United

The powerful nature of sexuality is both a gift and a challenge. As Fourqurean says, "It is an emotional, spiritual and physical fire permeating our whole life that is as beautiful as it is dangerous." If sexuality were not so powerful, we would not be so wonderfully transformed and enlivened by it. On the other hand, the intensity of sexuality can be difficult to channel into responsible, loving choices. Furthermore, the misunderstandings of sexuality promoted by the media do not help us to integrate sexuality into a whole and healthy way of life. **19**

In spite of the dilemmas that sexuality can present to us, we know that we were created as sexual persons, whose destiny is to be united with others. Whether we eventually marry, remain single, enter religious life, or become ordained, our sexuality will be with us, moving us to break out of our separateness and to seek loving relationships as whole persons.

Dear God,
You created us male and female,
    eager for love like you are.
Thank you for the good sexual energy you give us—
    energy for relating, for reaching out to others.
Help us to treasure our sexuality carefully,
    not to throw it around thoughtlessly.
Lead us to find the right way to express our sexuality
    chastely, passionately, sincerely,
So that we can grow to be the fully alive persons
    we are meant to be. Amen.

18
In writing, compare and contrast the need to have a permanent commitment as the context for sexual intercourse, with the attitudes toward sex that prevail in our culture.

19
Identify two areas of sexuality that most people your age have questions about. Do some library research and also interview teachers, parents, or helping professionals to gain insight about these areas. Prepare a written report.

7

Love:

Seeking Good for Others

What Is Love?

What could be more mysterious than love? It is the essence of much music, poetry, and literature—classical and contemporary—and the subject of endless speculation. People fight and die for it; blood has been spilled because of it since the start of humankind. Love of God has inspired missionaries all over the globe to die as martyrs. Sexuality may be the energy behind our reaching out to others, but love is what we ultimately long for.

Many Forms of Love

Love appears in the human condition in so many forms that at first it might seem impossible to speak of love as one reality. The word *love* encompasses both the passionate love of "lovers" and the familiar, almost unspoken love of two close friends.

Consider, on one hand, the kind of love expressed in Elizabeth Barrett Browning's "How Do I Love Thee?":

How do I love thee? Let me count the ways.
I love thee to the depth and breadth and height
My soul can reach, when feeling out of sight
For the ends of Being and ideal Grace.
I love thee to the level of every day's
Most quiet need, by sun and candlelight.
I love thee freely, as men strive for Right;
I love thee purely, as they turn from Praise.
I love thee with the passion put to use
In my old griefs, and with my childhood's faith.
I love thee with a love I seemed to lose
With my lost saints—I love thee with the breath,
Smiles, tears of all my life!—and, if God choose,
I shall but love thee better after death.

The fires of passionate love have dazzled and energized people throughout time. However, "lovers"

are not the only ones who love. Consider, on the other hand, the love of a friendship that has endured for many years:

Ted and Iggy walked into the diner together at exactly 7:00 a.m., just like they had for the last nine years since retirement. Every Friday morning they met at church for Mass and then headed to the Chat 'n' Chew Diner for what they both called a "high-cholesterol, one-my-wife-will-never-fix-me" breakfast.

"Hi, Margaret!" they both chimed in.

"Must be Friday at 7:00 if you two are here!" she chided, friendly.

"You bet!"

"Margaret, I believe you get prettier each Friday morning."

Margaret beamed. "You old jokers just sit down. I know what you'll order, so don't even say it." She bustled around, readying their standard.

Ted and Iggy eased into "their" booth. If a stranger had walked in and seen them, that person would have thought at one minute that they were planning a bank robbery—their heads bent close together as they talked furiously fast—and at another minute that they didn't know each other—their faces still, in calm repose.

The two men had gone to high school together and had grown up in the same neighborhood. Ted had taken a job as a postal worker after high school, and Iggy had sold men's clothing at one of the big department stores downtown. Each had been the other's best man and godfather to the other's first child.

During World War II, Iggy had been left behind at home because of a rheumatic heart. Every fifth of July since the war, Iggy would tell his wife that that same day in 1942 had been the worst of his life. He had gone with Ted down to meet the train that would take him to San Francisco and then to the war with Japan. Iggy had grieved because Ted was going to war without him.

"Agnes," Iggy would tell his wife, "that's one of the few times I ever cried. I thought I'd never see Ted again."

When Ted had returned from the war, Iggy had been there at the station. The two old friends had shaken each other's hand, but becoming overwhelmed with emotion, they had hugged each other joyfully. "I didn't think you would make it without me!" Iggy had yelled happily.

Then, just for a moment, the smile had left Ted's face. He had looked at his friend seriously, "I wasn't so sure that I would make it either."

After Ted's return, they never talked about the war. With only a few short absences from each other, the two men had stayed close, watched their children grow up and move away, argued about sports, consoled each other when they felt hassled, fished together, and called each other regularly to see what was up.

At age sixty-five, Iggy had "got religion," as Ted said, and he had started going to Mass almost every morning. Now Ted would join him on Fridays, mumbling that once a week was "okay for Jesus, why not for us?" Then the pair would head for their breakfast at the Chat 'n' Chew Diner. **1**

Passionate love and the love of a friendship that has endured a lifetime—both are love, and both give life zest and meaning. The range of possibilities for love is expressed by F. J., a student at Mercy High School in Riverhead, New York, in a series of "equations":

Love squared = gold
Love + one = family
Love - one = mourning
Love halved = heartache
Love divided by one = commitment
Love divided by many = friendship
Love times zero = loneliness
Love times two = faithfulness
Love times infinity = God

The Core of a Christian Lifestyle

Love is the center of meaning in a Christian lifestyle. Love is not a given; we do not automatically love. Nor is love simply a feeling that comes to us, something that just happens. Rather, we must *decide* to love; we must choose it as the focus of our life. This is the essential choice in a Christian's life.

The Law of Love

Jesus gave this blunt answer when asked by a scribe (someone who was an expert in interpreting the Jewish Law) which was the most important commandment:

"The first is . . . 'you shall love the Lord your God with all your heart, and with all your soul, and with all your mind, and with all your strength.' The second is this, 'You shall love your neighbor as yourself.' There is no other commandment greater than these." (Mark 12:29–31)

Jesus' answer was direct: Love is what the Christian life is all about. Jesus lived out this love by giving up his own life for us. No greater love exists than to lay down one's life for others. **2**

Christianity is a religion of love, even though Christians are not always the best models of caring. The religion of Christians—that is, its ultimate concern or focus—is love. Love is at the heart of Christ's mission and is the only real measure of following him.

God Is Love

The First Letter of John says that God and love are one and the same:

God is love, and those who abide in love abide in God, and God abides in them. . . . Those who say, "I love God," and hate their brothers or sisters, are liars; for those who do not love a brother or sister whom they have seen, cannot love God whom they have not seen. (4:16–20)

The whole of Christian tradition has made it clear that love of God and love of human beings are inseparable.

1
When you are about seventy-eight years old, who might be your Ted or Iggy? Could you build such a lasting relationship with anyone you know right now? Write a brief paragraph about the possibilities.

2
Describe an experience when you applied this principle: *Do the good to others that you would have them do to you.*

Nothing Without Love

Saint Paul stressed the importance of love in one of his letters to the Corinthians:

If I speak in the tongues of mortals and of angels, but do not have love, I am a noisy gong or a clanging cymbal. And if I have prophetic powers, and understand all mysteries and all knowledge, and if I have all faith, so as to remove mountains, but do not have love, I am nothing. If I give away all my possessions, and if I hand over my body so that I may boast, but do not have love, I gain nothing. (1 Corinthians 13:1–3)

In these scriptural passages, Jesus, John, and Paul help us get down to the basics: The most important life decision we will ever make is the choice to love.

A Definition

A definition of love needs to encompass the full range of ways of loving—from the passionate love expressed in "How Do I Love Thee?" to the familiar love of friends like Ted and Iggy. One of the most inclusive definitions may be this one:

- **Love** means to seek and then foster the good of others in the context of their concrete situations.

This definition may not sound very romantic, but it will serve us well after some explanation. Let's consider the definition in three parts:

To Seek and Foster

First, love means *to seek and then foster*. Seek and foster are active terms; love demands activity. That is, love entails finding out what another person needs and then doing something about that need. To love means to be active, to exert our power for another.

The Good of Others

Second, love means to seek and then foster *the good of others*. The good of others is the same good we would want for ourselves. Jesus made this very clear when he said, "'You shall love your neighbor as yourself'" (Mark 12:31). If we like to hear affirmative remarks about our accomplishments, we must compliment other people about what they do. If we wish that someone would listen to our problems, we should gladly listen to the persons we love. The good of others is, in one sense, whatever we would wish for ourselves. **3**

3
Brainstorm a list of ways of finding out or seeking what would be "the good" for another person. Compare your list with the lists of two other students.

In the Concrete Situation

Third, love means to seek and then foster the good of others *in the context of their concrete situations*. Love respects a person as he or she is—not as we might wish him or her to be. Each of us is unique, and we wish to be seen that way. So love must take the uniqueness of the other into account. For example, if the person you love does not like bowling but you insist that bowling would be good for him or her, you may be overlooking the concrete situation.

Loving within the concrete situation may require that we take painful or difficult steps for the good of another person, as in the following instance:

Rosemary had been afraid of her father for years; he ruled the family with an iron hand. However, now that she was in her twenties, Rosemary could see that it wasn't just the force of his personality that made her fearful; it was the fact that her father was drunk on almost every occasion that she visited home. He was wildly unpredictable when he had been drinking. This was a man who was in terrible trouble.

In spite of her fear, Rosemary loved her father. She had always been the one he could joke with and show his best side to, in between the fearful times. Her sisters and brothers also loved their father, each in her or his own way. Unfortunately, their mother was too afraid to intervene in order to help her husband with his alcoholism. Because of their mother's own need to escape, she also was becoming dependent on alcohol.

After building up her courage for weeks, Rosemary finally came to this conclusion: Love required that she and the other children, if they were willing, confront their father and mother about his alcoholism and her growing dependency. Regardless of the conflict and

upset feelings that no doubt would be kicked up, Rosemary had to try to help her father get the treatment that he needed so desperately but could not ask for on his own.

When we love another person, as Rosemary loved her father, we affirm that the other has value and that his or her development and needs are as important as our own. However, we do not surrender our uniqueness, our identity. The situation is quite the opposite: In love, the identity of each person is strengthened. Love affirms the beloved. It is power shared. Love creates new possibilities for a relationship. It starts with respect for another person as uniquely valuable and filled with potential. Rosemary could not have made the difficult decision to help her father without believing deeply in the possibilities within him. **4**

Saint Paul: What Love Is Like

Saint Paul summarized many of the characteristics of love in his advice to the Christian community in Corinth:

Love is patient; love is kind; love is not envious or boastful or arrogant or rude. It does not insist on its own way; it is not irritable or resentful; it does not

4
Have you ever known someone who confronted another person out of love? If so, describe in writing what happened.

rejoice in wrongdoing, but rejoices in the truth. It bears all things, believes all things, hopes all things, endures all things.

Love never ends. (1 Corinthians 13:4–8)

Love persists patiently—in times of convenience and inconvenience. Love never ends. But the world we inhabit has become accustomed to looking for quick solutions, immediately fulfilling experiences, and always gratifying relationships. However, people really are thirsty for the witness of those who love deeply.

Why Care?

We are compelled by our very nature to love; we are created to reach out to others. The desire for intimacy is rooted deeply in us. We feel incomplete, limited, and threatened without love. We may try to replace love with frantic activity, superficial socializing, group happenings, work, or the oblivion of drugs or alcohol, but finally we discover that caring relationships are the only ways to fill the emptiness inside us. **5**

In one Gospel story, Jesus raises Lazarus from the dead (John, chapter 11). Jesus' love for his friend brings Lazarus from the tomb and back to life. In our own time as well, love can snatch people from death—whether physical, social, or spiritual death. The wonderful quality of love is that it brings life to everyone involved.

Here is an example of a woman who discovered the truth that love is life-giving, both for the one loved and the lover:

As Carolyn sat at Dave's bedside watching his labored breathing, she pondered, as she had many times be-fore, the miracle that had brought Dave into her life—although at the time she wondered if she had not made a terrible mistake.

Two years before, Carolyn had gotten out of bed one Monday morning and wondered why she had even bothered. Ever since retirement and her husband's death, Carolyn felt lifeless. She enjoyed her old friends and waited expectantly for her daughter to call from Dallas, so that she could hear the little voice of her grandson. But day by day she realized that she needed more, more of something in her life. She was bored.

At Mass the day before, she had spotted a curious notice: "Needed: Mature People to Be AIDS Buddies" and then a phone number. At the time, Carolyn thought it odd that this should be in the bulletin. But as she toasted her English muffin for breakfast, she decided to call the number just to find out what it was about. "Doggone it, I need something to get me going. There's life in this sixty-eight-year-old gal yet," she mumbled to the canary, who answered with an affirming chirp.

Then an unspoken memory pierced her consciousness: the anguish of her friend Martha, whose son had died from AIDS, alone and uncared for. Martha would never forgive herself for having so alienated her son that they had severed all ties. Tears formed in Carolyn's eyes. "Too late, God, too late."

Later that morning Carolyn called the number and, without a lot of thought, signed on for the training. The training itself shocked some of her sensibilities. She had worked hard all her life and raised three kids, but she realized now that her world had been narrower than she imagined. She had never had to talk about her feelings about homosexuals before. After meeting some of the other Buddies she wondered

5
Describe in writing your most recent experience of emptiness or loneliness. Include the following factors:
- **what led up to the lonely time**
- **what may have caused it**
- **how you felt during it**

- **what you did about it**
- **any beneficial effects of this experience**

what everyone was so afraid of—what she had been afraid of. Then she was asked to be Dave's Buddy.

The first meeting with Dave had not gone well. Buddies were asked to visit the person with AIDS on a regular basis mainly to be a support. But Dave demanded more. He was angry at Carolyn, Bill (the program coordinator), the clinic, the medical profession, gay people, straight people, the federal government, the world. Dave wanted someone to heap his anger on. Carolyn caught the brunt of his rage on the first visit. After absorbing an hour-long harangue, she left confused, mad, and hurt.

Even so, Carolyn gritted her teeth, determined to care for Dave. She thought about his gaunt looks, wasted body, shabby apartment, and evident friendlessness. During his tirade Dave had complained about having to move back here from Chicago, about being deserted by his partner, and about his "useless, so-called friends."

For the first year, Carolyn visited once a week. She cooked anything she could think of that Dave could keep down. Despite his persistent grumbling, Dave ate and even gained some color back in his cheeks. Gradually, among the usual angry denunciations, Dave sprinkled stories about the pain of his parents' rejec-

tion, running away at age sixteen, drug addiction, recovery, and all the frustrated relationships. Carolyn began to see the warm, funny, clever sides of Dave as more of the bitterness flowed away in their talks.

After a year, Dave began having one infection after another. AZT, DDI, DDC, and other drugs had lost their effectiveness. Then he lost sight in one eye. Carolyn spent increasing hours with Dave. She often brought flowers to perk up the apartment. Once Carolyn had coaxed him into a support group, he began to have other visitors. She had even managed a reconciliation between Dave and one of his sisters. And Dave and Carolyn talked.

Now he lay dying. Two months ago she had gathered his few belongings to bring to the nursing home. His sight had gone completely. He could no longer get out of bed and had extended lapses into semi-consciousness.

Most of the time Carolyn just came, plumped up his pillows, and sat holding his hand. Her heart was breaking. She was losing her friend. Dave had always thanked her whenever she ended her visits over the past two years. Then as she prepared to leave him that first night at the nursing home, she leaned over and kissed his forehead. His hand tightened on hers.

"Thank you, Carolyn. You've given me more love than my mom ever did. I would've died long ago if it weren't for you. I love you so much."

So now she waited. Grief would take its toll on her, she knew that. But she also knew that Dave had made the last two years of her life vivid, challenging, and alive. **6**

Life becomes centered and purposeful when we use our talents, skills, intellect, and emotions for the ones we love. Giving away love never deprives us; it is the only way we gain life. As Saint Paul reminds us, without love for others, "I am nothing" (1 Corinthians 13:2).

For Review

- What is the most important choice in a Christian's life?
- What did Jesus say were the greatest commandments?
- What people are called liars by Saint John in his letter?
- Give an inclusive definition of love, and briefly explain each part of the definition.
- Supply an answer to the question Why care?

Types of Love

Love is concerned with the good of the other, affirms the other, is patient and enduring with the other. But who is "the other"? Specifying that "other" gives us a good way to categorize the types of love.

Self-love

Self-love may be the least understood of the types of love. It is neither selfishness nor conceit; rather, self-love is essential to loving anyone else: "'You shall love your neighbor as yourself'" (Mark 12:31). Think of it this way: You *will* love your neighbor *only if* you love yourself.

Self-love begins with self-acceptance, that is, the discovery and valuing of the qualities we possess and of who we are. Self-love fosters our best qualities in the context in which we find ourselves. Then we can esteem or value ourselves. We must try to see ourselves from God's vantage point. God loves us unconditionally—even (perhaps especially) when we make a mess of things.

False Messages About Worth

Most people have a hard time loving themselves. A variety of social and psychological factors accounts for this lack of self-love. One significant cause is the false messages given by our culture about what constitutes worthiness. People are told that their worth is measured by ungodly standards, such as how much money they make, how well they do in school, where they live, how beautiful or handsome they are, how much attention they receive, and so on. These things have nothing to do with God's view of human value. All they do is create a big gaping hole that we try to fill with illusions of all kinds to make ourselves feel better— clothes, possessions, bragging, status, power over others, al-

6

Tell the story of a time when someone's care gave you life. This might be presented in writing, as a collage, or as a watercolor painting.

cohol and other drugs, casual sex. God created us and loves each of us just as we are. We do not need any of these false props to make us worthy. **7**

Problem Signals

These signs of having difficulty with loving oneself may sound somewhat familiar:

- She would never go out with me. She probably thinks I'm the lowest form of life.
- I'm too tall! I hate looking down at guys.
- This speech is going to be terrible. The B on my last one was probably just a gift to encourage me.
- I would rather go along with what he wants than let him know what I really think. I cannot let him get mad at me. That would be awful.
- What a bunch of creeps. I wouldn't want to be seen with them.

In each of these statements, the individual is worrying about how she or he will come across to others—in other words, how she or he is "packaged"—rather than simply accepting and esteeming the gift of who she or he is, including flaws. The last example illustrates that a wound in the ability to love ourselves can be evidenced in a conceited or superior outlook, which is another form of worrying about how we look to others. The person who puts others down is usually having a problem with self-love.

Volumes have been written on self-love and self-hatred; psychologists stay busy treating people who do not seem able to love themselves. Despite the appearance of loving others (generous behavior, giving in to others' wishes, and so on), these people do not really love freely from their core, but instead act out of the desire to look better or be liked—a way of feeding the gaping hole of self-doubt and self-loathing. The realization of God's unconditional love enables many believers to break through these barriers to care genuinely for themselves as God cares.

Friendship

Friendship is universal. Saints and criminals have friends. **Friendship** is characterized by mutual caring between two people, usually involving loyalty, support, and a shared view of the world. Friends are capable of helping each other to achieve what is good.

The stories of Ted and Iggy, and Carolyn and Dave demonstrate what friendship is all about. Such deep intimacy is experienced with only a few friends in life. Besides loyalty and support and sharing a similar view of the world, friendship involves self-disclosure, the letting down of our guard to allow the other person to know what is really going on inside us. Our self-disclosure is deeper with our dearest friends, and we are far more vulnerable. Other friends may know a lot about us,

---

7
Complete the following statements in writing with as many comments as you can think of:
- The comments that others make to me that increase my feelings of self-love are . . .
- The comments that others make to me that decrease my feelings of self-love are . . .
Then think about this question and answer it in writing: *Do I love myself as much as God loves me?*

but our closest friends know almost as much about us as we know about ourselves—the good and the not so good, the interesting and the boring. A friend lets us pull off our mask and be ourselves.

When two people can enjoy being together without having to do anything in particular, and when they stay close through disagreements and separation, they have real friendship—the kind that lasts, holding on stubbornly through adversity and always hoping that new life and growth will come forth.

Friendship is so important that it is the subject of an entire chapter in this course. **8**

Erotic Love

Erotic love is the desire two people have for union of their bodies and souls, hearts and minds; it goes beyond mere sexual attraction. This is the love described in many passages from the Song of Songs. Erotic love, like all types of love, fosters the good of the other person; it has nothing to do with lust— treating the other as an object for one's own satisfaction. The specific element that distinguishes erotic love from other types is the yearning for sexual expression of that love. In erotic love, lovers make their own relationship the central foundation upon which to love other people.

From a Christian point of view, the nature of erotic love is such that expressing the love in sexual union implies total commitment of the partners. Unlike simple friendships (of which we may have many), erotic love is meant to be exclusive to the two persons. Saint Paul, echoing the Creation account in Genesis, described erotic love in this picture of what marriage means: "'For this reason a man will leave his father and mother and be joined to his wife, and the two will become one flesh'" (Ephesians 5:31).

Not all married couples reach the depth of commitment, passion, and intimacy that ideally is involved in the union of erotic love. This kind of love will be treated more completely in later chapters on preparing for marriage and marriage itself.

Romantic Love

Romantic love may come most readily to mind when we think of the word *love*. After all, most of the poetry and songs about love throughout history have described this kind of love.

The wonderful feeling of falling in love is probably one of life's peak moments. You may have experienced it already, and you may likely experience it again. Here is one young woman's description of falling in love:

All I can do is think of him. I can't wait to be with him all the time, and what's so fantastic is that he feels that way about me, too. Just thinking of him makes my heart race. We find all these special ways to say I love you—little gifts and surprises. All that matters is that we love each other. This feels so right, so *forever*.

Eventually, this "falling" phase passes into a less intense form of romantic love (no one could stand the intensity of falling in love for very long!), and this carries people into periods of dating steadily and even into engagement. Romantic love can be beautiful and energizing.

However, romantic love is not the whole story— or even most of the story—about what brings and keeps a couple together for a lifetime. Romantic

8
Many times small acts of love and concern from our friends are overlooked. Love often comes to us in small gifts. List ten specific expressions of concern that were extended to you in the last twenty-four hours.

love, precious as it is, cannot by itself sustain a relationship forever. This is why you may fall in and out of love several times with several different people. Although romantic love feels incredibly intense, eternal, and destined, it is not necessarily or even probably so. Most romances will fade in time.

In a marriage, romance will certainly reappear as time goes on, bringing zest and joy to the couple's relationship. But it should not be counted on as a constant to keep the marriage alive, because the feeling of romance comes and goes. A deeper and more solid kind of mature love, based on knowledge of and care for each other over the years, has to sustain a lifelong relationship through good times and bad. When people convince themselves that the only real love is romantic love and they set out on a perpetual quest for romance, they are apt to be disappointed—perhaps even divorced—many times. **9**

Pitfalls of Romance

Infatuation. A pitfall of romantic love is that it tends to set us into an emotional whirlwind that hinders clear perception and good judgment. Infatuation and love at first sight are varieties of romantic love that may provide roots too shallow for love to grow from. The two persons may be so enamored with the thrill of infatuation that they fail to really discover each other. Infatuation is like a roller coaster. It zooms along with everything passing in a blur, and when the cars go plunging downhill, people get dizzy. Infatuation can be a thrill a minute, but like most rides, it ends, leaving us a bit shaky on our feet.

Idolizing. Another problem related to romantic love is the phenomenon of idolizing another person—seeing him or her as perfect, wonderful, the answer to all prayers and dreams. The failure to acknowledge faults in the other person is as unfair

and hurtful as the failure to acknowledge his or her good qualities. In treating someone as an idol, we do not really love the person, we love our *image* of the person. Someday that image, that idol, will probably crumble in the face of evident flaws, and both persons will be hurt badly, particularly if they are married.

Thus, romantic love, rich and joy-filled as it can be, needs to be seen with a certain objectivity.

9
Do you agree that romantic love alone will not sustain a marriage? Support your response in writing with examples.

Student art: Untitled, collage and paint by Mylene Vergne-Lopez, Academia María Reina, San Juan, Puerto Rico

Nurturing and Parental Love

Nurturing Love

Fostering the good of needy, poor, homeless, hungry, or helpless persons is **nurturing love.** Carolyn's care for Dave is an example of nurturing love, although it eventually became a friendship, too.

Nurturing love starts with the belief that all people are our sisters and brothers, so we treat them as we would wish ourselves to be treated if we were in their situation. The Christian Testament is filled with stories of Jesus healing the blind and the lepers, feeding the hungry, and raising the dead. Jesus stated that nurturing love will be the chief criterion for separating the "sheep" from the "goats" at the last judgment, when he will speak these words:

"'Come, you that are blessed by my Father, inherit the kingdom prepared for you from the foundation of the world; for I was hungry and you gave me food, I was thirsty and you gave me something to drink, I was a stranger and you welcomed me, I was naked and you gave me clothing, I was sick and you took care of me, I was in prison and you visited me.' . . . 'Truly I tell you, just as you did it to one of the least of these who are members of my family, you did it to me.'" (Matthew 25:34–40)

Nurturing love is not merely an option for Christians; it is a requirement. As Latin American theologian Segundo Galilea wrote, "Christianity comes to be the only religion where we find God in human beings, especially in the weakest of them. There is no Christianity . . . without a sense of the poor" (*Following Jesus,* page 31).

Parental Love

Closely related to nurturing love is parental love. **Parental love** is the affirmation of one's children and the care and responsibility for them. As in nurturing love, parents exercise their power for the good of children who cannot feed, clothe, and shelter themselves. Additionally, parental love fosters children's intellectual, spiritual, and emotional growth. Of course, parental love, as with all types of love, makes returns to the giver.

Although much of the great love literature is of the romantic sort, some of the wonder and joy of parental love has been described by writers as well. In his poem "Romping," John Ciardi celebrates his small son, Benn:

Student art: "Faces of the Past," clay sculpture by John A. Drago, Holy Cross High School, Louisville, Kentucky

Silly. All giggles and ringlets and never
about to stop anything without fussing:
get down I say! Do you think I took your mother
to beget me a chimp for my shoulder?
I'm forty, boy, and no weight lifter.
Go find some energy your own size.
Get down!—Well, just once more.
There. Now get down, you baby-fat incubus.
Go ride your imagination. No, I don't care
how many kisses you'll write me a check for.
A million? Some banker you are. Still—
a million of anything is a lot of something.
All right. Once more, then. But just once. You hear?

In nurturing and parental love, persons give because the ones they love have such an aching,
sometimes urgent, need for what the givers of love
can provide. But it is not entirely a one-way street.
As the quote about the last judgment and Ciardi's
poem demonstrate, those who need us are gifts to
us as much as we are gifts to them. **10**

Love of Nature

In centering our life in love, we should not assume
that love is confined to people. God has created
the earth as a home for humankind. Just as a married couple want to provide a fitting home for their
children, so we are called to **love of nature**, caring

for the earth as the fitting home of all God's children. In loving the earth, we love all human beings
as well.

When God created the world, God declared that
"it was good" (Genesis 1:18). The earth is worth
loving not only as a home for human beings but
also as a good in itself. In his poem "As Once, So
Were We," Raymond Hamilton speaks of the elements of creation as his family members, with
whom he feels closely connected:

The Earth is my Mother,
She will always be near.
The Sun, my Father,
I have nothing to fear.
The Moon is my Sister,
Standing with me at night.
The Stars are my Cousins
Who guide me in flight.
The Great Spirit is my God
Of life and of love.

Just as with all forms of love, loving the earth
means that we give it respect, understanding, and
protection: we seek to foster the good of the earth.
Loving the earth means that we love it as we love
ourselves. **11**

Love of God

Love of God is almost unimaginable unless we
love ourselves, our neighbors, and creation. As
Saint John said, "Those who do not love a brother
or sister whom they have seen, cannot love God
whom they have not seen" (1 John 4:20). Seeking
and fostering the good of other people and of creation is the school in which we learn to love God,
the creator of all that is.

10
Parental love is a wonderful gift
to parents and their children, but
it demands self-sacrifice. Describe
five sacrifices that your parent or
parents, or your guardian if you
are not living with a parent, have
recently made for your benefit.

11
Describe the following situations
in writing:
• two ways you have cared for
 the earth over the last two
 days
• two ways you could show more
 respect for the earth

A Discovery

Love is the very nature of God. God is like a friend, lover, parent, and creator, but also so much more than we can imagine. One teen expresses her way of discovering and loving God in her life:

I'm writing because I found the answers to my most perplexing questions in life. I'm writing because I found God in myself—I found God in the simplest word I know: *love.* It suddenly dawned on me that all creation was created for a purpose, and all was created out of love. And the human soul—the essence of life—is 100 percent love. And God is love. So, God is present in all of us.

Love is what keeps us together, what binds us, what challenges us. It can't be held or captured—it's as free as the air! And yet it is full and overflowing, but it doesn't strangle us, doesn't kill us. To say "I love" is to say "God is here with me." Every time someone professes love it is a testimony to the existence of God!

I used to believe that to feel the presence of God you had to be meditating. But I've found that in just simply being alive—acknowledging your soul—God is *actively* present. Here, now, inside of me! And it's no cause to feel alarm. It's the warmest, deepest, most secure feeling I have ever known. Because, for once, it feels *real,* and *alive.* I feel loved from *within* myself. For the first time in a long time—love comes from within. It binds me, it overflows, and it's free.

And now I understand why one must love oneself before one can truly love another. It's simply over-whelming. No lights, no spectacular drama. Just simply "being." I understand now that God was always within me. I just needed to learn how to look at God.

(Adelaide Juguilon,
Magnificat High School, Rocky River, Ohio)

Time and Presence with God

This God who is always present to us invites us into a personal relationship. Like any relationship, one with God requires time and attention. If developing a friendship with another person takes time and attention, so does love of God. This act of giving time and attention to being with God is **prayer.**

Sometimes we find God with us in a moment when we are caring for someone. Our time of presence with that person then becomes a prayer or a meditation. Karen DeFilippis shares this reflection on her time with God while caring for her baby:

I've always treasured 2:00 a.m. feedings. It seemed to be the only time that I got to hold my baby without having to divide my time between the other children. . . .

One night as I sat in the dark of my living room holding the baby that had fallen asleep at my breast, I marveled at the gift of life. This gift of life *given to me.* This child, so fragile, so dependent, is loved unconditionally simply because he exists. He grew in my womb and was brought forth in living water, making me so vulnerable, making me see life brand new all over again. . . .

Student art: "World Youth Day: The Lost Group," ink drawing by Nicole Krayneski, Mercy High School, Omaha, Nebraska

. . . I began a dialog with God. I knew in my head that God's love was even more perfect than mine. . . . Two o'clock became a sacramental moment, for I was able to see that the child asleep in my lap was a perfect container for God's love. To look at the face of God and know God's love would be too awesome for me to handle. In the image of my child I could safely encounter the unconditional love of God.

The early morning feeding and the baby became the sacred time and place in which I could connect with God. At some point I became acutely aware of God's love enveloping me. I became the baby lying in the lap of God. . . . At the 2:00 a.m. feeding, I was being fed. Sometime between the dark of night and the light of day I was called by name, and I came to know what it means to be a daughter of God. **12**

All the types of love discussed in this chapter are just facets of the one reality of love, which is God. When we love, we are truly living in God.

For Review

- What is self-love? Why do people have a hard time loving themselves?
- What is erotic love?
- Briefly describe two pitfalls of romantic love.
- In what Gospel story does Jesus identify himself with the poor and the weak? What does he say about how we treat the poor and the weak?
- What does loving the earth mean for our actions?
- Describe the parallel between developing a friendship and loving God.

Love Is a Challenge

Love certainly challenges us, calling us to use all our human potential and all the help and inspiration that God gives us.

When *Love* Is a Trivial Word

Before we consider the challenges of love, we need to step back and think about how the word *love* has become cheapened in our culture. It is not just a matter of using the wrong word; our very understanding of real love has been trivialized by the language we use for things that are clearly not love.

On television, radio, or in everyday talk, we hear comments like these:
- Don't you just love this new shade of red?
- I love pepperoni pizza!
- I love to drive around in the state park.
- I love the view from up here.
- Wouldn't you love to go to the Rockies for vacation?
- If you loved me, you'd do it.

The use of the word *love* in each of these cases cheapens the meaning of real love. The word has been used to sell products and manipulate people so long that it has almost lost its power and true meaning. This situation can be dangerous when we start using *love* not simply to describe things or products or places we like, but to equate the way we feel about objects ("I love pizza") with the way we feel about a person ("Hey, I really love you!"). Thus we need to be careful not to use the word lightly or sloppily, but to recognize the great responsibility and precious gift that is entailed in saying that we love a person. **13**

12
Have you felt God's love? Like Adelaide or Karen, write your story of love. Or if you are not so sure about God's love, write a story of your doubts.

13
Find a printed advertisement that uses the word *love* in connection with a product. Summarize in writing how the word *love* is used in the ad. Does the ad distort the meaning of love as defined in this chapter?

To Love or Not to Love

The most basic challenge of love is whether to choose it, both as a whole way of life and in small, everyday instances. Even though Christian lives are meant to center on love, we often choose against it. We commit violence in big and small ways; we lie, we gossip, we overlook serious wrongs in society. In short, we sin.

To sin is to turn our back on God, who is love. **Sin** is the opposite of love. If love is fostering the good of others, then sin is harming others. But the decision to sin may not be truly conscious or deliberate. Sin may happen through passion, blindness, insensitivity, or sheer inertia. Nonetheless, it is a decision not to love.

Some acts are obviously sinful: for example, physical abuse to another person, stealing, cheating, slander. These are acts of **commission**, which involve actively doing something to harm ourselves or others. But sin can also take the form of **omission**—in other words, the failure to act for the good of ourselves or others and thus causing harm. In the description of the last judgment (Matthew 25:31–46), those who have neglected to feed and clothe the needy are guilty of sins of omission, for, when given the opportunity, they have failed to love those who needed love.

Sins of omission can be collective, or social, as well as individual. For instance, if as a society we neglect to clean up our lakes and rivers now, we are allowing the next generation to drink polluted, carcinogenic (cancer-causing) water, and we are condemning many species of wildlife to extinction. We are failing, collectively, to love creation and our fellow human beings.

The basic challenge of love is to choose it consciously in thousands of daily choices that together make up a person's response to life.

On the Way: Life Skills of Loving

Even with our best efforts, we can reach toward loving relationships but never attain them perfectly. The Christian life, however, does not demand perfection; it asks us to set out on a journey toward loving others as God loves us—to choose a path toward love. Along the way, we need to develop some life skills of loving.

1. Knowledge of the other person. We try to understand the other person in depth so that we can respond to his or her real needs.

Beth thinks about her friend Jim at lunch: "I know he's feeling really awful about that remark Phil made; I could just see it in his face. I think maybe I'll check out if he wants to talk about it by mentioning what I saw. If he doesn't want to, I'll just change the subject and we can at least eat lunch together."

2. Practical knowledge. We develop the skills and know-how that are useful in the ways we want to serve—whether in car repair, listening, or organizing a fund-raiser for hunger.

Gary says to himself before he goes to the hardware store: "I better get things straight. If I make a mess of this plumbing job, Grandma will be worse off than she was before she asked me for help."

3. Flexibility. We are able to respond to change in the other person and to shifts in the relationship.

Len explains to a friend how things are going since his wife began college: "With Barbara in college now, I have to spend a lot more time on housework and taking care of the kids. And she's not as available to me as she used to be. But I want to help. I know how important a college education is to Barbara."

4. Conflict resolution. We bring out in the open what bothers us in a relationship and try to resolve problems in a way that respects the value of both persons.

Jenny says to her friend Maria, "When you say you'll be here to pick me up at a certain time, it's up to a half hour later when you get here. It's been irritating me because I could be doing other stuff while I'm waiting if I know you won't be here for thirty minutes."

5. Patience. We hang in there with the other person through difficult times, and we respect the other person's timetable for growing.

A mother describes to a friend the behavior of her two-year-old daughter: "Lately Alissa has been throwing tantrums when we're in stores. It used to drive me crazy when little Mark did that; I would holler and threaten to spank him to make him calm down. But now I know that this tantrum thing is just a phase for Alissa. So when it happens, I say firmly, 'No, Alissa,' and take her out of the store."

6. Honesty. We are genuine in our caring and do not put on masks to pretend we are something we are not.

Dawn tells her friend about a discussion she had with her boyfriend's mother: "I was afraid that Kurt's mother would think I was a terrible person if she knew about my family and all the trouble we've had. But one night we talked about it, and it felt good to tell her where I've come from. Now we're really close friends."

7. Trust. We let go of our concern about constantly protecting our own interests in a relationship so that the other person can grow.

Don confides to a friend about what hard experience has taught him: "I learned my lesson about trust when Mindy broke up with me. I was trying to hold on to her. I wouldn't let her be with other people

Student art: "The Kaleidoscope of Dreams," ink drawing by Toby McGlinn, Santa Fe Catholic High School, Lakeland, Florida

because I was so afraid of losing her. Now I see that she felt mistrusted and smothered." **14**

8. Trustworthiness. We can live up to the other person's trust in us.

Linda talks with a friend about her relationship with her parents: "After I got caught shoplifting, I thought my parents would never trust me again. They knew I had lied to them several times, too. But instead they told me that they forgave me, that they believed in me, and that I could turn around from this. Now I'm totally honest with them. I wouldn't dream of breaking their trust."

9. Humility. We acknowledge our real situation—our accomplishments as well as our limits and flaws—and recognize that we are like all human beings, no better and no worse. We treat others as dignified and deserving of respect.

Jeremy describes his work at a local shelter for the homeless: "The people who come to the shelter teach me more about life than I ever learned in school. They're remarkable; they know about enduring, suf-

fering, and trying to cope. I feel fortunate that I've had the chance to know them."

10. Hope. We are ready at each moment to foster new growth in a relationship and are open to new relationships without putting heavy expectations on another person.

Julie thinks to herself about getting to know Justin: "I have a feeling that something really special may eventually come out of this friendship—what it will be, I'm not sure. Meanwhile, it's so much fun just getting to know Justin."

11. Courage. We have courage to face the unknown—possible rejection, conflicts, separations, the death of the other, abandonment, and the day-to-day demands of working at a relationship.

Wayne hasn't heard from Arturo in over a week. Wayne is a bit anxious about the possibility of being left out: "Maybe Arturo's tired of getting together with me. On the other hand, maybe I should take the initiative and call him for a change. That's what I'll do." **15**

14
In writing, describe how you have experienced each of the following skills of loving:
- practical knowledge
- patience
- honesty
- trust

15
Write a paragraph from your own experience describing why courage is needed in any caring relationship.

12. Forgiveness. We do not hold the other person's hurtful behavior or wrongdoing over his or her head. We talk about it with the person; then we go forward in the relationship with a generous spirit of forgiveness.

Sally says to her younger sister Megan: "I understand what you did and why you did it. I know you didn't mean to hurt me, even though it did hurt. I forgive you, and I don't hold anything against you. I think we should put this behind us and just get on with things."

We have the resources within us to love, and God's grace is always present in us. After all, God created us to love! However, the skills of genuine loving just described do not come instantly; they develop over a lifetime. When we make the choice to love, we do not automatically possess these skills, but we choose to try to develop them, being patient with ourselves in our attempts just as God is patient with us. **16**

For Review

- What is the definition of sin? What is the difference between sins of commission and sins of omission?
- List twelve life skills of loving.

A Vocation to Care

We are made by nature to love and to seek love. The Christian vocation, or call, is to love. Loving challenges us in ways that draw upon all our resources, but it also energizes us and brings us to life. We have much to learn about love, and at times we all fail at it. Even so, God has claimed us as lovable. If we believe in God's love for us, perhaps we will believe in our own ability to love. **17**

God,
We ask of you guidance—and a little more:
guidance in relationships,
guidance in decisions,
guidance in love,
and guidance in worshiping you.

To love just as Jesus,
to decide just as Jesus,
to relate just as Jesus
is our goal.

We thank you, God, for all your blessings—
for everyday blessings,
for the people we love,
for the sun to shine
and the ground to walk on.

(Peter Murray,
Fordham Preparatory School, Bronx, New York)

16
List two or three skills you would like to develop in your ability to love and care for others. Specifically describe what you would like to work on for each skill.

17
Compose your own prayer for the ability to love and for the gift of love you have been given.

8

Friendship:
Loving with Give and Take

The Goodness of Friendship

What is life without friends? Friends listen to us, take us seriously, make us laugh, lend a hand, have fun with us, pray for us, admire our accomplishments, and console us in our sorrow. Life without friends is lonely and desolate. They are as necessary to the spirit as food and water are to the body.

Through the ages, the praises of friends and friendships have been sung by bards around smoking campfires and written about by poets and novelists. The Christian tradition also tells of many great friendships. In the Scriptures, for example, the friendships of David and Jonathan, Ruth and Naomi, Mary and Elizabeth, and Paul and Timothy are famous. Church history, too, is full of accounts of saints who had deep friendships: Francis and Clare of Assisi, Teresa of Ávila and John of the Cross, Ambrose and Monica, to name just a few. These saints saw the importance of the kind of love that cares for others without any thought of what will come back in return—nurturing love (see page 134). But they also were aware of their need for the mutual love and caring of friendship.

Jesus, the Friend

It might be surprising to think of Jesus as having such give-and-take relationships. We may imagine Jesus as totally giving, not really relying on others to care for him or give him comfort. Yet Jesus had friendships that were significant to him.

One set of Jesus' friends that we know about from several Gospel stories was a family of two sisters and a brother—Martha, Mary, and Lazarus. Jesus used to go to their home in Bethany, a short distance from Jerusalem, to relax and get away from the pressures of the crowds of people who constantly wanted something from him. With

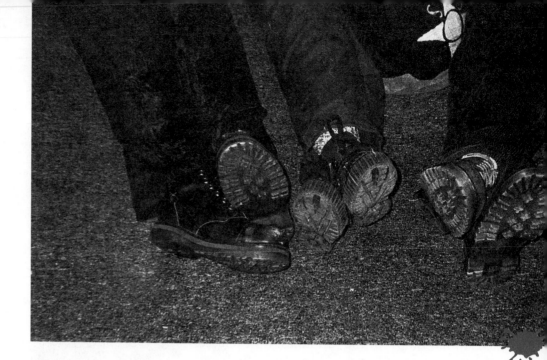

Martha, Mary, and Lazarus, Jesus obviously felt cared for. Martha typically would bustle about taking care of practical things like meals, and Mary would sit with Jesus and simply be present, chatting a bit or listening in her quiet, supportive way. Jesus felt refreshed by being with this family, and he even wished that Martha would stop waiting on him for a while and just sit and be with him as Mary did (Luke 10:38–42). He loved their companionship; it was good for his soul. **1**

Only twice do the Gospels record an account of Jesus weeping: one of them is when he cries over the death of his dear friend Lazarus. Jesus goes to Bethany to be with Martha and Mary in their time of distress. Arriving at the tomb, he sees Mary weeping, and then, "greatly disturbed in spirit and deeply moved" (John 11:33), Jesus weeps. The bystanders remark, "'See how he loved him!'" (John 11:36). So great is Jesus' love for Lazarus that he shows the power of God by raising him from the dead, and Lazarus does indeed come forth from the tomb in a dramatic, triumphant moment.

In another Gospel passage, Jesus speaks of his tender love for his disciples, whom he calls his friends:

"This is my commandment, that you love one another as I have loved you. No one has greater love than this, to lay down one's life for one's friends. You are my friends. . . . I do not call you servants any longer . . . but I have called you friends, because I have made known to you everything that I have heard from my Father." (John 15:12–15)

For Jesus, calling his disciples friends meant that he was sharing everything closest to his heart, indeed his very self, with them.

Someone to Be *Real* With

Jesus' friendships had some things in common with the friendships of many young people today. In the following conversation, several high school students share their thoughts about what friendship means to them:

1
Read Luke 10:38–42. As a friend, are you more like Martha or more like Mary? Explain your answer in a reflective essay.

Stephanie: I know my friends because they let me be me. I don't have to be fake. I want to hang out with people who let me be mad if I'm mad or funny if I want to be funny. Being someone you're not is a pain.

Adolpho: Yeah, and friends are around when you need them, and you are there for them, too. I have a good friend, Sam, who if I have to talk about something is always willing to listen, even if I'm really mad. And he won't spread around what I say.

Chrissy: The other thing about friends is that they always seem to understand what you're trying to say. Sometimes almost better than I understand myself. Jamie's that way, particularly when I'm having trouble with a boyfriend.

David: Friendship is a key factor in an adolescent's sanity. I would be a seriously disturbed kid if my social life wasn't secure. (You might say it's my social security.) I used to depend on my parents for company, learning, entertainment, and problem-solving. Now they are mostly just there for loving. My friends are the building blocks of my independence and self-satisfaction. (*Among Friends,* page 349)

We all need someone we can count on, someone who understands us, someone we can share our closest concerns with. Jesus needed that, too, and he looked for it in his friends. **2**

Friendship as Mutual Caring

As a way of loving, friendship is characterized by mutual caring between two people, usually involving loyalty, acceptance, honesty, availability, generous help, and equality. Its give-and-take quality sets it apart from nurturing love and parental love, which care for those who are needy with no expec- tation that they will love back in the same way. But friendship is a strong foundation for just about all other types of love, including (and especially) the erotic love of persons who commit themselves to each other in marriage. If two "lovers" are not friends, they are not really lovers at all.

An "I-Thou" Relationship

Essential to friendship is that each person see the other as an end, not as a means to an end. In other words, one person sees the other as having value and worth *in himself or herself,* not simply because he or she is useful in bringing about some desired result. The Jewish philosopher **Martin Buber** called the first kind of relationship an "I-Thou," and the second kind an "I-It." When we treat another as a subject with an inner life, we are encountering a "Thou," a word that carries a hint of the sacred quality of the relationship. When we treat another as an object or thing that can be used for whatever purpose seems desirable, we are relating to him or her as an "It." The relationship of friends ought to be an **"I-Thou" relationship**, and that is what intimacy is all about.

A Glimpse of the "Eternal Thou"

Buber saw the "I-Thou" relationships we experience with others ultimately as ways of relating to God, the "eternal Thou":

The extended lines of relations meet in the eternal *Thou.*

Every particular *Thou* is a glimpse through to the eternal *Thou;* by means of every particular *Thou* the primary word addresses the eternal *Thou.* (*I and Thou,* page 75)

2
Ask three people to tell you the qualities they associate with true friendship. Write down their lists and a list for yourself. Compare all the lists and determine the most agreed-upon qualities.

Buber saw encounters with other persons as grace-filled moments, times when we are actually encountering God. Contemporary Christian theology likewise emphasizes that God and the sacred are found in the midst of life, not apart from life or above the everyday. In this understanding, our friendships can be sacred experiences, opportunities for grace. To the extent that we relate to our friends as precious subjects, not objects to be used or manipulated, we are also relating to God. **3**

For Review

- Did Jesus have friends? Give two examples.
- What characterizes friendship? How is it different from nurturing and parental love?
- According to Buber, what is an "I-Thou" relationship, and what does it give us a glimpse of?

3
Complete the following phrases in writing: *I am most treated as a "Thou" in my relationship with . . . An example of that is . . . The person I most treat as a "Thou" is . . . An example of that is . . . .*

Who Are Our True Friends?

We can tell when someone is relating to us as a "Thou" rather than an "It." We know that the person who sticks her or his neck out for us, challenges us, supports us, and brings out the best in us is our friend. The following story of Jorge and Kevin demonstrates what friends are all about:

Being Mexican American in a small town in Montana did not usually present problems for Jorge, but when he became the starting quarterback on the football team, racism reared its ugly head—especially because he won the position from the son of the school board president.

The Buffaloes had not won a single game the season before. The team had been losing for years. The new coach felt pressure to turn things around. When he picked Jorge to start the first game of the season instead of Tim Perkins, the coach knew that he would catch flak. Nevertheless, Jorge had what it took. Tim's main qualification was being the son of J. J. Perkins, school board president, but Tim was also whiny and spoiled.

After the first half of the opening game, the Buffaloes trailed by seventeen points. Jorge had completed five of nine passes, despite having little protection, and he had run for forty-one yards. Even so, when he ran past the stands for the second half, he heard some parents chanting, "Get the greaser out of the game" and other racial slurs.

Even though Jorge served as the entire offense, the yelling and baiting continued during the whole second half. In the middle of the hecklers stood J. J. Perkins, obviously drunk. Jorge looked at Tim on the bench; he just sneered back. By the end of the losing effort, twenty or thirty people had joined Perkins's assault on Jorge. Between the chanted racial slurs, they began yelling, "Tim, Tim, Tim."

Jorge stormed into the locker room, hurt, furious, embarrassed, and sickened. When he hurled his helmet at the wall, Kevin knew he had better intervene.

Kevin was a mediocre guard and an average student, but he was a leader type. He was also the first guy to befriend Jorge when Jorge's family moved into town three years earlier. He and Jorge advised each other on girls, kidded each other incessantly, argued over everything, hung out together, and backed each other up.

"Kevin, I'm quitting the team if Tim's father doesn't apologize. Can you believe it, the school board president yelling 'spick' and 'greaser' out there? I don't care if he *was* drunk." Several of the other players tried to humor Jorge, but Kevin realized that Jorge meant it and had every reason.

At the start of practice the next day, Jorge made his announcement that he would quit unless J. J. Perkins apologized. Some of the players were sympathetic; some were angry at Jorge. The coach remained neutral. The team's lack of outright support angered Kevin. "Well, we'll go to the principal, then," Kevin declared.

The principal tried to smooth things over, but Jorge and now Kevin would not be so easily calmed. They decided to bring their case to the next school board meeting. Quickly word spread through town. Some people divided into camps, but most were embarrassed by the whole thing and wanted it dropped.

By the night of the meeting, both Kevin and Jorge had been harassed by students and parents who just wanted things left alone. For Kevin, not being liked was a new and unpleasant experience, but it strengthened his resolve and his appreciation for Jorge, who had dealt with bigotry all his life.

The school board meeting was packed. Perkins attempted to stack the agenda, but a couple of members stood up to him. Finally, Jorge was asked to speak. His message was simple: He had been abused for being who he was; the school board president should be above such things and serve as a good example; Perkins owed him and everyone in town an apology. He stopped and sat down. Some patches of clapping broke out.

Then the board called on Kevin. He began: "During the last few days I've learned a lot from Jorge about courage, self-esteem, and dignity—things that our school board president could learn. I've also learned a bit about being ridiculed, disliked, and harassed. But it's all been worth it because, you see, Jorge is not just a star football player and a good student. He's my friend. So . . ." Kevin's voice trailed off, and he quietly returned to his seat.

Eventually, the issue was resolved, but not that night. It was not until Jorge, Kevin, and some of the other players refused to play in the next game that J. J. Perkins finally issued an apology. For a long time, some people wouldn't talk to Kevin. Jorge lost some of his enthusiasm for football, but he played as hard as he could. One thing continued to grow—their friendship. **4**

We can determine who our real friends are by asking these questions:

- Do we bring out the best in each other?
- Are we loyal to and honest with each other?
- Is our relationship mutual and equal?
- Do we accept each other for who we truly are?
- Are we generous with each other?

4
Pretend you are either Jorge or Kevin ten years after this incident. Write a letter to the other person, reflecting on what the incident meant to your friendship and how it has affected you these past years.

As is probably obvious from this list of questions, the way that we *get* true friends is to *be* a true friend ourselves. So the questions we can use to consider whether the people we spend lots of time with are really our friends are the same questions we need to ask of ourselves.

Bringing Out the Best?

Friendship—like all love—means seeking and fostering what is good for the other person. Friends encourage us to be the best person we can be. They urge us to use our talents, to make positive decisions, and to grow into the most dynamic, loving person we can be. And we do the same for them. As one of the biblical proverbs says, "The righteous gives good advice to friends" (Proverbs 12:26).

A thirty-two-year-old woman who became an anthropologist attributes her achievements to her friend:

"I didn't really know I was smart until I became friends with Myra who's a brilliant woman. I'd say something to her and she'd look impressed, like, "Wow, that's clever," and I used to be surprised. It was my friendship with her that enabled me to go back to graduate school, get my Ph.D. and become a college professor. I still have to pinch myself to make sure it's real." (*Just Friends,* page 40)

Friends see our potential and tell us about it. They let us know that we can be more than we may imagine. They are people who prompt us to say to ourselves, "I like who I am when I'm with that friend!"

Friends who bring out the best in us do things like these:

- remind us that we actually prefer to dance rather than get smashed
- point out the best features of our compositions for English class and tell us to "write some more, just like that"
- let us know when a better job has opened up and encourage us to try for it
- urge us to take a hard course that will challenge us instead of a snap course that will bore us
- compliment us on good decisions, even if they are not popular **5**

5
Complete this statement in writing: *My close friends have brought out the best in me when* . . . (Be specific.)

Loyal and Honest?

Newspaper columnist Walter Winchell said that "'a friend is someone who walks in when the rest of the world walks out.'" A real friend will not desert us when the going gets rough. As Jesus told his disciples, "'No one has greater love than this, to lay down one's life for one's friends'" (John 15:13).

This little fable by Aesop praises loyalty among friends:

Two friends were travelling together when a bear suddenly appeared. One of them climbed up a tree in time and remained there hidden. The other, seeing that he would be caught in another moment, lay down on the ground and pretended to be dead. When the bear put its muzzle to him and smelt him all over, he held his breath—for it is said that a bear will not touch a corpse. After it had gone away, the other man came down from his tree and asked his friend what the bear had whispered in his ear. "It told me," he replied, "not to travel in future with friends who do not stand by one in peril."

Genuine friends are proved by adversity.

Lots of "bears," or adversities, threaten us and our friends: pressures to drink excessively, disapproval of a powerful clique at school, small acts of betrayal, family breakups, and broken promises. Friends loyally try to help each other out along the way.

When a friendship is honest, the friends can be open and frank with each other and expect confidentiality. Even when the truth seems ugly, a real friend will listen, try to understand, and respond with what is on his or her mind. He or she will not reject us for telling the truth about ourselves, although our friend may urge us and support us to make a bad situation better.

Honesty may also include telling our friend a painful truth about herself or himself. Bill, a carpenter, makes clear what a loyal and honest friend did for him: "'A friend is someone who tells me the truth about me. I want to know when my work stinks or I'm being hurtful or stupid. I expect my friends to save me from myself'" (*Among Friends*, page 44). **6**

A loyal and honest friend does things like these:

- listens to our interminable tale of woe when the love of our life tells us to take a hike, but then eventually suggests when we have beaten this dead horse enough
- drives us to the hospital at three o'clock in the morning and stays with us when a family member has a heart attack
- indicates that we have had one drink too many and should not drive, and when we get angry, stays, persuades, listens to our ranting and raving, and drives us home
- tells us without shame about his or her need for help in chemistry and then accepts our help

6
Briefly describe a time when a friend "saved you from yourself" by being loyal and honest.

Mutual and Equal?

To be genuine, friendship must be a two-way street. We give and receive mutually and, over time and through various ways, equally. When a relationship becomes one-sided or lopsided, then it ceases being true friendship: it might be nurturing love or an acquaintanceship, but it is not friendship.

One woman said of her friendships, "'In my close friendships there is a high degree of giving and receiving. What I mean is that things that are important to each of us are expressed and reacted to by each of us'" (*Worlds of Friendship*, page 16). Essential to true friendship is giving and receiving.

Friends with a mutual, equal relationship must do the following:

- each initiate getting together: one friend will call and invite the other to a baseball game that night, and a week later the other friend will say, "Let's go . . ."
- talk together about where to go for lunch rather than one person deciding all the time
- give each other gifts without being reminded that a gift might be appreciated
- tell each other what is on their mind and in their heart so that each knows about an equivalent amount about the other—for example, if I tell you about my fear of failure, at some point you will tell me about your fear of being too skinny; or if I tell you my dream of becoming a volcanologist, you dream out loud about becoming a world-class windsurfer. **7**

Accepting of Who the Other Is?

These two students explain the importance of acceptance in a friendship:

Patrick: If a friendship is a real friendship, both people know and accept each other's good and bad qualities. That's a real test of friendship because it's easy to deal only with someone's good qualities.

Annie: I try to turn my friend's bad qualities into something funny as a way to accept them. It's like seeing the glass half-full instead of half-empty. Lou Anne is always forgetting things. Then she does this, "Oh, God, I did it again" and sort of jumps up and down. Now we call it her Loulou dance. When she starts the "Oh, God," I start jumping up and down with her. Then we laugh together, making a joke of it. It helps both of us not feel frustrated so often.

Student art: Untitled, watercolor painting by Catherine Williams, Mercy Academy, Louisville, Kentucky

7
Think of your closest friend and then answer this question in writing: *Is my relationship with [name] mutual and equal? How so?*

All of us have our foibles and faults. Our genuine friends accept the total package of who we are, "warts and all."

However, acceptance does not mean tolerance of just any type of behavior. For instance, if a friend tells us she is going to kill herself, we do not just say, "Okay, I accept you no matter what." Our friendship demands that we do everything possible to talk her out of it, stop it however we can, and help her find alternatives and hope. Acceptance means helpful and wise support.

In situations less serious than a potential suicide, acceptance also may include some confronting or challenging of the other person on certain behaviors that cause a problem. For instance, "I know you didn't have a chance to study, but I don't feel right letting you copy off me on the test." We need to remember the first criterion of true friendship, too: Do we bring out the best in each other?

Friends accept each other when they do things like these:

- overlook annoying foibles that are not hurtful
- refuse to condemn each other for past mistakes or even new ones
- see each other's essential goodness and overlook superficial things like fashion, size, shape, hairstyle, and popularity
- offer alternatives to problems, realizing full well that the other person must freely make his or her own decision **8**

Available and Generous?

Generous acts may come from people other than our friends, but they are especially important between friends. Nowadays, when people's schedules tend to be so full, one of the most appreciated acts of generosity is the gift of time. A young woman tells of her friend:

I had just broken up with my fiancé. I found out he was running around with one of my best friends. So I not only lost him, but her, too. I was livid and so deeply hurt. What a wreck! I would go from crying my eyes out to throwing things around my apartment.

Then Brian called. He's one of my oldest friends—ever since we worked together on a ministry team in college. We call each other once a week, even though it's long distance, and he doesn't make much money. I started blubbering and then just wailing loudly. I must have sounded at the end of my rope, not my usual confident self at all. So he drove down from San Francisco—about an hour's drive. You have to understand, it was like nine at night when he called.

8
Make a list of three things about you that a close friend might find difficult to accept. Then list three things about one of your friends that you find hard to accept, but do accept anyway.

Anyway, he got there about 10:30. I went through my whole crying, ranting, hurt, angry tirade. Used up a box of Kleenex and must have drenched the shoulder of his shirt. He just hugged me when I needed it, listened, agreed that my ex was a jerk and my friend just as bad. By the time I finished getting the whole mess out, I was exhausted, but felt much relieved. He left at 3:00 a.m. and had to work the next day.

I hate to think what I would have done if Brian hadn't come. Phone calls are nice, but there's nothing like a real shoulder to cry on, that physical presence of someone who I know cares for me. Brian's a sweetheart. I'd do the same for him, but I'll always be grateful for what he did. Anyway, I sent him some gift certificates for the mint fudge ice cream he adores; I owe him a lot more, but friends like us don't need huge things to say thanks with.

A generous friend will do things like these:
- make a detour on a trip just to see a friend
- make her or his house the other one's home away from home
- take a friend to a job interview when the friend's car breaks down
- lend favorite clothes to the other
- go to see the other in a game or performance instead of doing something he or she prefers **9**

Two people choose to be good friends, although we are not always aware of what draws them together. Friendship, like much that is holy in life, is often a mystery that defies analysis.

When we choose to be good friends, we take on the responsibilities of being loyal, accepting, honest, available, generous, and good for each other in a mutual and equal way. Friendship is a great gift, and not given lightly.

The poem "Friendship," by Kathryn Crossley, paints a picture of the tentative first phases of risk taking in a friendship that grows:

My milieu is the shallow end of the pool
along with the cowards and children.
So what am I doing in the deep end,
treading water and calling your name?

Because you emboldened me with a smile
and spoke encouraging words
is no reason for me to be in over my head—
striving to be better than I am.

Still . . . because I know your hand is near
and ready to reach out to me,
my fears are ebbing away.

Look at me—
I'm swimming. **10**

For Review

- List the five qualities that can help us determine who our true friends are. Give an example of each quality in action.

9
Think of four instances when you have been a generous friend and four instances when your friends have been generous to you. Even if you have thanked them before, thank them again today, in person, over the phone, or in a note.

10
In one page, describe a time you took a risk to initiate a friendship, or wanted to but did not.

Student photo, facing page:
Untitled, black-and-white photo by Joseph Emmons, St. Viator High School, Arlington Heights, Illinois

Levels of Friendship

Close Friends

Most of us have only a handful of friends who meet the criteria we have been describing for true friendship. In fact, we are fortunate if we have even one person in our life that we consider a deep friend. Ask yourself, Is there *one* person in my life—whether a classmate or team member, a teacher, a family member, or whatever—to whom I could disclose *anything* about myself? (Remember, the important thing is that you *could* disclose anything about yourself, not that you have already or should). If you can answer yes to that question, you are certainly blessed.

Beyond such a **close friend**—and everyone needs to have at least one—are the other friends who meet the criteria of a true friend in varying degrees. No one is perfect, and our friends certainly cannot be expected to be. But we can look at least for inklings of those qualities in them.

Other relationships—acquaintances, collaborators, or buddies—may have some of the qualities of friendship, but lack some important elements. These relationships may become true friendships, but they are also valuable just as they are; they play different and important roles in our life. Not every relationship can grow to a deep level, and we should not expect that of every relationship.

Acquaintances

Coworkers, schoolmates, neighbors, and social contacts with whom we touch base occasionally may be **acquaintances.** We know who they are and a little about them. We say hello to each other and might make small talk with them. Other acquaintances might be the school secretary, a gas station attendant, a hairstylist or barber.

In trying to describe his acquaintances, one young man said:

"There are many people that I like but I wouldn't call them friends. I guess acquaintances is a better description. These are people that I see and do certain things with. Like some of the people I work with. We pass the time of day and joke around. But we never get personal in any way." (*Worlds of Friendship,* page 22) **11**

Collaborators

People who have a common interest or project that they are working on together are called **collaborators.** In these relationships the people come together because they each contribute something useful to the task. The relationship may be lopsided—that is, one person may have more power, money, prestige, or intelligence than another. Or the collaborators may be about equally matched. But when the project is done, the play performed, the season over, collaborators do not necessarily continue the relationship.

Here is an example of a collaborative relationship:

Dean and Pam had been acquaintances at Lourdes High School, but did not hang around with the same people very much. During freshmen orientation at college, Dean spotted Pam waiting in line. He was desperate for a familiar face. As it turned out, so was Pam.

Even though it soon became apparent that they had little in common, they attended events and met at the student union to eat together. Pam, ever the extrovert, soon became acquainted with many of the other freshmen. She also quickly found her way around the college bureaucracy. Even though she got somewhat tired of Dean's enthusiasm for football and computers, he did introduce her to some of the people in his dorm.

For his part, Dean liked Pam well enough. However, as he slowly felt more comfortable with the new people, he called her less often. By early November, Dean and Pam seldom made contact.

Collaborative relationships are most often like this one: we form the relationship, find it helpful for a while, and then it ends when the collaboration seems no longer necessary. For Dean and Pam, it was useful to "collaborate" on the task of getting accustomed to college, but their relationship was not headed for deep friendship. It is okay to acknowledge that some relationships have limits. **12**

Buddies

Buddies usually form around a mutual interest or activity. For instance, two men who might never have crossed paths, one an African American pediatrician and the other a Polish American plumber, play on the same YMCA basketball team for several

11
Draw up a list of five acquaintances. Which one of them might become a close friend? How could you nurture that relationship?

12
In a short paragraph, describe a collaborative relationship you have been in.

years. Occasionally they will go out for a beer together, but their relationship always revolves around basketball. They are buddies.

Activity-based

A buddy or pal relationship relies on activity. If one of the buddies cannot take part in the common activity, the relationship often dissolves. This happened to Connie and Michael, whose relationship focused on tennis. When Connie broke her ankle, her tennis days were put on hold for several months. Michael liked Connie, but he quickly found another tennis partner. By the time Connie was back on her feet, Michael was friendly but never asked her to play tennis again. Buddies like Connie and Michael need some shared activity, or the relationship evaporates.

When Buddy-ism Reigns

Many men, more so than women, depend almost exclusively on buddy relationships. Friendship in the sense we have been describing it in this chapter requires more time and emotional commitment than some men wish to make. A lot of men also back away from being vulnerable with anyone other than their spouse or girlfriend. As a result they stick with buddy relationships, as this thirty-two-year-old man describes:

"A buddy is a guy you can have a beer with and kibbitz around. We mostly talk about sports and cars. . . . I don't think of these buddies as really close friends. I don't have any close friends and neither do most of the guys I know. I think a friend is a guy you get close to, someone you can really unload with. But that's not part of my life and I don't feel like I am missing anything. With buddies it's all out in the open and you don't owe anybody anything." (*Worlds of Friendship*, page 143)

Unfortunately, many men in our culture are raised with this man's attitude about close friendship. Affected by a false sense of independence, they feel that they should not owe anyone anything or be close to other men. This would make them vulnerable and show them to be "weak" to their male peers. As a result, men who have no close male friends grow almost completely dependent on a wife, a girlfriend, or some other woman for emotional support. This dependency can strain the relationship unbearably. **13**

Buddies are fine, and it is wonderful to have lots of them with whom to have a good time. But they cannot fill the need we have for listening, understanding, and emotional support as life goes on and we face crises and limits. Many middle-aged men find themselves isolated, lonely, and empty, especially as they grieve over a deceased spouse or parents, diminished physical ability, and all the other losses that build up with age. A close male friend could supply the help to get through those times, but men who have had only buddy relationships all their life will be hard-pressed to shift into developing deep friendships.

Relatives as Friends?

An old adage says, "You can pick your friends but not your relatives." This is quite true, but some **relatives** can be friends, too. Our relationship with a brother, sister, or cousin may seem to have all the characteristics of a friendship, except choice. Even then, our friendship with that person is still a

13
Agree or disagree in writing:
Young men of my generation know how to be close friends, not just buddies.

choice. Sisters who have a close relationship are fond of this saying: "Chance made us sisters; hearts made us friends."

Members of a family have a lot of history tying them together. Even painful parts of the story link members of a family. This common story can be the foundation of a wonderful relationship, or it can be the death of it. Another facet of family is that seldom is equality achieved in a family relationship, especially due to age differences among family members.

However, relatives can have a special friendship with each other in a way that others cannot. A young woman comments about her relationship with her brother:

"It's the shared experience that makes for a kind of closeness that's different than with friends. There's a special sense, even if it's not always the kind of intimacy you have with a close friend, that comes with sharing that much, with having so many shared memories—this house and that dog, and a mutual relationship to parents. And we look like each other too. There's something there that's intangible. Imagine, someone who's recognizably your brother; that's pretty special." (*Just Friends*, pages 25–26) **14**

For Review

- Describe three kinds of relationships that have some of the qualities of friendship but lack some important elements.

Developing Friendships: Types of Intimacy

Friendship does not happen automatically. It begins and is developed in moments of **intimacy**—that is, close association and contact that results in bonding between two persons. Intimacy can develop in just about any life activity or context that the two people share. Intimacy in one area of their relationship may lead to closeness in another area, and then genuine friendship may grow between

14
Do you have a family member with whom you share a special bond? Describe your relationship and how it is like or unlike your other friendships.

■
Photo: Men who became friends under the crisis conditions of war gather by the statue of the three servicemen near the Vietnam Veterans Memorial in Washington, D.C.

them. Acquaintances, collaborators, buddies, and relatives can become close friends as they find intimacy of various types, such as the following:

Work intimacy. When people share tasks that bond them to one another in affirming ways, they experience work intimacy. Sharing responsibilities, decisions, and the satisfaction of a job well done brings people together because they can appreciate one another and feel mutual support. Think about how much time you spend talking about your work—which is being a student—with the people around you. Schoolwork is a point of contact and a shared experience that can bring people together.

Emotional intimacy. Persons who share significant experiences and feelings that touch them in important ways have emotional intimacy. Most of us need—and perhaps have—someone with whom to communicate our sorrows, joys, angers, disappointments, and exhilarations, someone who will accept these feelings as important and maintain our confidences. Emotional intimacy can become the core of our deepest friendships.

Intellectual intimacy. People who can talk about ideas and opinions, and challenge one another to stretch their minds know the rewards of intellectual intimacy. They might exchange ideas about a movie, a book, or an exciting new computer program.

Crisis intimacy. Imagine that you are a photographer for the yearbook staff. You finish developing the photos for the whole book—including the final photos of graduation and all the year's activities—and you and the editor put them with all the layouts in the overnight mail to the publisher, just in time for the deadline. Two days later you find out the photos and layouts were apparently lost or destroyed in the mail. You and the editor turn to some people you trust, and you all stay up until the wee hours to develop the photos again and to try to reconstruct the layouts. As you work together, everyone talks. You begin to see the strength of these people. You have experienced crisis intimacy, which happens to people in disaster situations. For example, lifeboat survivors of a sinking ship, victims of war, and soldiers in the same platoon during battle frequently experience some of the most intimate moments of their lives. Veterans who come to the Vietnam Veterans Memorial in Washington, D.C., to see and touch the names of their dead comrades may weep openly, illustrating that crisis can bring a tremendous depth of intimacy.

Common-cause intimacy. The commitment of people who fervently share an ideal or cause often produces common-cause intimacy. For example, people in the environmental movement experience a genuine closeness with other members of the movement because of their strong, personal involvement in the common cause of the earth.

Spiritual intimacy. The intimacy between people who share a relationship with God or a similar sense of the meaning of life is spiritual intimacy. It may be expressed in religious practices—worship and shared prayer—or in simple conversations

about life and purpose. Young people who have gone on a retreat together may find that they share spiritual intimacy.

Aesthetic intimacy. Watching a brilliant sunset, admiring an oil painting, or listening to a jazz quartet—when two persons appreciate beautiful scenes, music, art, literature, or movies together, they experience aesthetic intimacy.

Recreational intimacy. Two women who jog together every morning might become close on the level of recreational intimacy. Doing something playful together can allow individuals to drop their masks and be themselves. This honest way of relating also fosters intimacy.

Creative intimacy. Two avid gardeners can talk about miraculous varieties of cucumbers or roses with such enthusiasm that they find each other's company exhilarating. Likewise, parents, who are nurturing new life in their children, find much to talk about—with each other and with other parents. The process of creating together brings about creative intimacy.

We can appreciate the opportunities for intimacy that exist in almost all areas of life: at work, in church, at school, in the library, in a restaurant, during a misty morning jog, or at an art gallery. Intimate relationships can be nurtured into loving ones—true friendships—if we use some initiative and a little imagination. **15**

For Review

- List and briefly describe nine different types of intimacy.

15
Write down the names of six of your friends in a column, skipping a line after each name. Next to each name, indicate the type or types of intimacy that you share with that person. Next to the names of your three closest friends, answer this question: *What types of intimacy could I further develop with this friend?*

When a Friendship Ends

Even good friendships can come to an end. Sometimes the ending is peaceful, natural, and positive; at other times, it is painful, bitter, and hurtful or resentful.

Buddies, collaborators, and acquaintances may just slip out of our circle of contact without setting off alarms or causing significant ruffles. But the end of a true friendship does not go by without notice. We feel the friendship ending with a heavy heart. Here is one inexplicable but poignant account of the end of a friendship, by poet Langston Hughes:

I loved my friend.
He went away from me.
There's nothing more to say.
The poem ends,
Soft as it began—
I loved my friend.

Why End?

The reasons that friendships end are many, but the most common are these:

Distance. Despite phone calls and letters, friends five hundred miles apart may find it very difficult to maintain their closeness. Over the years the intensity of the relationship diminishes.

Changes in each person. People naturally learn and grow beyond where they were. Sometimes a friendship ends when one person changes and the other person does not, or when both people change in different ways. For example, if your friend begins to be absorbed in country music and car racing, and you have turned to musicals and ballet, your friendship might melt down.

Competition and envy. Friends should applaud and honor each other's successes, but sometimes they are threatened by each other's achievements or good luck. Maybe they are insecure about themselves or afraid of being left behind. In any case, the worm of envy and competition invades the relationship, eating away at it and eventually destroying it.

Money and favors. Friends may help each other out financially, but the arrangement can turn sour. Unpaid or slowly paid loans or unreturned favors can lead to resentment and endanger a friendship.

Overdependence. A relationship in which one person conforms to every wish of the other simply to hold on to him or her can masquerade as a friendship, but it is actually a form of destructive dependency. Devotion to another person may look like love. However, in an overly dependent relationship, the uniqueness and individuality of each person is not respected. One person twists his or her personality and interests to coincide with the other's. The dependent person may fear that if he or she does not conform, the other will reject him or her. This is not friendship. It does not foster the good of both people. There is no mutual respect or care.

Betrayal. Your closest friend starts dating your girlfriend. A secret you shared with a friend is suddenly making rapid headway through the student body. You happen to overhear your friend making humiliating, sarcastic, and untrue comments about you to a circle of other people. Betrayal is equivalent to guerrilla war in a friendship. You do not know where it will hit next, but if you worry about it, it can destroy your sanity. **16**

16
Recall one of your important friendships that ended. Describe the forces at work that caused your friendship to end. Then answer this question: *Knowing what I know now, could we have saved our friendship?*

Letting Go

Listening, understanding, and forgiving might patch a friendship damaged by envy, loans unpaid, and even a betrayal. Indeed, friendships have to be worked at. They demand some self-sacrifice. On the other hand, sometimes we have to let go so that we can get on with living.

It helps some people to let go if they formally close the friendship. For instance, at lunch they may thank one another for what was good in the relationship and wish each other well. One friend may write a letter, expressing her or his sadness about a betrayal, forgiving the betrayer, but ending the relationship. If a friend has simply withdrawn and does not want to communicate, you may choose to wrap things up by putting away reminders of the friendship, such as photos and souvenirs.

A key to recovering from broken friendships is to remember that the lost friends once cared for us and gave us part of their life. If they were true friends, even though distant now, they live on inside us in the confidence they gave us, the fun and laughs we shared, the acceptance we found. And we will always have the treasure of knowing that by being a friend and investing in friendship, we ourselves have grown. Friendship is ultimately a gift that cannot be taken from us, even though our sadness may tell us otherwise for a while.

For Review

- Explain the six factors that can contribute to ending a friendship.
- Give two suggestions for enabling a person to let go of a friendship.

A Priceless, Sacred Gift

Our friends bring out the best in us, accept us, and support us. They can be trusted for their loyalty and honesty. Our relationship with friends is mutual and equal. When we are in need, our friends are available and generous. They give us a gift that transcends our ability to thank them. Even so, we have to work at these relationships because friendships can be fragile, destroyed by insensitivity or just neglect. We need to treat friendships as sacred, as encounters with a person we love, a "Thou"—but also as glimpses of the "eternal Thou," God.

If a friendship ends—no matter what the reason—we still have been given a priceless gift that cannot be taken away. For a short or long period of time, someone has shared their life's energy, their talents and wisdom, and their heart with us. Friendships bring us to life, and even when we have lost a friend, we have gained life.

Gratitude for our friends overflows into the desire to be a good friend to others, as in this prayer:

Today I acknowledge the joy that friends bring into my life. I give thanks to God for the friends with whom I share joy, laughter, companionship, comfort, and understanding. Thanks for my friends who welcome me, who make me feel comfortable in just being me. I think of myself as a friend to all, reaching out and welcoming. I can reach out to others by showing a sincere interest in them. Thank you, God, for making me feel welcome in you. Help me to make others feel welcome too. Amen. **17**

(JulieAnn DeSantis,
Notre Dame–Bishop Gibbons School,
Schenectady, New York)

17
**Write your own friendship prayer
for your friends.**

9

Communication:
Sending and Receiving Messages

RT WASHINGTON
SOUTH OAK
115, MO 63155

JOHN DAVIS
1842 WEST L
COREY VILLE

ROSE SANCHEZ
49 EAST ALAMEDA
SANTA FE, NM 87501

KATIE BROCK
324 NORTH OA
APPLETON, ME 0

JEFF WHEELER
R.R. 2, BOX 67
NORFOLK, NE 68701

Our Need to Communicate

Friendship relies on communication, the sending and receiving of messages, to help it grow. When we can talk freely and honestly with someone about our feelings and thoughts, ambitions and problems, we know that we have a close friend. Intimacy of various kinds, even the kinds that involve less self-disclosure, like recreational intimacy and work intimacy, depends on the sharing of thoughts, feelings, and meaning that makes up communication. The everyday business of life—the activities of shopping, learning, going to work, helping someone with directions, and so on—requires that we send and receive messages.

In fact, communication is a crucial bridge between people—friends, acquaintances, enemies, members of different social groups, nations. When communication breaks down, relationships break down. The dynamics of communication are complex, and psychological experts are often called upon to help groups and families figure out how their communication has broken down (if it ever existed) and how it can be repaired or established.

When Communication Breaks Down

At the extreme end of the spectrum, where relations between people or groups is negative or actively hostile, we see small instances of antagonism flaring up into major episodes of violence. A high school student from New York City wrote this account of an incident between groups that were not used to communicating with each other in a constructive way. A relatively minor provocation, supposedly just "having fun," turned into a violent racial incident, fueled by prejudice on both sides:

Splat! An ice cube slams into the neck of one of two Chinese students on their way home from school.

"Hey, what's going on?" one boy shouts angrily as the other one wipes the back of his neck.

"Just kidding. Just kidding, man," laughs one of the students walking behind them. The two boys behind, one an African-American and the other an Hispanic, are fooling around, throwing ice from the fruit stands of a Korean market. The Chinese guys don't go along with the fun.

". . . Nigger! . . . Spik!" they grunt.

The laughter stops. Battle lines based on race are quickly drawn. "Fu Manchu! Geek! Chink! Go back to where you came from," the black and Hispanic boys reply.

By the time the four kids reach the Twenty-third Street subway station, fists replace the words. Punching, kicking, jabbing. Books and papers spray across the sidewalk. One of the Chinese students hits the concrete and the African-American jumps on top of him. The other Chinese boy exchanges karate punches with the Hispanic. "Kick him. Get him. Hit'm again," shout the crowd of teenagers who circle around the fighting boys.

A squad car, siren screaming, roars up the avenue. The police officers break up the fight without much difficulty and haul the kids back to the school.

In her office, Dean Barbara Williams, an assistant principal, history teacher, and the adviser to the African-American Club, calms everyone down and listens to the boys' complaints. She offers a simple choice: mediation or suspension. They choose mediation. . . .

All four boys involved . . . air their grievances and with a little prodding come to an understanding. (Kuklin, *Speaking Out,* pages 53–54)

Fortunately, this conflict was temporarily defused with the intervention of a wise school official. But without a sustained effort to build bridges of communication across antagonistic groups, such inci-

dents are bound to come up again. Conflicts are fueled by the unwillingness to listen or to try to understand the other. They are inflamed even more when stereotypes and prejudice are influencing the way people see one another. In our society we have witnessed minor conflicts escalating into violence, as people armed with mutual misperceptions shut down communication with one another. **1**

What Is Communication?

Communication is an exchange of ideas, feelings, or meaning between two or more persons. It implies that these persons give and receive information. Each person must pay attention to the other. A person who is communicating well knows and feels, even if only partially, what the other person knows and feels.

Communication takes place in many ways. We are accustomed to thinking of communication as words, but words are only part of the picture. The exchange of ideas, feelings, and meaning happens through body language, listening, and verbal language. Though people tend to emphasize the last method, which involves words, the other two methods are just as significant, if not more so. We will focus on these three methods later in this chapter.

Hard-won Lessons

Our deep need to communicate stems partly from the drive to love and be loved and partly from the simple desire to express ourselves and to gain from hearing others express themselves. In the exchange of feelings and ideas with other human beings, we learn what being human is all about. This situation illustrates what can be learned through communication:

1
Briefly tell a story from your experience of a time when miscommunication or refusal to communicate led to anger and even violence.

Nick was a transfer student who had quickly gained the reputation of being a snob. He made straight A's, always raised his hand to answer questions in class, and even took a first-place prize in the state speech competition. Added to that, Nick defeated the junior class president for the position of starting shortstop on the baseball team. His classmates thought that he was snobbish, not because of what he said (he never bragged about his accomplishments, never even talked about them), but because he walked around with his head tilted up in the air. When students talked to Nick, he had the appearance of looking down on them.

One day at lunch Nick overheard two guys talking. One of them said that Nick was "such a snob, always walking around with his nose in the air." Nick was hurt and angry. Even though he was extremely shy, he walked over to the student and confronted him.

"I heard what you said," Nick snapped. The boy who had made the remark began to turn flaming red. "I can't help walking around with my nose in the air. I have an eye problem, and to see okay I have to hold my head the way I do. I don't like this problem, but I have to live with it and with people like you who make no attempt to understand." Nick turned on his heel and stormed off to his next class.

The two students were deeply embarrassed. Soon word got around that everyone had been perceiving Nick unfairly. Nick's classmates began to view him in a new way. Before long, he had the reputation of being a very generous guy who knew how to have a good time, too.

The students in this story learned a few hard-won lessons about the need to communicate:

- Having accurate knowledge about an individual is the key to opening up a relationship with that person. **2**

- Body language is important—all the nonverbal signals that people give off about how they are feeling or what they are thinking. But in this case, Nick's body language—the way he tilted his head—was misinterpreted. The way he held his head was not really a way of communicating an attitude or feeling, but a way of coping physically with a vision problem.
- Communicating directly with an individual is better than speaking behind the person's back.
- Confrontation can lead to a welcome shake-up in stale patterns of thought and behavior. In this story, Nick's confrontation with the gossiper was risky for him. It took courage because it made him vulnerable to further ridicule. But Nick's act gave the students a chance to throw off an old and destructive pattern of thinking and behaving—slanderous gossip.

2
Recall an incident when you did not check to see if your perceptions of another person were correct but instead acted on an incorrect assumption. Write a brief description of what happened.

By trying to understand what Nick felt due to his eye problem, his peers developed **empathy**, the ability to walk around in another person's shoes, to see and experience the world as that person sees and experiences it. Empathy comes through communication.

Attitudes: Avenues and Roadblocks to Communication

Nurturing relationships through communication requires a receptive and open frame of mind. Picture communication as a car that carries information, feelings, and opinions back and forth from one person to another. The ideal situation is one where the car moves freely on wide avenues, with no kinks and twists in the road. To move easily, the car must not encounter any roadblocks.

The attitudes that make up our frame of mind when relating to others can be either **avenues** or **roadblocks** to communication. Attitudes that are avenues can ease the passage of information, feelings, and opinions. Attitudes that are roadblocks can throw up all kinds of barriers that make communication nearly impossible. The following paragraphs describe several of the most significant avenues and roadblocks.

Trust Versus Self-protection

The avenue of trust. With an attitude of trust, we act on the assumption that the other person will not disappoint us or hurt us; we do not demand evidence that the other person is trustworthy and will not let us down. In the Bible, Sirach warns: "Woe to the fainthearted who have no trust! / Therefore they will have no shelter" (Sirach 2:13). If we do not trust anyone, we will not have the shelter of friendship. Trust involves risk, and communication requires this willingness to take risks. Although we need to be wary of known liars and cheats, our relationships should typically begin with a trusting spirit. **3**

3
Briefly describe two things about a person that indicate you can probably trust her or him.

The roadblock of self-protection. The opposite of trusting others is overprotecting ourselves. We insist on seeing evidence that communication will involve no risk before we attempt to relate to another person. So we might not talk to certain people because we think that they are too intelligent for us. Or we may share very little of our thoughts and feelings because we think that people would not like us if they truly knew us. This risk-free, self-protecting approach tends to create a self-fulfilling prophecy; that is, when we protect ourselves because we think people are not interested in us or do not like us, those people stop trying to communicate with us.

Hope Versus a Win-Lose Attitude

The avenue of hope. We enter into dialog with someone because we hope that our conversation will have a desirable outcome. Hope in communication is a readiness to respond to a person without necessarily knowing exactly what the outcome of communicating will be. With a spirit of hope, we treat communication as an adventure. In other words, we take a trip through another person's experience and ideas, taking a chance that positive results will happen between us but not insisting that the results happen *our* way.

The roadblock of a win-lose attitude. Conversely, carrying a win-lose attitude into a relationship is bound to bog down communication. With this approach, being right is more important than understanding or relating. Instead of listening and getting to know the other person's ideas in a hopeful spirit of adventure, we use the conversation to establish that we are on top or better. This need to win can push us to distort the ideas of others, become sarcastic, or preoccupy our mind with impressing others. A person with this attitude quickly shuts down communication.

Acceptance Versus Stereotyping and Judging

The avenue of acceptance. We need to accept people as they are, in their uniqueness and specialness, in order to have an interchange of experience and understanding with them. We do not have to like all their attitudes, ideas, and mannerisms, but we do need to respect their right to be different and try to see the world through their eyes. Jesus told his followers: "'Be merciful. . . . Do not judge, and you will not be judged; do not condemn, and you will not be condemned'" (Luke 6:36–37).

When people feel accepted, they usually react by being more open, by revealing more of who they are. They communicate more freely because they

feel that the other person is not about to make swift judgments about them or evaluate their every word. People grow and become their best selves in a genuinely accepting relationship.

The roadblock of stereotyping and judging. "He's a dumb jock!" "She's a nerd." "He's one of those low-life types; you can't trust anything he says." Such statements are evidence of stereotyping, the tendency to put people into a neat role that does not take into account their individuality and then to judge them on the basis of that role. Once we have stereotyped someone, we presume we do not have to treat that person as the complicated and interesting individual he or she is. We also may develop a judgmental attitude toward a person based on some behavior of his or hers that is a pet peeve of ours. As surely as the acceptance of an individual helps him or her to communicate openly, stereotyping and judging will cut off communication with that person. **4**

For Review

- What is communication, and why is it important to us?
- Briefly describe the attitudes that are avenues and roadblocks to communication.

Body Language

Earlier in the chapter, these three ways of communicating were identified:
- body language
- listening
- verbal language

Most of the remainder of this chapter will focus on listening and on several aspects of verbal language that can present problems for people. First, however, we will turn our attention to the area of body language.

4
List eight of your pet peeves about people. Rank them from 1 (most bothersome) to 8 (least bothersome). Ponder your list for a few minutes, then place a check mark next to the items that you are guilty of yourself. Finally, answer this question in writing: *When I am bothered by someone because of a pet peeve, how does that influence my ability to communicate with them?*

"Speaking" Without Words

We often give messages even when we are not speaking words. Usually we are not conscious that our body as well as our words are speaking to other people. In fact, this **body language** is often more significant in communication than verbal language. Much of what we understand from others comes through nonverbal cues. Such things as bodily gestures, facial expressions, posture, tone and pitch of voice, rate of speech, clothing, and the use of physical space form a language of their own. Here are some examples:

- *A wink.* Depending on the context, a wink could mean "This is a joke" or "Let's get together after the party."
- *A hug.* A hug usually communicates affection, but its specific meaning may vary from "I'll protect you" to "I sure do need you."
- *A scowl.* A scowl can indicate "I'm disgusted with you" or "This situation is making me furious."
- *Crossing arms.* Crossing one's arms can often signal "I need to protect myself," but it can also indicate that "I'm cold."
- *Looking away from the speaker.* Depending on the situation, looking away from the speaker may mean "You are boring me," "I'm anxious about what you're saying," or "I'm preoccupied with other concerns."

Often we can tell from the context of the situation or by the slightest shade of difference in nonverbal behavior what the person really feels or thinks. Of course it is always possible to misinterpret body language (recall how Nick's classmates mistook his way of tilting his head up and thus looking down as evidence of snobbery). But if we are sensitive and intuitive, we can be right on target in "hearing" what someone is saying with their body. **5**

Directing What We "Say"

Most of the time we do not need to consider our body language. We act naturally, and that is fine. However, just as with our use of words, the situation sometimes calls for us to direct what we "say" with our body.

Becoming Conscious of Our Signals

When you are giving a speech, if you wave your note papers around anxiously or sway from side to side you can make your audience uneasy because these movements give them the feeling that you are nervous. In more intimate communication—for

5
Observe people's body language and list as many nonverbal signals as you can. Write down your interpretation of what people are "saying" with them.

Student art: "Mixed Messages," colored pencil drawing by Mandy Rager, Holy Cross High School, Louisville, Kentucky

instance, in trying to help someone open up and talk—sitting behind a desk will put a physical and psychological barrier between you and the other person. Sitting behind the desk tells the other person, "I am protected from you; there is a distance between us." If you want the other person to talk freely, sit across from him or her at eye level—on equal terms—with no physical barrier.

What to Believe?

Body language is important because people tend to believe these nonverbal messages more readily than verbal messages. Nonverbal behavior is less conscious, less subject to control. So when there is a discrepancy between words and nonverbal messages, the nonverbal behavior has more credibility and therefore is seen as the "real" message. Because body language can be misinterpreted, though, it helps to look for other signs of the "real" message as well, and even to ask the other person directly about it.

Here is an example of nonverbal behavior conflicting with verbal:

Lynn had planned to go to a movie with Maura on Friday night. But when another girl whom Lynn had been trying to be friends with offered her a chance to get together, Lynn suddenly changed her plans and told Maura that she was busy. Maura now feels hurt and tells Lynn so. Lynn's response is to cross her arms, tap her foot, purse her lips, and say in a somewhat heated tone of voice: "Listen, I'm *sorry!* I didn't think this would hurt you!"

If you were in Maura's place, would you believe Lynn's words or her body language? As Maura, how would you respond?

Moving Toward Integrity

We can consciously tune in to nonverbal behavior—in ourselves and in those with whom we are relating. We may find ourselves saying one thing with our words and another with our body; we may discover that we have even fooled ourselves into thinking we feel a certain way when in fact we feel the opposite. Our body language tips us off as to what we are truly feeling.

Lynn, for instance, probably thought she really felt sorry. But if she had paid attention to her own nonverbal behavior, she might have concluded to herself, "Wow, I must feel really guilty and I'm just denying it, because I'm acting so hostile and defensive!" Once Lynn is in touch with her feeling of wanting to lash back out of guilt, she might calm herself down, admit her sense of guilt to herself, and say to Maura: "Look, I feel really rotten about this. You know, I could hardly look you in the eye when I saw you the next day. This whole thing must have hurt you bad, and I apologize." Awareness of her own body language could make Lynn a more sensitive communicator and a person with greater integrity.

The Human Need for Touch

The area of **physical touch** deserves special mention in our consideration of body language.

Most children love to crawl into a parent's lap to be held, cuddled, and kissed. Children thrive on this physical expression of affirmation and affection. As mentioned in the discussion of power in chapter 1, infants whose cries go unanswered and who are therefore deprived of regular, caring touch have been known to withdraw and even die. Touch as a means of communicating love can be intensely meaningful, especially in circumstances where words cannot be found. For instance, at funerals close friends often console each other simply by embracing; in the face of death, words seem hollow.

As children get older they often become more wary of touching. For instance, sons and fathers may cease to hug each other. The need for signs of affection remains, but the fear of being thought of as weird or the desire to appear independent may make affectionate touch taboo. Teens and adults can also be touch deprived. Several psychologists have even noted that what compels some young people to premarital sexual relations has more to do with a need for touch than a desire for sex.

In any case, most human beings of all ages relish simple, affectionate touch. Persons and relationships suffer without any physical signs of caring. A popular saying from the field of family therapy is, "We need four hugs a day to survive, eight hugs a day to be maintained, and twelve hugs a day to thrive." Although these numbers are just hypothetical, the saying does get across the point that human beings desperately need physical affection. **6**

Interestingly, cultures vary widely in their norms about who may touch whom. In North American culture, a man and a woman walking hand in hand are considered acceptable, but two men or two women walking this way might be suspect. However, in many places in Asia and the Middle East, just the opposite is true, because in those cultures, sexual interest or intimacy (signified by a man and a woman holding hands) should be expressed only in private.

6
In a brief paragraph, explain your agreement or disagreement with this statement: *Most people my age want affectionate touch that is not geared to romance but do not know how to give or receive it.*

Touching without love or care is meaningless and may be exploitative and abusive. Perhaps the best guideline when the situation is questionable is this: *Touch to give, not to get.* Though the person who offers a caring hug or a stroke on the arm may certainly benefit from that touch, her or his motive for reaching out physically should be to offer sympathy, encouragement, or friendship. Whenever one person is simply trying to "get something" from the other through touch, that is manipulation, not genuine affection.

At times, though, we may need to ask for touch from another person. Generally this is not manipulative, but simply honest caring for ourselves. For example, if we feel deep sadness or the need for consolation, we might ask someone we care about and trust: "Can I have a hug? I feel really bummed out." In certain situations we have to let go of our own emotional needs, but to *always* stifle our needs can take us down a road of long-term frustration and emotional shutdown.

Because communication tends to be equated with speech, the highly significant area of body language is often overlooked when people are considering how they communicate. We must remember that our body sends off a constant stream of quiet but powerful messages.

For Review

- What is body language? Why is it more readily believed than spoken language?
- Describe the human need for touch and its role in communication. What is a good guideline for when touch is appropriate?

Student art: "Let's Just Talk," painted clay sculpture by Nizxaliz Campos, St. Michael Academy, New York, New York

Listening

Listening may be as overlooked as body language when we consider all the ways we communicate. We are not accustomed to fine-tuning our listening skills, perhaps because we think of listening as simply the absence of speech. But listening is much more than that.

An Overlooked Essential

If you are like most people, you have often wanted to say: "You're not listening! No one ever listens to me." It is not a nice way to feel. We want to be taken seriously. We prefer to think that what we have to say is important and that how we feel is worth attention. Indeed, one characteristic of friends is that they listen to each other. Susan understands this well:

Susan looked around at her classmates at graduation. She thought about all the people with whom she had trudged through four years of high school. So many characters, so many laughs, so many crazy memories. Now everyone would be going their separate ways. Who would she miss, and what would she miss the most? Susan realized with a pang how much she treasured her friendship with Carl—Carl, who listened to her heartaches, her plans, her worries, and her exciting news in a way that made her feel wonderfully understood. Susan knew deep down that she and Carl would always be friends.

Listening is important not only in friendships but in all other relationships as well. Top-caliber students tend to listen in class better than other students do. Successful salespersons usually listen carefully to customers' wants and needs. The most effective managers usually listen well to their employees. Listening is crucial to success. What is more important from a Christian perspective, though, is that listening is essential to caring and loving. **7**

Guidelines for Listening

You are probably listening well if the other person keeps talking and tells you about what is important to her or him. Good listening is *not* advice giving, problem solving, or a time for you to tell your story. These three things may happen later, after you have listened. But for the time being, the listener's job is simply to let the other person talk. If the listener does speak, it should be only to encourage the other person to continue talking or to clarify something she or he said. Listening well involves both body language and spoken language.

Here are some helpful guidelines for good listening:

Quiet your own speech and be attentive. Being quiet does not necessarily mean that you are listening, but it is almost impossible to listen and talk at the same time. So do not interrupt the speaker out loud, and also hold back the inner talk that may be trying to race through your mind. That is, do not formulate your response mentally while the other person is still talking. In effect, that is the same thing as interrupting the speaker, and it conveys disrespect. Besides, if you formulate your response halfway through the conversation, that response may be appropriate only to the half of the conversation that you were listening to.

Communicate an open attitude with your body language. Sit up attentively and face the other person, being aware that your facial expressions, posture, and positioning can convey either openness or a closed feeling. If you sit too far away, frown, or tap your fingers impatiently on the arm of the chair, the other person will probably clam up rather quickly.

Stay in eye contact. This tip is closely related to the last one. Look at the other person. This shows that you are focusing your attention on him or her, not on the sun peeking through the clouds or the painting hanging on the wall. However, do not stare; just be sure that your eyes meet the other person's eyes regularly and attentively.

Avoid assuming anything about what the other person will say. When someone starts speaking and you assume that you know what the person is about to say, your mind may race in a direction different from that of the actual conversation. **8**

7
Out of all the people you know, who is the best listener? Describe in writing what makes him or her a good listener.

8
Briefly describe in writing five things that make listening hard for you. Then describe five features of listening that you enjoy.

Give signals that you are listening. When it feels natural to do so, nod and say "yes" or "okay" or "uh-huh." These little signals let the speaker know that you are following carefully.

Help by summarizing occasionally. A speaker sometimes becomes stuck or confused, especially if she or he has been talking for a long time or is very upset. If it seems appropriate, you might say something like, "Let me see if I have it straight. What you just said is . . ." Your summary may or may not be accurate, but your attempt to let the person know what you understood will encourage her or him to clarify thoughts, perhaps overcome confusion, and keep talking. However, avoid the temptation to use the speaker's concerns as a takeoff point to talk about yourself. Stories that begin "That reminds me of when I . . ." or "You think you've got it bad . . ." derail the conversation and do not help the speaker.

Ask clarifying questions. Help the other person to say more by asking questions that clarify what the problem or feeling is: "So how did you react when he did that?" Or you may simply want to ask a question to clear up your own confusion: "I'm not sure I understand what happened, Jake. Could you go over the last part of what you said?" Such clarifying questions are especially important in disagreements, where differing uses of words sometimes lead to misunderstanding.

Check your perceptions of the speaker's body language. If a speaker is red-faced and clenching his or her teeth but is talking in a hushed tone, he or she might be looking for an opening to express some stronger feelings—or maybe not. So perhaps say something like, "You look uncomfortable. Is there something else you wanted to say?"

Let the person know if you cannot listen at the time. It is better to let a person know you have something else you need to do and you do not have time to listen than to agree to listen and then spend the time thinking about what you have to do. Honesty conveys respect for the other person. **9**

Being listened to well is a priceless gift, one that should not be taken for granted. If you are on the receiving end of some good listening, be sure to express your appreciation to the listener.

In the following poem, Donna Webb, a student at Our Lady Academy, Bay Saint Louis, Mississippi, expresses the need we all have for good friends who are good listeners:

Wanted:
Someone who will talk to me,
Let me listen, let me learn.

Wanted:
Someone who will listen to me.
A kind ear that will not turn.

Wanted:
Someone to say "It's all right,"
Who will be there when the nightmare stops.

Wanted:
Someone to say "I love you,"
Who will help fill the emptiness inside.

Wanted:
Someone whom I can trust,
Someone who will stay by my side.

Wanted:
A pair of arms willing to give a hug,
A voice to whisper, "The nightmare will end,"
A hand to wipe the tears away.

Wanted:
A friend.

9
What grade would you give yourself as a listener: A, B, C, D, or F? Write down your grade and your reasons for giving yourself this grade. Then write one specific goal you might work toward to improve your listening skills.

It is safe to say that our best friends and the world's best communicators are also the best listeners. Listening skills are indispensable to communication. But some of us are more skilled at listening than others. We need to accept that we are not perfect listeners while we make an honest attempt to develop our abilities in that area. Listening is a very concrete way of following the commandment of Jesus to love your neighbor as you love yourself.

For Review

- Why are good listening skills important?
- How can you tell when you are doing a good job of listening?
- List the nine guidelines for good listening.

Verbal Language

At this point we will turn to several aspects of verbal language that can be particularly challenging in communication, especially the kind that aims at nurturing intimate relationships. We will cover the following aspects of **verbal communication:**

- self-disclosure
- "I" messages versus "you" messages
- setting and respecting personal boundaries
- handling conflict

Although all these topics certainly involve body language and listening, we will concentrate on the verbal dimensions of these areas of communication.

Self-disclosure

Friends share something of themselves with each other. They share facts about themselves and, perhaps a bit later, their ideas and opinions about what matters to them. But for the friendship to move to a deeper level of intimacy, the friends must begin to communicate about what is most personal to each of them—their own feelings. This gradual, mutual process of **self-disclosure**, all the way from sharing facts to sharing feelings, is what builds lasting, intimate relationships.

Communicating Feelings

When we open up to a friend and talk about our emotions, we are offering a special gift to the other person. We are saying, in effect: "I trust you with this very personal information about me. I'm telling you how I feel because I want you to understand me, to appreciate me—all of me, including my deepest feelings."

Communicating or disclosing our feelings, however, can be threatening. We might be afraid that others will take advantage of us if they know that we are sensitive about a particular issue. Or perhaps we are afraid that if we share our emotions, others will think of us as weak. So maybe we keep a stiff upper lip: we push all our feelings inside and hope that they will go away. In Judith Guest's novel *Ordinary People* (also an Oscar-winning movie), Conrad is a young man who is troubled and haunted by his brother's accidental death. Dr. Berger, the psychiatrist whom Conrad has been seeing, tells him this:

"People who keep stiff upper lips find that it's damn hard to smile.

". . . Feeling is not selective, I keep telling you that. You can't feel pain, you aren't gonna feel anything else, either. And the world is full of pain. Also joy. Evil. Goodness. Horror and love. You name it, it's there. Sealing yourself off is just going through the motions, get it?" (Pages 225, 227)

Those who cannot acknowledge and express their painful feelings can find themselves denying almost all their feelings—even the joyful ones. Sharing feelings with a friend not only builds the friendship but also enables us to experience the richness of life.

The wonder of self-disclosure is that it most often leads to more self-disclosure. However, we cannot and should not open up to *everyone*. Some people will use our self-revelations against us. We have to choose carefully those with whom to share our inmost self. But to share our feelings and deepest experiences with no one condemns us to a lonely life, a life in which we never feel solidarity with other people. The trust necessary for love or friendship is built on mutual self-disclosure. **10**

Confidentiality

A key principle about communicating personal and important matters is this: Maintain the privacy and the **confidentiality** of your conversations with other people unless they give you permission to discuss what they have revealed to you. Physicians, counselors, lawyers, priests, rabbis, ministers, and spiritual directors are expected to keep confidences because people need to feel secure that whatever is said to these helping professionals will be held private. In this way, people can confide sufficiently to solve their problems or to free their souls of the burdens of sin.

Confidentiality in a friendship is just as important as it is in the professions cited. Friends without a mutual deep respect for and protection of self-disclosures begin to distrust each other and to hide significant areas of life from each other. Unease grows between the two people. Because few people like to be around those with whom they feel uncomfortable, the relationship usually comes to an end.

Think about how true friends were described in chapter 8: they bring out the best in us, are loyal and honest, are mutual and equal in their relations

10
List one or more persons with whom you feel you communicate most openly and deeply. Explain in a paragraph why you trust these people as you do. Then write a short prayer of thanksgiving for these confidants.

with us, accept who we are, and are available and generous to us. These are the kinds of persons who we will want to disclose ourselves to and who we can trust with our confidences. Self-disclosure and confidentiality form the soul of a friendship. **11**

"I" Messages Versus "You" Messages

You probably remember *Alice's Adventures in Wonderland,* by Lewis Carroll, as a zany tale of a girl who alternately shrinks and grows huge, making her way in a world of weird characters and bizarre, dreamlike situations. *Alice* can provide us with a fine example of a tendency that we too often see in communication. Consider this bit of dialog between the Mad Hatter and Alice:

"Your hair wants cutting," said the Hatter. He had been looking at Alice for some time with great curiosity, and this was his first speech.

"You should learn not to make personal remarks," Alice said with some severity: "It's very rude." (Page 94)

First the Hatter made a subjective judgment about Alice's hair, which he pronounced as a fact. For her part, Alice defended herself by scolding the Hatter and making the subjective judgment of her own that the Hatter was rude.

The problem in this dialog is **"you" messages.** A "you" message is a comment that we make to an-

other person that implies a negative judgment of that person. "You" messages seem to be designed to annoy and anger. Here are some typical "you" messages:

- You ought to listen more carefully.
- You don't care.
- You should ask for others' opinions.
- You must be nuts.
- Your clothes are weird.

The above remarks usually evoke responses like the following:

- *You're* a worse listener than I am.
- No, *you're* the one who doesn't care.
- Well, *you* never ask for other people's opinions.
- *You're* the one that's nuts.
- *You've* got no taste in clothes.

"You" messages typically force people to defend themselves. Instead of fostering communication, these messages make others close their gates and guard their fortress.

In contrast to "you" messages, which label other people with our own judgments about them, **"I" messages** tell another person: "Here I am; this is the way that I feel, think, and see things. These are my reactions, and I hope you will listen and understand them."

For example, Alice might have responded to the Hatter's remark with an "I" message: "I feel quite insulted when you say things like that." That would be an "I" message because Alice would not

11
Reflect on the last month, remembering a time when you needed to and did talk to another person about something important to you. Maybe you were angry, happy, worried, full of plans, or confused. Describe the situation in a paragraph, addressing the following:
- what you needed to talk about
- who you talked to first
- how the talk was or was not helpful

"You" messages

- You ought to listen more carefully.

- You don't care.
- You should ask for others' opinions.
- You must be nuts.
- Your clothes are weird.

"I" messages

- When you interrupt me while I'm speaking, I don't feel listened to.
- I feel left out.
- I wish that I had the chance to give my opinion.
- I am very upset.
- I have different tastes.

be blaming or accusing the Hatter. She would be expressing her own reaction as just that—her *own*.

Consider the way each "you" message from the dialog has been changed to an "I" message:

Notice that the "I" messages state observations, feelings, thoughts, and wishes. They do not blame, judge, or belittle the other person. "I" messages communicate the speaker's concerns, but they leave the other person free to respond or not to respond.

Two Dialogs

Observe what happens to communication in this dialog between Amy and Jay:

Last night Amy waited for Jay to pick her up to go to a movie. Jay never showed up, despite having called Amy yesterday afternoon to decide on a time. Jay did not even phone afterward to explain why he had not picked her up.

Amy sees Jay ten minutes before their first class, looks at him icily, and says, "You expect me to even *talk* to you after what you did to me? You've taken advantage of me once too often, Jay. I don't need people like you in my life."

"If you were a real friend, you'd trust me. I don't need your whining and complaining, either, when I've done nothing wrong."

"What do you mean, 'nothing wrong'? I've had it with your excuses! You're always so ready to blame everyone else. I've never seen you take responsibility for your own mistakes."

"Okay, *be* that way, but it's the last you'll see of me!" At this point Jay storms off.

Obviously, "you" messages are flying everywhere in that interaction. Compare that dialog with the following one:

"Jay, we were supposed to go out last night. I waited. What happened?"

"It's a long story. I could have used a friend last night."

"I wish it could have been me—but I was pretty upset when you didn't come. Tell me what happened."

"I hate to talk about it, so I've never told you. My dad gets drunk all the time, and last night was the worst ever. He was throwing things at Mom and screaming at both of us. He finally passed out, but by then it was past ten and I'd forgotten all about the movie. I feel awful for you; you must have been mad."

"Well, I have to say I was really wondering, and I did get irritated, but then I figured something was wrong. This thing with your Dad sounds terrible. Are you worried?"

The second dialog begins with statements of fact and a question; Jay does not have to defend himself because Amy simply asks him to explain. Amy expresses how she feels, but she does not blame her feelings on Jay. Consequently, Jay feels he is not under attack, so he shares his burden about his father with her. Amy does not need to feel embarrassed at having made an accusation, and Jay does not have to feel humiliated. Jay may go on to say more about his concerns for his father and his whole family. **12**

A certain humility underlies an "I" message. It is not arrogant. Instead it implies that what the speaker says is simply his or her reaction, opinion, or version of a story—not the whole or absolute truth. "I" messages imply a willingness to *take responsibility for owning one's communication.* In other words, with an "I" message, a person says, "This is how I am reacting," not "You shouldn't be that way." Recall the earlier discussion of avenues and roadblocks to communication. "I" messages travel on those wide, spacious avenues of trust, hope, and acceptance.

Assertiveness and "I" Messages

An "I" message is an accurate description of the speaker's own feelings about what happened, yet it permits the other person to explain. Allowing the other to explain and withholding judgment take a good deal of courage, for in doing so an individual gives up the illusion that she or he can control the other. "I" messages do not imply weakness in the speaker. To say, "I am very angry because I had to wait" instead of "You are always late" is not feeble

behavior. Far from being a sign of weakness, "I" messages are a crucial part of being assertive.

Assertiveness shows a healthy respect of self and other people. To be assertive means to respect the rights and dignity of others but also to communicate our own views, feelings, and needs. Assertiveness should not be confused with **aggressiveness**, the attempt to dominate others by making them do what we want them to do. Assertiveness indicates strength of character; aggressiveness illustrates the character of a childish bully who has to have his or her own way and who cannot permit other people to be themselves. It is probably obvious to you now that aggressive people pepper their speech with heavy doses of "you" messages.

Besides aggressiveness, the other extreme to avoid in communication is **nonassertiveness.** Nonassertive persons devalue themselves; they find life frustrating because they assume that their own feelings, ideas, and wants are not as worthwhile or as valid as those of other people.

Of course we all behave with a combination of assertive, nonassertive, and aggressive behaviors,

12
Imagine that you have to talk with a friend about something she or he did that really bothered you. Write what you would say, using "you" messages. Then change your complaints or criticisms into "I" messages.

depending on the circumstances and on the particular relationships we are in. But we can aim to nurture a healthy, assertive style of communicating. These general guidelines are helpful:

State in specific terms what you want to say. Avoid generalizations. Say, "I feel taken advantage of when the only time I hear from you is if you need a ride someplace," not "I just don't feel right about things."

Do not apologize for what you say and do. (This presupposes that what you say and do is legal, moral, and reasonable.) Say, "This feeling of being taken advantage of is beginning to make me resentful when we get together," not "I know I probably shouldn't feel this way, but I do."

Make specific requests. Indicate what you want from the other person. Do not leave the situation unclear. Say, "Can we talk about this? I'd like to figure out a way to stay friends without my feeling resentful," not "I don't suppose there's anything that can be done about this situation because you don't have a car." **13**

Listen. Hear what the other person has to say, recognizing that her or his feelings and ideas may be different from yours but that they are valid, too. Say, "Do you have any reactions to what I just said?" not "Well, I've said what I wanted to say. You can take it or leave it."

People need to behave assertively in order to be healthy. Sitting on feelings and wants and stuffing them inside ourselves (nonassertiveness) or operating as if our own feelings and wants are the only ones that count (aggressiveness) can only bring havoc to our well-being. The skill of using "I" messages wisely is a key to a healthy, assertive lifestyle as well as a loving one.

Setting and Respecting Personal Boundaries

In relating to others, we need to be aware that we have a certain dignity that must not be violated. Behaving and communicating assertively involves the ability to set personal boundaries for oneself so that others will not violate that dignity.

A Necessary Line of Separation

A **personal boundary** is a kind of invisible line that separates us from others, so that we know where another person "ends" and we "begin." A person has good boundaries if he or she does not allow others to "overrun" him or her with their own agendas—emotional, physical, intellectual, and so on. A person with good boundaries is not easily manipulated. People who tend to be nonassertive have particular problems setting and maintaining their boundaries.

On the other side, we need to be careful that we do not violate other people's boundaries, or try to

13
Recall a relationship with a friend. Do you ever have a need for a particular response from him or her? Name the need, and write how you would assert this need. For example, "I need to know how you feel about having to wait for me after school."

do so. Others have lines we should not cross, and if we find ourselves constantly crossing those lines, we are not respecting their dignity. Even if they are not aware of those lines, we should be. Here are several examples of violating another person's boundaries:

- manipulating or making decisions for someone, especially by using threats or guilt or even compliments
- speaking for another person
- not honoring another person's refusal
- incessant questioning and badgering someone to divulge information
- going through someone's belongings
- touching another person without asking
- giving unasked for advice
- violating a confidence
- verbally, sexually, physically, or emotionally abusing someone

Response to a Red Flag

When we find ourselves doing any of these behaviors or being the object of these behaviors by others, a red flag should go up in our head: "Danger: Boundary being violated!" Then we need to take steps to correct the situation, as in this instance:

Eduardo has the feeling he's going to collapse if he doesn't get some sleep. He's been getting only two hours of sleep a night for the past two nights because of papers and assignments he had put off; when the deadlines came crashing in on him, he just stayed up most of the night to get them done.

At seven o'clock the evening after the second short night of sleep, Eduardo's friend Greg calls, reminding him: "Hey, you said you'd help me fix my car, and man, I gotta have it for tomorrow. No way can I get along without a car tomorrow."

Eduardo says: "Wait a minute, I thought we were going to fix the car this weekend. Don't you know I'm ready to drop dead? I've been up for two nights."

"Okay, pal, next time you're desperate for a loan, I'll remember this."

Eduardo, recalling the many times Greg had lent him money, was about to cave in. Then something clicked in him, and he responded: "I appreciate all the loans, Greg, but if I came over to help you with your car, I wouldn't be alert enough to do a good job. This is one time I gotta say no." **14**

Setting our own boundaries and respecting others' boundaries is not easy, especially if we have been in an atmosphere where people are accustomed to overrunning one another's boundaries. But it is essential to healthy relationships.

Handling Conflicts

Inevitably, value disagreements, misunderstandings, competing interests, complaints, or criticism will cause conflicts in a relationship. Pain and frustration often result. However, conflicts can be handled in a way that minimizes anger and hurt; these occasions can even become growth points for the relationship.

Anger in Itself Is Okay

Everyone gets angry sometimes—even saints and even Jesus. Seeing merchants taking advantage of poor people at the Temple, Jesus "entered the temple and began to drive out those who were selling

14
Pick from the list of behaviors one that you have personally experienced (either someone violated your boundaries or you violated someone else's). Write a reflection on how that situation could have been changed.

and those who were buying in the temple, and he overturned the tables of the money changers and the seats of those who sold doves" (Mark 11:15). Jesus felt angry because of the injustice he saw, and he expressed it—not by attacking people but by driving out the crass, exploitative activity.

Like all emotions, **anger** just *is*. It may be caused by some injustice, as with Jesus' anger toward the money changers. Often anger is triggered by fear that arises when we perceive a threat from some source. For example, two people begin arguing. Suddenly the argument leads to anger when one person calls the other stupid. Feeling a threat to his ego, the second person says, "If I'm stupid, you're so ugly you have to sneak up on sleep." Anger becomes a problem at this stage because it can escalate into violence.

Anger can also create havoc when we constantly swallow it, stifle it, suppress it. Soon it starts eating away at our insides. Anger needs some expression. Here is a helpful story about anger:

"On a path that went by a village in Bengal, there lived a cobra who used to bite people on their way to worship at the temple there. As the incidents increased, everyone became fearful, and many refused to go to the temple. The Swami who was the master at the temple was aware of the problem and took it upon himself to put an end to it. Taking himself to where the snake dwelt, he used a mantram to call the snake to him and bring it into submission.

"The Swami then said to the snake that it was wrong to bite the people who walked along the path to worship and made him promise sincerely that he would never do it again. Soon it happened that the snake was seen by a passer-by upon the path and it made no move to bite. Then it became known that the snake had somehow been made passive, and people grew unafraid. It was not long before the village boys were dragging the poor snake along behind them as they ran laughing here and there. When the temple Swami passed that way again he called the snake to see if he had kept his promise.

"The snake humbly and miserably approached the Swami, who exclaimed, 'You are bleeding. Tell me how this has come to be.' The snake was near tears and blurted out that he had been abused ever since he was caused to make his promise to the Swami.

'I told you not to bite,' said the Swami, 'but I did not tell you not to hiss.'" (Boyd, *Rolling Thunder*, pages 105–106)

Just because we are angry, we do not have to be aggressive, "biting" others; but neither must we be passive, letting ourselves be abused or taken advantage of. When we feel anger, it can be released in dozens of harmless but helpful ways. We can wax our car furiously. We can chop wood, run laps, bang on the piano, write unsent letters, or organize a nonviolent protest. We can talk with the person with whom we are angry. In other words, we can hiss all we want, but we need not bite. **15**

15
In one or two sentences, describe something about which you are angry and in conflict. Then outline a plan in which you can hiss but not bite, a plan that allows you to express your displeasure but keep communication open.

Useful advice for dealing with our anger and other powerful emotions comes from Saint Paul's letter to the Ephesians: "Be angry but do not sin; do not let the sun go down on your anger, and do not make room for the devil" (4:26–27). Notice that Paul does not say, "Do not be angry." He knows that people get mad. His advice is to deal with the anger constructively as soon as possible so that it does not eat away at us and turn into a monster.

When we resolve conflicts using the following principles, we will be dealing constructively with any anger we might feel toward the other person in the conflict.

Do Unto Others

An essential principle in a conflict situation is to treat other people as we ourselves would want to be treated. If we do not like being spoken to in a condescending manner, then we should not use a condescending tone with others. If we like being reasoned with, then we should reason with other people. If we expect some compromises from others, we must be willing to compromise.

Go to the Source

Another principle in handling conflict is to go directly to the source, the person with whom you are in conflict, and talk about the matter. Going to a third person or talking about the problem to everyone but the individual involved usually accomplishes little and makes the situation worse. Eventually, if the direct approach breaks down, you may need a third person or a higher authority to intervene. But starting with the other individual involved in the conflict is important.

Get the Facts Straight

A third principle in handling conflict is to have the facts straight before rushing into battle. For example, if we think that someone is spreading a rumor about us, we should do some careful verification before making accusations. Many of us have had the embarrassing experience of charging into combat only to find out that we have accused someone of doing something that she or he did not do.

Take a Problem-solving Approach

The final principle in handling conflict is to treat the conflict as a problem to be solved by both persons, not as a win-lose situation. These suggested steps will help to solve a conflict:

1. **State the problem clearly.** Use "I" messages, not judgments or accusations, and allow the other person to state his or her perceptions about the problem, too. Sometimes no conflict exists once both parties have tried to define exactly what they think the problem is. Limit the conflict under discussion to a particular issue; try not to bring a whole history of conflicts into the discussion.

2. **Brainstorm for solutions.** It takes two people to create a conflict and therefore two people to create a solution. Brainstorming together means coming up with as many ways to solve the problem as possible—from the lofty to the ridiculous. You will be surprised at how often a creative solution emerges.

3. **Evaluate carefully each proposed solution and choose one.** Reflect on the solutions together and talk about which will work best for the two of

you. Then choose the one most acceptable to both of you. Sometimes the only solution seems to be for one of the parties to give in—a win-lose outcome. This is a sad situation because a win-lose outcome ultimately harms the relationship. A solution that both persons can at least live with—a win-win outcome—is always preferred.

4. Let go of the outcome. After doing steps 1, 2, and 3, you have done all that you can to resolve the conflict. Now it is time to let go of the outcome and get on with life. This is not always easy, but holding on to one definite outcome in a conflict can lead to more conflict and little peace.

Sometimes resolving a conflict requires a mediator—someone who can step in and help the two people to agree. This mediator must be trusted by both persons and must be a good listener. Although a mediator helps two people to work out their conflict, he or she does not impose a solution. Often the best result is a compromise.

Conflicts are not always bad; they are normal. If two people are committed to finding a solution to a conflict, their relationship can be stronger in the end. After all, wrestling through a problem together, with all the listening and talking involved, can lead to greater self-understanding and mutual knowledge. This knowledge can support and build friendship. Conflicts also push us to clarify our thinking, sharpen our principles, and test our skills of communication. **16**

For Review

- How is self-disclosure sometimes threatening?
- Why is confidentiality important in relationships that involve self-disclosure?
- What are "you" messages and "I" messages? Give two examples from the text of each type.
- List the four guidelines to assertive communication.
- What is a personal boundary? Give three examples from the text of violating personal boundaries.
- Give the perspective on anger illustrated by the passages from the Christian Testament.
- List and briefly explain the four principles of conflict resolution.

A Rich Harvest

Communication requires patient effort as we try out different approaches, stumbling at times and feeling accomplishment at other times. But a conscious attempt to become more aware of body language, to develop skills in listening, and to use language carefully yields a rich harvest of friendship, intimacy, and self-respect. In our own small part of the world, we may then experience something of Jesus' dream for us, becoming fully alive.

Lori Bykowski, a student of Bishop George Ahr High School in Edison, New Jersey, shares this prayer for the gift of communicating well:

God, grant me the gift of understanding to really be able to communicate with those I love and to be able to accept the unexpected burdens that life sometimes brings. God, let me continue to believe that everything happens for a cause and that "good" will always show after "bad." **17**

16
Recall a recent conflict that you had with someone. Answer these questions in writing:
- Did you use any of the principles for handling conflict, and if so, which ones?
- Which principle is hardest for you to follow?

17
Describe the most significant realization you have had in this study of communication. In what ways do you think that you will be a better communicator?

10
Dating:
Befriending and Romancing

What's Up with Dating?

As a high school senior, perhaps you have been dating for a few years. You probably have heard all sorts of comments about dating from friends.

Different Perspectives on Dating

The following reactions may be like some that you have heard or even had yourself, or that you may hear in the next several years:

- Whenever I go out with Vanessa, we just enjoy being with each other. I hardly even think of us as dating; we're just friends.
- When I met José, it was love at first sight. We've been going out together for a year now. We'd be married, but we just don't have the money to get started yet.
- When I'm with Brad, there's only one thing he wants.
- I just want to have fun and not get too involved. I went out with this guy last year. He was very nice, but when he started talking about visiting his mom and dad, I knew he was getting too serious. I'm not ready for that, so I broke off the relationship.
- Joni and I go out dancing because we really enjoy it. Well, if you want the truth, we are great dancers. But otherwise we don't do much together.
- I wasn't attracted to Richard right away. In fact, the first time we went out was a disaster. He actually nodded off during dinner. I thought, "What a jerk." Later, the woman who had arranged the date explained that Richard had just driven across Tennessee after spring break and was exhausted. As I've gotten to know him over the last ten months, I've come to like him a lot. We just match. We'll see what happens when he finishes pharmacy school.

- *Getting out of ourselves.* Talking with another person, actively listening to him or her, and being sensitive to his or her feelings and ideas are wonderful ways to stretch ourselves beyond our own narrow concerns and interests. It feels good to get out of ourselves.
- *"The thing to do."* Peer pressure to date can put a tremendous burden on a shy person or a person who would rather do such things as study, work, or play tennis. The individual may feel forced to date to avoid being judged as strange—taking on one form of discomfort to avoid another.
- *Companionship.* We seek someone with whom to share experiences. Talking with someone after a movie usually feels better than walking home alone. The companionship of dating counteracts our loneliness. This poem entitled "Unique," by Mary Paquette, expresses this well:

"I" is such a slender word,
a selfish word.
"We" is broader and enchanting
for it doubles the outlook.

- *The joy of give-and-take.* We may want to offer our talents, skills, and affection to another person, realizing that she or he has talents, skills, and affection to offer as well. We enjoy the adventure of a give-and-take relationship.
- *Finding a marriage partner.* Marriage may not be a strong motive for dating if a person is recently out of high school, but as an individual reaches the late twenties and thirties, the desire to find a lifelong partner may take on an urgency that he or she had not known before.

Self-awareness about our motives for wanting to date a particular person, or for wanting to date at all, can help us to become more genuine in those relationships. We may question our own motives if they seem primarily negative, or we may wonder why certain motives are absent in a given relationship. Understanding our motives also can help us to appreciate the gift that we have in a very satisfying relationship. **4**

Friendship Between the Sexes

Perhaps the best reason to date is to develop a friendship. Recall the earlier definition: "Friendship is characterized by mutual caring between two people, usually involving loyalty, acceptance, honesty, availability, generous help, and equality." Friends can bring out the best in each other.

4
Consider someone you have dated or would like to date. Which of the motives given in this chapter is dominant for you? Are you comfortable with this motive? How do you think this motive might affect your relationship?

Relating as Friends

As mentioned earlier in this chapter, people today are more comfortable having close friendships with members of the other sex than they used to be—friendships without necessarily the agenda of romance.

For many men, women friends provide them with accepting companionship not as easily found among male friends. Often men can more readily open up emotionally and spiritually with women friends. A young lawyer confirms this:

"Right now, and I am sure in the future, my female friends are far more important to me than my male friends, although that was not true in the past. I am beginning to think that "macho" threatens male friendship and that is not a threat with women friends. It gets down to the bottom line of there being trust with the woman that is often not there with the man." (*Worlds of Friendship,* page 111)

Besides this kind of trust, women friends help men understand life from a woman's point of view, thus expanding men's appreciation of living.

Men offer women valuable companionship, too. Novelist and screenwriter Rita Mae Brown says this about her own male friends:

"My best friend, Bill, identifies with my career. If I take a beating on a book, Bill is right by my side. He's on my team. He'll threaten to punch out a critic or he'll say, 'Come on, let's ride up in the Blue Ridge and forget these turkeys.' . . . [My men friends] are able to draw closer to me through an activity. In other words, we usually don't sit and chat, we do something. . . . I need my men friends. I learn something from them that I can't learn from women, namely, what it is like to be a man." (*Among Friends,* page 338) **5**

Friendly Guidelines

Friendships between men and women have wonderful possibilities. However, if they are to work, four guidelines need to be remembered:

1. The woman and the man need to see each other as human beings first, and as man and woman second. Both have to consider each other as persons with needs, interests, talents, experience, and as persons worthy of respect and honor.
2. They must view each other as equals. True friends treat each other as they wish to be treated. No one wants to be seen as inferior or incompetent.
3. Both need to see beyond stereotypes of their respective sex. For a male-female friendship to thrive, the woman as well as the man should be able, for example, to initiate activities to do together. Both should be able to listen well and share feelings.
4. Finally, they need to refrain from sexual relations together. There are good reasons for two unmarried persons to abstain from sexual relations (see pages 117–121). In addition to those, sex takes friendship in a different direction and frequently ends it. A young social worker comments on this reality:

"I have had friendships end because sex entered. This is because the sexual dimension took precedence over what we had before. What happened was that once sex entered our relationship it was not kept in the proper perspective and all sorts of emotions, jealousies and so on came forth." (*Worlds of Friendship,* page 107) **6**

Dating with the hope of becoming good friends makes the whole process less pressured and prob-

---

5
For women: List all the benefits you can of a friendship with a man.
For men: List all the benefits you can of a friendship with a woman.

6
Complete each of these sentence starters and then write a one-sentence explanation after each:
- **The guideline easiest to follow is . . .**
- **The guideline hardest to follow is . . .**

lematic, and more comfortable and open. A solid friendship, in fact, is the best foundation for a dating relationship and for a relationship that becomes the "going out" kind. Ultimately, friendship is the most essential ingredient of a marriage relationship. So those who want to cultivate the skills of being a marriage partner would do best to improve their ability to be a friend.

For Review

- Briefly explain how North American dating practices have evolved over the last few centuries.
- List eight motives for dating.
- Summarize four guidelines for friendships between men and women.

Pressures and Problems of Dating

The Pressure to Make It Perfect

Although dating is ideally fun and an adventure, it can put tremendous pressure on us. Few people getting ready for a date—especially if it is their first date with each other—are calm and serene. What they experience is a bit like stage fright, and they are plagued by a swarm of doubts. The pressure to have everything turn out perfectly creates these doubts (which is another good reason to aim for friendship first, rather than romance—it creates less anxiety).

It is natural to want to be thought of as likable and attractive, and understandably, we may feel anxious about our image when dating someone new. The problem is that such anxiety turns our attention inward—How am *I* doing? How do *I* look?—rather than outward to the other person. What we may forget is that if we are anxious, the other person is probably anxious also. Maybe if we stepped back and realized that neither of us is perfect and that both of us are somewhat nervous, we could relax and enjoy each other. **7**

The pressure to have everything go perfectly shows itself in at least two ways:
- high expectations
- concerns about being attractive

High Expectations

Having hope is not the same as having expectations. Having **hope** implies that a person is ready to respond when an opportunity presents itself. Having **expectations**, on the other hand, indicates

7
From what you have seen of the dating scene, are teens pressured by their peers to date? If so, list the various sources of pressure. Describe in writing how you feel about the pressure to date that is put on you or other people.

that a person thinks a certain outcome is probable. When we expect something to happen and it does not, our disappointment can be great. Notice what happens to Laura when she expects too much of her date:

Laura is feeling very down. Her classes have been a drag, teachers are piling on homework, and she is worried about next week's midterm exams. Her parents are irritated with her, and her best friend has been giving her the cold shoulder.

Luckily, Laura is looking forward to a date with Eddie on Friday night. It will be her first time out with him, and he has the reputation of being a very funny guy. "I just know he'll pull me out of this slump," she thinks.

However, when Friday evening is over and Laura realizes that Eddie has *not* cheered her up, she feels even worse. She wonders: "What went wrong? Was Eddie bored with me? Why wasn't he as much fun as I thought he would be?"

Laura's high expectations invited disappointment; they put pressure on the situation and on Eddie. A sense of hope instead would have opened Laura to the kind of mutual sharing with Eddie that marks real friendship.

Concerns About Being Attractive

Besides expecting too much, another pressure may be our concern about the attractiveness of our physical appearance and our personality. We may think that having a perfect experience means that *we* must be perfect. This kind of thinking leads to anxiety that prevents us from enjoying the other person.

We are who we are—shy or sociable, overweight or thin, imperfect but also lovable. Certainly we can grow and improve ourselves, but we also need to like and accept ourselves as we are today. It is true that good looks may initially attract attention and admiration, but appearances become less important as people come to know each other. **8**

What to Do, Where to Go?

Routines are easy to slip into when dating. The old standards of entertainment are always available and do not require much imagination: movies, restaurants, games, dances, and school activities. In

Student art: **Untitled, acrylic painting by Emily Burns, St. Peter's High School, New Brunswick, New Jersey**

8
List in rank order the ten characteristics that you consider most important in someone you would wish to date. Then make another rank-ordered list of characteristics that you consider most important in someone you would wish to marry. Are the two lists different? If so, write your reflection on why there are differences.

college the old standards do not change much, although going to bars might be added. It is helpful to remember that many other dating possibilities are available.

To make a date interesting and beneficial for both of you, it helps to ask, What does this person like to do? Then be open to new ideas. Recall the nine types of intimacy on pages 156–158. One way to think ahead about a date is to ask yourself how your relationship with the other person can become more intimate—intellectually, recreationally, aesthetically, creatively, or spiritually. It also helps to think of things that will engage you actively, rather than encourage passivity.

Here are some different date activities that might sound appealing:

- *An orchestra concert.* If your friend likes this kind of music, try it out.
- *A soup kitchen date.* Maybe your friend volunteers at a soup kitchen or in some other facility. If so, accompany her or him to volunteer someday. You will get a better sense of who your friend is and will have a lot to talk about later.
- *A canoe trip.* Take your friend canoeing on a river or a lake for an afternoon. It is fun to see each other in a different light, out in the natural world.

- *A tennis match.* Any sport suitable for two will do—tennis, bowling, swimming, cross-country skiing, and so on. What can be particularly fun is to have your friend teach you a sport that you do not already know.
- *A photography expedition.* Head out across town together to capture your favorite sights on film. Put each other in the pictures.
- *A different kind of dancing.* Go country-western dancing or learn to samba. Dancing is a great way to be together, use your energy, and express yourself.
- *A meal cooked by two.* Work on creating a dinner together and invite friends over to share it. Cooking is a great skill. If you have never tried it, you will definitely learn something. The adventure of learning together is always interesting.

So when deciding what to do on a date, consider mutual interests. Use some imagination. Become engaged in some mental or physical activity. Be open to new adventures. Intimacy can grow in many ways. **9**

Problems with Romance

Romance, discussed in chapter 7, is one of life's great thrills. When a simple dating relationship

9
Come up with three creative ideas for what to do on a date. Write them up as "recipes for a great date."

illusion in romance is **infatuation.** We see the other person through a distorting lens; we may perceive the romance's effect on us in a skewed way as well. We lose objectivity. Losing objectivity is part of the thrill of infatuation, of course, but it can also wreak havoc on us.

When we are infatuated with someone, we imagine the person to be more than he or she is. We idolize, rather than simply admire, the person. We are oblivious to his or her faults.

The case of Stephanie and Paul contains some of the main characteristics of infatuation:

When Paul sat down next to Stephanie in Intro to Philosophic Inquiry that first day of class, she was afraid that he would hear the pounding of her heart. She thought that he was about the most gorgeous guy she had ever seen. He had lazy blue eyes that seemed to size up everyone. Paul slouched in his desk with an easy confidence that none of the other freshmen could muster. When he passed her a copy of the syllabus, he grinned. She was smitten, even though a little voice inside told her she was just a bit loony.

Over the next week, Stephanie managed to sit next to Paul in philosophy and English comp. She manipulated her work-study schedule so she could hang around the computer lab where he worked. After another week of longing, Stephanie finally asked Paul if he would like to go see the show in the Pub on Friday. "Sure," he said. "Great."

Stephanie dropped by Paul's room in plenty of time for them to walk over to the Pub. The sounds of hard rock and shouted profanities vibrated the door of Paul's room. Somebody yelled, "It's open, damn it!" when she knocked a third time.

As Stephanie peered in, the stench of stale beer and grungy clothes whacked her every inhalation. Paul

blazes into a romance, and the couple now claims to be "going out" with each other, lots of wonderful feelings flow, along with a generous surge of sexual energy. It is no wonder that romantic plots and themes are central to so many movies, TV shows, novels, songs, and poetry: romance is captivating!

Yet along with the rush of romantic love can come illusions; we are particularly vulnerable to them when we have "fallen hard." This sense of

was sprawled on his futon, rubbing a cold beer on his head. With a string of expletives, he griped about a headache. Undeterred, Stephanie asked if he was still going to the Pub. "Of course," he said, though he walked in a heavy silence next to her all the way across campus.

All during the songs, Paul talked loud and drank. By the last song, Paul was weaving and obnoxious. He hardly noticed her, and when he did he called her Tina once.

Stephanie managed to set aside whatever negative reaction she had to Paul by the time she saw him the next Monday in class. She felt her heart flip-flop every time he looked at her.

It wasn't long before they were "going out," and Stephanie's misgivings were chased away by a rush of elation that she was the lucky one chosen by such a fabulous guy. Never mind that most times when they were out together, Paul drank too much. And he would ignore her but then make up for it by giving her that incredible, sexy look of his. He still was the most gorgeous guy on campus, and the funniest besides, and she was the envy of all the women in her dorm. Maybe, Stephanie thought, she just needed to loosen up a little and learn to enjoy herself like Paul. **10**

Infatuation, like Stephanie's feeling for Paul, presents us with several problems: it is superficial, overpowering, fickle, and short-lived.

Superficial. Infatuation has its origins in a person's looks, a few nice words, a certain magnetism. Romantic feelings either vanish or change to real love if two people get to know each other better. But infatuation thrives on superficial knowledge of each other; it avoids the truth.

Overpowering. The feelings associated with infatuation are so powerful that they can overrule our judgment. Their intensity tends to blind us, so that we cannot make wise decisions.

Fickle. When we are battling our own better judgment and fighting very hard to avoid seeing a situation clearly, we tend to go through a roller coaster of emotions—from optimism to pessimism, desire to repulsion. Rather than the steady affection, affirmation, and new discoveries that a truly good relationship can bring us, we feel exhaustion, punctuated with thrilling moments. Even these may disappear over time.

Short-lived. Recall certain celebrities who are famous for the number of marriages they have had. As each romance and marriage is breathlessly reported in the tabloids, we are struck by the way these celebrities seem convinced that this relationship, more than any other before, represents "true love," that this is the bond that will last forever. We cannot judge these individuals from the outside, but chances are that the short-lived nature of their marriages has to do with the restless quest for the powerful, exciting experience of infatuation, which lasts only a short time.

Particular Hurdles for Regular Pairs

When a woman and a man start "going out," they may enjoy the security of having one person they can depend on for companionship. They may feel a certain contentment that they do not have to prove themselves to someone new. Perhaps they are beyond infatuation in that they are realistic about each other's good qualities and weaknesses.

10
What advice on male-female relationships would you give to Stephanie? to Paul? Write up your advice.

A KWIK HISTORY OF DATING

On the other hand, they still need to clear several hurdles if this relationship is to be a true friendship: jealousy, dependency, and exclusivity.

Jealousy

When two people start seeing each other steadily, any perceived interference in the relationship may be viewed as a threat. When **jealousy** is at work in us, we begin to suspect even our friends of being rivals. Kelly explains jealousy this way:

"I don't like this about me very much, but when somebody turns Jeremy and me into a threesome, I get jealous and real possessive. I feel like, "Watch it, he's mine." Jeremy and I have some common friends. That's okay, and I don't get jealous when they're friends to both of us."

When one person in a couple feels a "red flag" reaction every time certain other individuals come around them, jealousy is interfering with the relationship. In those instances it is best for the jealous person to ask herself or himself why she or he feels so insecure around those other persons, and to bring that awareness into the light, where it can be confronted.

Dependency

At various times we all need to rely on other people, and that is normal. The **dependency** being considered here, however, is different from that. It is an unhealthy centering of one's energy and meaning on one person. In a couple, one or both persons may depend on the other for all their social life, new ideas, and engagement in activities. Such dependency begins to weigh a relationship down, often to the breaking point. Matt describes how dependency began to ruin a significant relationship:

At first, being with Debbie was great, and we wanted to be together all the time. But after a while, it got a little old. I mean if I just wanted to do something with the guys or even stay home on a Friday night, she'd be on my case, telling me how depressed she was and how I should do something with her to get her out of it. She just didn't know what to do with herself when I wasn't around. I was her whole life. Eventual-

ly, I had to break off the relationship, but I felt so guilty about it, she made it sound like she wouldn't be able to survive.

Matt grew away from Debbie because she was centering her life and hopes on him. All our needs and desires can never be fulfilled by one person, let alone a person with whom we have no permanent commitment.

Exclusivity

Closely related to jealousy and dependency is **exclusivity**. This is the point at which a couple block out other relationships to spend time exclusively with each other. Experience shows that this eventually kills a relationship. One of the two persons begins to feel suffocated and pulls away. Exclusivity, too, can drive away other friendships and important relationships that we need over the long haul. This remark by Steve, a high school student, shows how exclusivity can hurt our friendships:

"When my two best friends and I went to the university together, we hung out all the time with each other during most of the first semester freshmen year. It was really strange when Tim started going out real often with this new girlfriend. Tony and I felt left out. I would make these sarcastic comments to Tim. He'd get mad. Then I realized that I was sort of jealous, so I stopped. Things are better now."

Genuine love between two persons has a way of fostering their capacity for friendship and love with others; it does not stifle their relationships with others. **11**

For Review

- What is the difference between hope and expectations? How do expectations put pressure on the dating situation?
- What helpful things might one consider when thinking about what to do and where to go on a date?
- Describe the effect that infatuation has on a person's perception. What are four problems presented by infatuation?
- Briefly explain three hurdles that couples must overcome to have a true friendship.

11
Briefly describe a case in which jealousy, dependency, or exclusivity has ruined a potentially good relationship between a man and a woman.

Dating and Sex: Decisions with Consequences

Dating may challenge us to make decisions about sexual involvement. The following story illustrates some of the consequences of decisions about sex:

When Wendy was a junior in high school, she started dating Tom, who was a freshman at a college in town. After their first date, Wendy knew that Tom had been around. From some of the innuendoes that his friends made, Wendy got the idea that he had been involved sexually with several women. Wendy was flattered by Tom's attention. She felt that she must be pretty special, someone worth caring about. As Tom's girlfriend, Wendy also became more interesting to her classmates, and she met many other college students at the parties of Tom's friends.

Eventually, Tom began pressuring Wendy to have sex with him. She found it difficult to say no. Wendy was afraid that if she did not have sex with Tom, he would reject her, and all the new friendships that she was making would evaporate.

Saying yes to Tom did not help matters. He became possessive and demanded that she be ready to go out whenever he wanted and that she do whatever he wanted. The pressure of Tom's demands, her neglected schoolwork, and her worry about losing him made Wendy feel like a slave. Even so, Wendy broke off her relationship with Tom only after she saw him flirting with another woman.

Wendy thought that was the end of the situation, but it wasn't. She didn't feel well and began to suspect that she had caught some sort of sexually transmitted disease from Tom. The symptoms were there, she had to admit. Wendy was petrified of telling her parents because then they would know that she had

Student photo: Untitled, black-and-white photo by Greg Ulankiewicz, St. Viator High School, Arlington Heights, Illinois

200

had sex with Tom, but she was equally scared about the possibility of disease.

During the next two months Wendy refused dates with two other guys she had always wanted to go out with. Her grades suffered because she was so worried. The isolation terrified Wendy, but she knew that if she told her friends, they would feel superior and might even tell others.

Finally, in addition to the symptoms of the sexually transmitted disease, Wendy developed a case of bronchitis. In a visit to the family doctor, tired of the worry and fear, Wendy described her other symptoms to the doctor. After some tests, her fears were confirmed. Fortunately, the disease was treatable. Wendy was relieved of her physical problem, but the feelings of isolation, betrayal, guilt, and anger would not heal so easily.

Premarital sexual intercourse—having sex before marriage—may not end in pregnancy, sexually transmitted disease, or bitterness, but nothing guarantees that it will not. The decision to become sexually involved with someone always carries consequences of one kind or another, so the decision must be taken seriously.

Premarital Sex: Why and Why Not?

Valid Reasons?

Consider some of the reasons that young people give for having sexual intercourse with their dates:
- I may lose her if I don't have sex with her.
- We just got carried away.
- I won't be a man [woman] until I've had sex.
- Once we start drinking, forget about self-control.
- If we're in love, why isn't it okay to have sex?

- What's the big deal about putting on the brakes? Sex is what makes life interesting.
- Most of the people I know do it.
- She'll think I'm gay if I don't have sex with her.
- Sex will prove whether we love each other.
- It's okay to have sex because we'll get married if I get pregnant.

Long-term Consequences

The trouble with all the reasons advanced by people who want to have premarital sex or by those who coax their reluctant dating partners to have sex is that none of these reasons recognizes the long-term consequences of sexual intercourse before marriage.

Pregnancy. The most obvious consequence is premarital pregnancy, which affects not only the two partners and their families but also the whole life of the child who will be born. A child needs to be raised and loved in a stable family. A teenage single parent is not well equipped to raise a child. And if the young couple should marry under the pressure of a pregnancy, the stability of their marriage would be in serious question. "Shotgun" marriages have a poor chance of success. Moreover, abortion as a solution to a premarital pregnancy carries other deeply harmful consequences. **12**

Sexually transmitted disease. No one should be naive about the long-range effects of AIDS (acquired immunodeficiency syndrome), which at this point is fatal and incurable, and the less serious but incurable genital herpes simplex. Of course, sexually transmitted diseases (STDs) like gonorrhea, syphilis, chlamydia, and genital warts, though treatable, are not what we would wish to

12
Using current magazines and other sources, write a report on one of the following topics:
- **teenage pregnancies**
- **teenage marriages**
- **AIDS**
- **herpes**
- **another sexually transmitted disease**

give to or receive from someone we love. If no established commitment exists between two people who have sexual relations, it is dangerous to assume that a sexual partner has not had sex with someone else. Comments by Jill Savitt, a young woman from New York City, to an interviewer give an indication of the uneasy atmosphere in much of the dating scene today:

"A few weeks ago, I got a message on my answering machine from someone I dated in college. I hadn't heard from him since he graduated. He just said, 'Hi, give me a call.' In the time before AIDS, I just would have been flattered and curious. Instead, I wondered why he would call me out of the blue—if that could be why he needed to speak to me. . . . Finally, I returned the call, with great dread. As it turned out, he was just coming to town." (*13th Gen,* page 155)

In the age of AIDS, indiscriminate sex can be deadly. At the least, it can insert an unnecessary and unwelcome specter of fear into life.

A diminished relationship. Young people who choose to have sex while dating often assume that sex will enhance and deepen their relationship. Instead, it often leads to a diminished relationship. Without a long-term commitment, the relationship can take on a one-dimensional, sexual character. Other types of intimacy may be crowded out of the couple's awareness in favor of sex.

In addition, the emotions stirred by having sex may be so strong that they obscure the young persons' better judgment about their relationship; they may no longer be able to evaluate whether the relationship is healthy and whether they would really want to marry each other. The couple may lose the perspective that love is proved over years and through many types of intimacy. **13**

The Church's Response

You probably already know the Catholic church's view on the decision of whether to have sexual relations before marriage: *no.* What frequently gets lost in the decision-making process is why the church has traditionally taken this position.

Mutual commitment. Having sex without a firm, permanent commitment to each other means that the couple are not pledged to mutually bear the consequences of sexual intercourse. The church sees sexual relations as an expression of deep love between two people—love so profound that the two individuals pledge themselves to mutual, life-long commitment in marriage. The sexual intimacy that expresses this deep love should be the full meeting and sharing of body, mind, and heart; it is not to be taken lightly, as mere recreation or affectionate expression for people who are not committed to each other.

13
Do you agree that premarital sexual relations can crowd out the development of other types of intimacy in a relationship? Write a rationale for your position.

A life-giving context for children. The most obvious result of intercourse is the conception of a child. As a senior man from a Milwaukee high school said, "People forget that sex is about having *babies;* it's not just for having fun." When a baby is conceived from a couple's sexual union, it is cause for great joy and celebration. But the baby deserves to be born into a family, with a mother and a father, and this family setting is the most life-giving context for raising a child. The church, along with many psychologists and social scientists today, believes that sex outside of marriage puts the child born from that union at risk.

Members of Christ's Body. Saint Paul condemned fornication—sex outside of marriage—in his first letter to the Corinthians, who certainly knew about sexual immorality. Corinth had a reputation for being a wild city. Prostitution and all sorts of other sexual activity flourished there. Paul warned the Christians in Corinth to refrain from extramarital sex because it would tear apart the loving community that he was trying to build. In addition, he told the Corinthians:

The body is meant not for fornication but for the Lord, and the Lord for the body. And God raised the Lord and will also raise us by his power. Do you not know that your bodies are members of Christ? (1 Corinthians 6:13–15)

As members of Christ's Body who care for one another, Christians who are dating are called to do only what will promote the total good of the other person. **14**

We are sexual beings, blessed with sexuality so that we can bring about new life—children, love between a man and a woman, and other relation-

ships that flow from creating. Sex, like all fragile gifts, must be handled with care. It requires stability based on commitment.

For Review

- List five reasons that young people sometimes give for having sex before marriage.
- Describe three long-term consequences of premarital sex.
- Explain the church's reasons for its stand against premarital sex.

14
Imagine that it is twenty-five years from now and you are the parent of a teenager (decide on either a son or a daughter). In a letter to him or her, write whatever advice you want to give about sex before marriage.

Letting Go of a Romantic Relationship

Most dating relationships and romances do not eventually lead to marriage of the two individuals. And most people at your stage in life are quite tentative about considering a permanent commitment, even when they are dating someone they feel very strongly about. So the chances are that if you are "going out" with someone, at some point the relationship will end, and you will move on with your life. How that ending happens can be the most stressful part of dating, but it can be made less painful for both persons.

When Boundaries Are Crossed

Recall the discussion of boundaries on pages 180–181 of this text, and of how we need to establish and communicate our boundaries to other people. In a dating relationship, boundaries are crucial.

Making a break from someone who has violated our boundaries may not be easy, but it is imperative. If someone has disparaged, manipulated, or used us, we owe it to ourselves to say no to the relationship and get out of it. The cleaner and more complete the break, the better. We are not obliged to be cooperative with a violator. However, if that person has not respected our boundaries during the relationship, she or he will undoubtedly not respect them when we want out of the relationship. It is tough to extract ourselves from this entanglement when the person refuses to hear our no. If necessary, refuse phone calls, send back notes, and avoid the person. **15**

When It's Going Nowhere

It is a more delicate matter to let go of a relationship that just seems to be going nowhere. There does not appear to be a clear violation on the other person's part; you simply sense that it is over for a variety of reasons. Here are some suggestions about how to make a break and let go while doing the least damage to the two of you:

- Be up-front and honest all during the relationship. If you have talked frankly about what you believe, think, and like, and have allowed the same from your friend, you will more likely come to a mutual understanding about when to break up when the time comes.
- Periodically talk about your relationship itself. Keeping in mind the importance of using "I messages," share with your friend how you think the relationship is going—what you enjoy and what tough spots you see. Again, such talks may give early indications that the two of you may want to let go of the relationship.
- When you think you should let go, talk to a trusted friend that knows you both. Check out your perceptions with that friend and listen to advice. **16**

15
Write a list of your boundaries, lines you would not want someone else to cross if you were dating or "going out."

16
Complete this sentence with five separate answers: *A good reason to let go of a relationship is* . . .

- How to break the news? Person to person is best. It may be a painful encounter, but it is a necessary part of the process. Letting another person know it is over in a note or phone call is insensitive—unless, of course, that person has violated your boundaries or refuses to get the message that you want to end the relationship.
- Let go as friends, but let go. Communicate what you need to say in a kind way, but do not leave the door open or waffle. If you call or send cards to ease the blow of breaking up, you may signal that you are still interested in "going out" together, and the other person may cling to false hope. Maybe at a later time you will see more of each other again, romantically or not. For the time being, though, it is probably best to let communication rest until healing has had a chance to take place in both persons.

For Review

- What is the main message this chapter gives about breaking up with someone who has violated our boundaries?
- Give three pieces of advice for ending a dating relationship or romance when it is going nowhere.

The Dance of Dating

Like most things worth doing, creating and nourishing relationships with members of the other sex is challenging and energizing. As sexual beings, women and men will always be drawn toward each other. Dating provides women and men with ways of becoming friends and, sometimes, life partners. It also helps us to learn about one another and expand our vision of the world. Despite the problems we may experience with dating, it is an adventure worthy of our creativity, care, and energy. We are all invited to the ancient dance of spirit and body that is friendship between women and men.

God, you created women and men
 to dance together in joy and hope.
Bring your presence to our relationships
 with persons of the other sex,
So we might be filled with the grace
 and happiness of good encounters.
Give us wisdom to make good decisions in our
 relationships,
 and lead us with your light,
So our friendships bring us to the full life
 that you want for us.
Amen to friendship. Thanks be to you, Holy Friend.

Student art: "The Tango," acrylic painting by Regina Jeanpierre, Mercy High School, Omaha, Nebraska

- Right now in my life I'm down on dating. I just can't be bothered by all the pain and pressure of getting caught up in a romance, and then, bam, it's over and I'm alone. I have to get ready for my MCAT [Medical College Admissions Test].
- I don't like to date more than one person at a time. When I date someone, I need to know pretty quickly whether we're serious enough to start going together. If not, it's no use dating.

Eight different people equal eight different perspectives on dating. Many of the above comments represent the thoughts of young adults beyond high school age. For some of them, dating is closely linked in their minds with the possibility of marriage. However, few high school seniors are aiming toward marriage with a particular person when they date someone. The median age for first marriage in the United States has been getting older; it is now age twenty-six for men and age twenty-four for women.

Certainly **dating** calls on our confidence, our communication skills, our sense of values, and our creativity in using leisure. But above all, dating calls us to take the opportunity, in a relaxed and unpressured way, to enjoy another person, possibly to come to know that person deeply, and to learn about ourselves.

Dating can be a joy and an adventure. God did not want human beings to be alone, so we were created male and female, drawn by our very natures toward each other (Genesis 2:18). Our sexuality invites us to the great dance of soul and body, the dance of relating together as women and men. **1**

Not Always This Way

Each era in history has shaped the ways unmarried young men and women relate with one another. In fact, dating as we know it today is a relatively recent phenomenon, and it is not universal. Some

1
Women and men relating is often compared to a dance. Write one other metaphor or image that describes relating between the sexes: Women and men relating is like . . .

Photo (facing page): **Prom night in the 1950s**

cultures still arrange marriages for their children. In various societies strict prohibitions regulate relationships between adolescent girls and boys, and between unmarried young adults.

In the "Olden Days"

During the first two centuries of North American life—the **"olden days"**—young adults did not do what we call dating. Young women and men met almost always in the company of other people. They would meet at balls, in shops, on the street—in public. If a young man took special interest in a woman, he would "call" on her, presenting his calling card at the door. If the young woman admitted him, they would visit in the presence of her parents. Women might see several "callers." The young woman controlled who she saw. Repeated refusals to admit a caller indicated that the young woman was not interested in the man.

If a couple became serious about their relationship, they might start **"keeping company."** The woman would see only the one young man, who would visit her at her home—now largely unsupervised. The purpose of calling and keeping company was to find an acceptable mate. This usually meant that a young woman would see callers only of her own social class and religion.

In the "Classical Era" of Dating

With the advent of the automobile, longer school attendance for both women and men, and increased autonomy due to income from part-time jobs, the **"classical era"** of dating began. Dating meant that two people paired off into a couple to enjoy each other's company. Marriage was not the

primary motivation; enjoyment was. Peer culture, not adults, set the rules for dating. Dates—going to dances, movies, or parties—were largely unsupervised. If two people became serious, they went "steady." This usually meant that the boy would give the girl his class ring. The purpose of dating was to learn how to relate to the other sex, as in, "I need to date to develop my skills at relating so that when I find the right person, I will know how to be successful at marriage." The dating culture switched control to men. Women were supposed to wait until asked for a date by a man. Men paid for the movies, the dinners, and transportation. **2**

Nowadays

Much different norms prevail around dating today, and some young people would not even think of their time spent with persons of the other sex as "dates." Also, high school dating is less oriented to getting married than it used to be, because young adults tend to marry later in their twenties, and a sizable number opt not to marry at all.

2

In a brief paragraph, describe one advantage and one disadvantage of dating as it was practiced in the "olden days" or in the "classical era."

One phenomenon around male-female relationships today is that young men and women tend to get together informally in the context of larger groups. Women can initiate dates, and the expectation has evolved that often each person pays his or her way on a date, rather than the guy paying for both. Norms around dating are certainly in flux. One young man nicknamed Crasher summarizes his experience of how different today's male-female relating can be from the conventional understanding of dating:

"I can't remember a single time in high school that I went on a real, honest-to-goodness one-on-one '50s-style pick-her-up-in-the-car, go-to-a-movie-and-talk-on-the-porch date. It was always about five guys and six girls, randomly going to the mall, and then to some goofy pool party, and then maybe pairing off at the end. My prom experience was like some gigantic square dance; ten guys in tuxes went with the same number of girls in dresses. When the photographer asked us to pair off in couples, we couldn't figure out who to stand with. . . . Picking one person seemed a trifle silly. (*13th Gen,* page 154)

One welcome change in young adults' relating is that women and men are more likely now to have close friendships with each other, without the expectation that it must be romantic. When a one-to-one, paired romantic relationship exists, it may be called "going out," what used to be called "going steady" (the terminology, of course, varies from region to region). **3**

Why Date?

Looking at what motivates people to date is one way to gain insight into the dynamics of dating. In any given situation, a person's motives naturally will be mixed, and some motives can lead to more satisfaction than others. Any of the following motives might be combined in a particular instance of dating:

- *Sexual attraction.* We long to seek completion as persons through relationships with other people. Sexual attraction, which in its best sense is more than just physical attraction, moves us to explore relationships. This kind of attraction can ignite romantic love.
- *Fun.* Some people are funny, spontaneous, and interesting. On a date with such a person, we feel comfortable, accepted, and entertained. Dating is for the fun of it.
- *Ego boost.* Sometimes dating a particular person can boost our ego because that person is physically attractive, wealthy, or powerful. Although we may not like to admit it or even be aware of it, we might be dating that person to draw others' attention and approval to ourselves.

3
Write your response to this statement: *Today women feel equally able to initiate a relationship with men as men do with women.*

11

Single Life:
A Path to Living Fully

Singleness:
A Lifestyle in Its Own Right

Most people lead the single life for at least some part of their adulthood, and in that sense, being single is common. What is not so common is an appreciation of living singly as a path to fulfillment and happiness, just as the other lifestyles—marriage, religious life, and ordained ministry—can lead to fulfillment. Being single is not simply a state of being *not* married, *not* a religious, or *not* a priest. It is that, but also more than that: the **single life** is a lifestyle in its own right with its own unique opportunities and problems.

A Variety of Situations

Statistics show a dramatic rise in the number of single people living in the United States:

- Today, nearly one out of four households is composed of a single person. In 1970, only one out of six households was composed of a single person.

- The age for marrying is getting older: In 1970 the median ages for marrying were 23 for men, 21 for women. In 1990 the medians were 26 for men, 24 for women.

Many situations account for the single status of millions of adults:

- Some people are single because of the death of a spouse.

- Other people delay marriage for further education or a career, or because they have not found a person they want to marry.

- With the divorce rate at about 50 percent (that is, about half as many divorces as marriages occur in a year), a large percentage of singles are divorced people.

- Some people choose to remain single, and the number of singles in this category seems to be increasing.

The following remarks represent various situations of the single life:

- *Jan.* I've always been single. I've dated a lot and even came close to becoming engaged once, but then the decision came down to whether I liked the way my life was going or I wanted to change it by marrying. I had to admit that I liked being able to travel as much as I do without feeling that I was neglecting kids or a husband. And now I'm next in line for a promotion. If I get it, I'll have to move to Pittsburgh. The promotion is a great opportunity that I might not have had the freedom to accept if I'd gotten married. Sure, I get lonely sometimes, and I may get married someday. But I'm just not ready to take on that type of responsibility. Maybe, because I'm thirty-three, I'm fooling myself that I might get married someday. For right now, though, I'm really happy with my life as it is. **1**

- *Alan.* If I couldn't use a can opener, and microwave dinners didn't exist, I'd be in big trouble. No, really I'm coping, but I'm also realizing all the stuff that I don't know about being a parent. Ever since my wife and I separated, I've come to appreciate all the work that she did. After four months of being a single parent, I still mess up the wash cycles on the laundry, occasionally forget what time Scottie gets out of day care, and on and on. The worst thing— I'll never forget it—was when I came home from work, still ticked off at one of the accountants, and I started dinner and completely forgot to pick up poor Scottie. I still get real emotional when I think about how I got there and found him sitting on the steps, crying his eyes out. I'll never forget to pick him up again. Like I say, things are rotten sometimes, but I'm much closer to my son now than I ever used to be, and that's great.

- *Cal.* I graduated from the U in May; I thought I would have a job by now. Last month I had to move out of the apartment that I rented with two friends. I just couldn't afford it. I'm still looking for a job, so I've moved back in with my folks. We get along okay, and they're glad to help out. It's a good thing I'm not seriously involved with anyone right now. I don't have a solid job, a place of my own, or enough money. But I have good friends, my family, and I'm working hard at finding a job. I'll be okay. **2**

- *Ruth.* I never thought Charlie would die so suddenly and so young. He was only sixty-three. We had talked a lot about things we would do when we retired. After three years, I've adjusted pretty well. Lucky for me, I had been working at the same job for fifteen years. Just having to get up and go to work helped me during those first months after he died. Since I quit work last year, I've gotten involved in local senior citizen activities. Next week my good friend and her husband and I are going to an Elderhostel program in New Mexico [Elderhostel is a summer program for older persons that consists of short courses offered at college campuses]. We attended one last year and took courses on the Civil War, the flowers of Virginia, and the Gospel of Mark. The program is only a week long, and the price is reasonable. I learn a lot, and it's a nice chance to meet other folks. I still miss Charlie, but he wouldn't want me to mope around. He would want me to enjoy life.

Whether chosen or the result of circumstances, temporary or permanent, the single lifestyle can be purposeful and rich in experience. But as is true of any path in life, singleness is not smooth all the way; it too has its potholes and bumps along the road.

1
In writing, share your reactions to Jan's comments.

2
How do you feel about Cal's situation? Write your reactions in a brief paragraph.

By Choice or by Chance?

For people who choose to remain single because of a conviction that this lifestyle represents the best way for them to grow and to make a contribution to the world, the single life is a vocation, a calling. Other persons who are single by force of circumstance and who do not wish to embrace the single life permanently still need to value their singleness as a lifestyle, even if their single status lasts only for a short time. They need not consider this phase of life as merely a "holding pattern" until something better comes along.

The story of a life's unfolding can be mysterious indeed, with events and circumstances eventually bringing forth unimagined fruits. By valuing the opportunities and challenges of singleness, even if this lifestyle is a matter of circumstance and not choice, a single person can make a valuable contribution to humankind and can develop his or her own life, too. Instead of waiting for life to happen, a single person can make decisions that give life joy, meaning, and direction whether the person marries later or stays single.

A Life of Loving

Central to the call for all Christians is the command to love God and neighbor. Love is essential to happiness and to a sense of meaning in life, and love can be given and received whether a person is single, married, religious, or ordained. The single life is as much a call to love as the other lifestyles are. The person who taught us most dramatically and effectively about the centrality of love was Jesus—a single person. Within a single lifestyle, Jesus answered the call to love, giving Christians for all time a model of how the single life can be a life of love.

Many single people love, create life and happiness around them, and live meaningfully in ways like these:

- having a circle of generous, supportive friends
- playing music or sports, cycling, dancing, running, acting in community theater, or traveling
- being good at their jobs—both in their dedication to the work itself and in the ways they treat their coworkers
- learning and developing skills such as drawing, painting, writing, or reading good literature
- caring about their family—spending time with brothers and sisters, cousins, aunts and uncles, nieces and nephews, grandparents, and parents
- doing volunteer work in parishes, soup kitchens, programs for the handicapped, and so on
- giving their time and talents to causes such as human rights and the environment
- working as a volunteer in places where people are in need—for example, internationally with organizations like the Peace Corps, Catholic Relief Services, and Maryknoll Lay Missioners, or domestically through groups like the Jesuit Volunteer Corps **3**

3
If you knew that you would be single for the next fifteen years, which three of these ways of living meaningfully would you find most appealing? Explain your choices in writing.

Jean Donovan:
A Call to Serve in El Salvador

In the late 1970s a young single woman from Cleveland, Ohio, found herself pulled from a rather comfortable life by a sense that she was meant for something more. At twenty-four years of age, **Jean Donovan** had a master's degree in economics, an executive position with one of the largest accounting firms in the United States, a nice apartment, her own car, and a motorcycle. She had close friends and a caring family. Yet she also had a belief that she was called to work with the poor people of El Salvador. So Donovan left the security of job, relationships, and possessions to join a team of Catholic missionaries who were distributing food and clothing to Salvadoran victims of the civil war that was tearing the country apart. She explained why she went into this dangerous situation:

"I have been thinking about this vocation for many years. Actually I think, that for a number of years, Christ has been sending various people into my life, that through their example and actions I saw a calling to missionary work. I have a gut feeling that my main motivation to be a missionary is a true calling from God." (*Salvador Witness*, page 67)

Death squads were killing anyone who showed the least sign of opposition to the Salvadoran government and to the powerful, rich elite. Some priests and religious had already been killed. Donovan knew this before she went to El Salvador. Once there, she wrote:

There's one thing I know, that I'm supposed to be down here, right now. Not that I'm going to be able to do anything, or contribute to anything, but it's just a feeling I have. And maybe—maybe I *will* be able to. . . . I read a very interesting article . . . about Tom Dooley hospital [Dooley, a single man, was a doctor who served in Laos in the 1950s and 1960s during a civil war]—and two of the things that really hit me in it were: first, that you can contribute a lot and make a big difference in the world if you realize that the world you're talking about might be very small— maybe one person, or two people. And the other thing it said was that if you can find a place to serve, you can be happy. I think, they're both really true. (Page 96) **4**

Because of their work with poor people and other victims of the civil war, Donovan and three U.S. women who were members of religious orders were targeted for execution. Donovan knew that she was in danger; anyone who helped poor Salvado-

---

■

Photos (left and right): Jean Donovan and Central American children, like those she went to serve in El Salvador

4
Do you agree with this statement by Jean Donovan? Think of instances when you have made a big difference in the world—even if that world consisted of only one or two persons. Describe one instance in writing.

rans or showed the slightest objection to the military was at grave risk. Death came in December 1980, when Donovan and the other three women were returning from the airport to the town where they worked. Their van was stopped by Salvadoran national guardsmen. The women were raped, murdered, and buried in a shallow grave.

Jean Donovan said yes to life, found meaning in caring for other people, and gave up her life for them. She probably would have felt that she was answering her call to serve even if she had contributed to the lives of only one or two persons. But Donovan could not have anticipated the inspiration that her life and death would give others. After the deaths of these four U.S. women, thousands of North Americans for the first time opened their eyes to the injustices being done in El Salvador and became involved in a huge, influential U.S. religious movement for justice. **5**

Christians are called to live out the mission of love in unique ways. For Jean Donovan, the way to live out that mission was as a single woman. A person who wants to discern her or his distinct call needs to ask the question How is God calling me to grow, to develop, to love, and to serve? For some people, the vocation will be to a single life.

For Review

- Summarize the reasons that Jan, Alan, Cal, and Ruth are single and how each of them feels about it.
- What is central to God's call for all Christians, including those who are single?
- What question does a person need to ask to discern his or her distinct call?

Being Single: Opportunities and Problems

The single life, like every lifestyle, has unique opportunities and problems. Built-in risks accompany opportunities. Whether a person is single permanently or temporarily, by choice or by circumstance, considering the various opportunities and problems can help that person consciously shape her or his decisions about how to live. **6**

5
What do you think of Jean Donovan's decision to leave her career and serve the poor people of El Salvador? Write your reactions.

6
List five single people you know over the age of twenty-two. Interview one or two to find out what they see as the advantages and the disadvantages of the single life. Then summarize each interview in a report.

Freedom or Egocentrism?

The Opportunity: Freedom

A single person has **freedom** to make decisions based on his or her convictions, needs, or goals. Lynn Cohen, an engineer and software developer, likes living alone for the freedom it offers. He told *Newsweek:* "'I come and go pretty much as I please and I don't have to explain what's what and where I'm going.'" Or take Jack's situation:

For several years Jack has been eager to move out of the city to the mountains. He wants to hike, fish, hunt, and breathe the clean air—not only on vacations but all year round. Jack knows that he can quit his job as a mechanic at the airport and support himself on less money with a highway maintenance job. He realizes that if he were married and had kids, the decision would have to take into account his wife's desires and job, and their children's needs. This decision is easier for Jack than it would be for a married person.

Single people have the freedom to choose for themselves—from simple choices like where to go for dinner, to complex decisions like cross-country moves or career changes. They can involve themselves in unpopular causes or take on volunteer tasks that might seem impractical or risky to some observers. For instance, Jean Donovan put her life in danger. A married person with young children would need to evaluate her or his decision to take such a risk against a very different backdrop of responsibilities and concerns.

Dorothy Day, cofounder (with **Peter Maurin**) of the **Catholic Worker Movement**, lived her single life with the freedom that she believed all Chris-tians are called to have. In the 1930s she began a newspaper that advocated peace and justice (which still sells for a penny a copy), and she started a network of houses of hospitality (staffed primarily by single people), which continue to shelter the homeless and feed the hungry. She was arrested many times in protests against U.S. involvement in three different wars, in marches for voters' rights, and in support of strikes by migrant farmworkers. Throughout these events, Day kept speaking out in print and in person, spreading the Gospel message.

What Day preached was a stirring call to leave behind the false thinking of the times—a thinking that trapped people into maintaining personal security rather than living the freedom of the Gospel. These words about security, written by Day in 1935, have a very contemporary ring:

Christ told Peter to put aside his nets and follow Him. He told the rich young man to sell what he had and

Photo: **Dorothy Day**

give to the poor and follow Him. . . . He spoke of feeding the poor, sheltering the homeless, of visiting those in prison and the sick, and also of instructing the ignorant. . . .

Paul Claudel [a twentieth-century French philosopher] said that young people have a hunger for the heroic, and too long they have been told: "Be moderate, be prudent." . . . **7**

In this present situation when people are starving to death [although] there is an overabundance of food, when religion is being warred upon throughout the world, our Catholic young people still come from schools and colleges and talk about looking for security, a weekly wage. . . .

Why they think a weekly wage is going to give them security is a mystery. Do they have security on any job nowadays? If they try to save, the bank fails; if they invest their money, the bottom of the market drops out. If they trust to worldly practicality, in other words, they are out of luck. . . .

What right has any one of us to security when God's poor are suffering?

Strong challenges, tough words. They came from a woman who gave up a career in commercial journalism to do just what she challenged others to do. She intended her message for Christians in all walks of life, not only in the single life. But her own single lifestyle gave her the freedom to live without the types of guarantees that many of us want.

The Problem: Egocentrism

At the same time that the single life offers the freedom to make decisions based on a person's own convictions, needs, and desires, it presents a parallel problem—the danger of developing **egocentrism**, a self-centered or selfish outlook.

Particularly if a single person lives alone, he or she may not have the constant opportunity for give-and-take relationships that are part of a community whose members are committed to one another, such as a family or a religious community. Such relationships rub off some of the rough edges of an individual's personality, enabling a person to adjust to other people's needs and ways of living. **8**

In the extreme, a lack of give-and-take relationships can lead to an inability to commit oneself to anything or anyone. The freedom to choose may become so distorted that an individual is absorbed only in choices that imply no involvement or commitment. When love is possible, an egocentric person might push away, saying that she or he does not want to be tied down. Responsibility in a group endeavor might be avoided because she or he "just cannot plan that far ahead." Some egocentric individuals literally wander from job to job, or city to city, continuously moving away from commitment. Such is the case of Pete:

7
List ways that people have told you to be moderate or prudent. Then answer in writing: *What can happen to people who live their entire lives being moderate—never being heroic in relationships or taking a stand on principle?*

Student art: **Untitled, mixed media relief sculpture by Alicia DiBenedetto, Boylan Catholic High School, Rockford, Illinois**

8
Do you have any rough edges in your personality that might become exaggerated if you lived alone? If you are unaware of any, ask your parents, brothers or sisters, or close friends.

I had a job out of college, but it was 9 to 5—crazy as far as getting up every day, so I quit. I figure if I can just do a little afternoon or evening temp work through an agency for a while and crash at my friends' apartment, I can get by. They're not too crazy about it, but . . . I've been thinking about moving out to California, but then I hear the job situation is even tougher there. Anyway, I'll get out of here soon enough, I guess. It's a good thing I got Mindy out of my life; she was trouble, always looking for some kind of "commitment." I kind of like hanging loose. I don't want to have to live up to anyone's expectations. I can just blow around wherever I want to go.

Flexibility and freedom are advantages of single life, but when a person makes no commitments and is rootless, life can lack purpose. Establishing a career and stable, intimate relationships does not necessarily become easier later in life. **9**

Another form of egocentrism appears as a narcissistic preoccupation with consuming things. The world, and even relationships, become just a vehicle for satisfying one's own needs and wants. Marcy is a case in point:

With my income, I can have the condo I want, plus a vacation-share place in the islands, a new car every year—and no headaches trying to work all this stuff out with some guy. When I want something, I just buy it. And I buy the best, the absolute best, whether it's clothes or jewelry or furniture, and I don't want any hassles deciding what to get. Why would I be crazy enough to consider marriage? I have a great life!

Solitude or Loneliness?

The Opportunity: Solitude

Some people assume that being alone is the same as loneliness, an emotionally painful condition. They fear being alone and dread being single if it means coming home to an empty apartment every night. Samuel Johnson, perhaps the grumpiest writer of the eighteenth century, declared, "The solitary mortal is certainly luxurious, probably superstitious, and possibly mad."

Actually, time spent alone can be full and renewing. **Solitude**—being alone for thought, creative pursuits, rest, learning, or prayer—is necessary for growth as a person. The single life generally offers a greater opportunity for solitude than the other

Student art: "Negative," white charcoal drawing by Shawn M. Beirne, Holy Cross High School, Louisville, Kentucky

9
Can you think of any other examples of people without commitments whose lives are shapeless? Write your reflections on how you think their life became this way.

lifestyles because a single person typically has more control over his or her time and space. **10**

Many creative single persons have had the solitude to develop their talents. Among such persons was **Flannery O'Connor,** one of the most original and respected U.S. fiction writers of this century. For many of her productive years before her death in 1964, she suffered from a disease that handicapped her. Her letters show her to have been feisty, witty, committed, and largely content with who she was. O'Connor learned to live with her illness and to use the solitude of her single life to think, write, and be creative. In one of her letters she wrote:

In a sense sickness is a place, more instructive than a long trip to Europe, and it's always a place where there's no company, where nobody can follow. Sickness before death is a very appropriate thing and I think those who don't have it miss one of God's mercies. (*Habit of Being,* page 163)

O'Connor did not readily express her emotions about her illness and the anguish that it caused her. But as she indicated in the same letter, her inner emotional world gave thrust to her creativity:

But the surface hereabouts has always been very flat. I come from a family where the only emotion respectable to show is irritation. In some this tendency produces hives, in others literature, in me both. (Page 164)

On another occasion, O'Connor wrote wryly about herself as a person of faith:

I am not a mystic and I do not lead a holy life. Not that I can claim any interesting or pleasurable sins (my sense of the devil is strong) but I know all about the

garden variety, pride, gluttony, envy and sloth, and what is more to the point, my virtues are as timid as my vices. . . .

However, the individual in the Church is, no matter how worthless himself, a part of the Body of Christ. . . . [But] I distrust pious phrases, particularly when they issue from my mouth. (*Habit of Being,* pages 92–93)

O'Connor's letters, written wittily in the midst of chronic illness, point to an advantage of being single: To live fully, we all must come to grips with who we are and accept ourselves. Single people have the space and time to encounter themselves and to reflect on their experiences. By living alone, they may have a harder time running away from themselves than do people who are surrounded by family.

Solitude can urge us to appreciate our relationships more. Sometimes we can see the beauty of good friends and family only when we have been away from them for a while. Shirley, a woman in her mid-thirties, remarks on a special annual opportunity for solitude that she takes:

I lead a very hectic life, usually committed to too many things at once. I can really get fried! But every year, the week after Christmas, I go off to this retreat center for a week of quiet in a hermitage, a little cottage for one person. I bring my own food and cook, and spend my days just being at home with myself, sitting and looking at the mountains, praying, writing

10
Describe in writing the last time that you wanted some solitude:
- **What made you want time and space to be alone?**
- **If you were able to be in solitude, did the experience help you?**

in my journal, talking occasionally with the sister who runs the center. It ends up being a significant time for me. I've made a lot of important decisions about directions for my life during those weeks. And I always feel restored being there.

People like Flannery O'Connor and Shirley remind us that being alone does not necessarily mean being lonely.

The Problem: Loneliness

Being alone is not always experienced in a positive way, as solitude. It may be experienced instead as **loneliness**, a feeling of sadness from being alone. Even when we are physically with people, we can feel lonely if we are psychologically isolated or alienated from them. Loneliness can exist in any walk of life, including marriage. It is part of the human condition. **11**

Single life perhaps presents more obvious occasions for loneliness. One experience that single people who live alone frequently have is the difficulty of coming home after a splendid day. No one is there to talk with about a great success, so the victory seems flat. Or after a bad day, a single person needs a willing listener to help make sense of a failure, but no one is there to talk with, and the trouble seems to grow even worse. Eating meals alone, especially in restaurants, can feel particularly awkward and lonely. In a 1993 *Newsweek* article, Dione Donnelly, a widow, spoke for a lot of single people when she said: "'The thing that bothers me the most is not having someone to share all the small everyday details that couldn't possibly interest anybody else.'"

This loneliness takes tangible form sometimes in its inconvenience. A woman quoted in a 1993 issue of the *Utne Reader* reflected on the situation she often finds herself in:

Nobody lends a hand. We can't say, "Would you get the door for me?—hand me the towel?—hold up the other end?—go see what's making that funny noise?—grab the cat while I shove the pill down her?—answer the phone?—mail a letter?—put your finger on this knot?" . . . We do it ourselves or not at all. . . . Only we will carry out the trash and carry in the groceries and cope with the IRS. . . . If the couch is too heavy for one person to move, it stays where it is, waiting for the next strong guest. And only we will answer when we speak.

As a single person grows older, the fear of being alone in old age also grows. Not having children or a community to take care of him or her during periods of illness can burden a single person with worry, physical distress, and loneliness.

11
Recall a lonely time. Then reflect on these questions in writing:
- **Why were you lonely instead of simply alone?**
- **What made loneliness different from solitude?**
- **How did you respond to it?**

Loneliness can be heightened for divorced or widowed people. After years of living intimately with someone, they are suddenly deprived of companionship, affection, and the challenges of living closely with another person. A huge gap exists in their lives. Even if the relationship had been a difficult one, it nevertheless provided shape and form to life, and the absence of that relationship leaves a person feeling disconnected.

Although loneliness can be a painful problem of being single, it can also be an opportunity. Painful experiences are not always to be avoided; sometimes they are the path to growth. Psychologist Clark E. Moustakas, who has done extensive studies on loneliness, drew this conclusion:

Loneliness keeps open the doors to an expanding life. In utter loneliness, one can find answers to living, one can find new values to live by, one can see a new path or direction. Something totally new is revealed.

. . . It is not loneliness which separates the person from others but the terror of loneliness and the constant effort to escape it. . . .

Loneliness is as much a reality of life as night and rain and thunder, and it can be lived creatively, as any other experience. So I say, let there be loneliness, for where there is loneliness there is also sensitivity, and where there is sensitivity, there is awareness and recognition and promise. (*Loneliness,* pages 102–103)

These may seem like strange words from a psychologist because the common belief is that loneliness should be escaped at all costs. But the pain of loneliness is also the pain of being human. **Dag Hammarskjöld**, a Swedish man who served as secretary-general of the United Nations from 1953 to 1961, understood this aspect of loneliness from his own life as a single person. This dedicated peacemaker wrote his personal reflections in a journal. After Hammarskjöld's death, his notes were published as a book entitled *Markings*. His book has inspired millions of people around the world. On loneliness, Hammarskjöld wrote:

What makes loneliness an anguish
Is not that I have no one to share my burden,
But this:
I have only my own burden to bear.

. . . .

Pray that your loneliness may spur you into finding something to live for, great enough to die for. **12**

(Page 85)

12
Have you found anything that is "something to live for, great enough to die for"? Write your reflections on this question.

The challenge of transforming the problem of loneliness into an opportunity involves using the loneliness, as Hammarskjöld did, to experience a deeper level of being human. Loneliness becomes hazardous when a person cannot grow by it but instead becomes completely paralyzed by it, falling into a downward spiral of depression and negative thinking.

Wider Friendships or Not Belonging with One Special Person?

The Opportunity: Wider Friendships

For a single person who has no children or the kind of intense involvement that family requires, the possibility of a wide network of friendships opens up. Married people, religious, and priests have friends too, but the particular commitments of their lifestyles tend to focus their relationships more on family, the religious community, and their ministry, respectively. A single person may have the time and space to pursue a much broader range of friendships and types of intimacy—recreational, intellectual, aesthetic, spiritual, work, common-cause, and so on. Because the single lifestyle does not provide ready-made relationships, a single person must exert a great deal of initiative to create a network of friends, but the rewards of those relationships can be great. **13**

Doris is an example of a woman who has taken the initiative in friendships during her single life, since her husband left her twenty-five years ago. A younger friend comments about Doris's life:

When I was growing up, Doris was the most exciting person I'd ever known. I would go to the big city to stay with her for a few days, and she would treat me like a princess, showing me the sights, buying me a new dress. Then we would pop in on her friends or bump into them on the street—what an incredible variety of human beings!

There was the old woman from Italy who made spaghetti for her, the security guard she became good friends with while serving on a jury, the priest she met in Vatican City who turned out to be the pope's assistant, the fatherless little boy whom she was teaching to ice skate, the nuns who had served with her in the refugee camps of Vietnam, the doctor from the Philippines and her elderly mother, a young Japanese couple for whom she was searching for housing. And that's only the beginning.

Doris knew everyone, not just casually but at some very significant level. Her friends seemed to look to her for a special grace. I think she brought a kind of magic into their lives. I know she brought it into mine. Her life has been all about friendship.

13
Ask a married couple about the role of friendships in their former single life versus in their present married life. Ask them how friendships have changed for them since they were single. Write up their answers.

The Problem:
Not Belonging with One Special Person

Even if a single person has a wide variety of friends, she or he is not immune to the ache of not belonging with one special person. Kent, a thirty-eight-year-old electrician, expresses this feeling:

You know, sometimes I come home and wonder what I'll be like when I'm seventy, if I live that long. Most single men die earlier than married men do. That's a sobering thought, eh? Anyway, what bothers me is that with all my good friends I still don't have anybody who is there all the time for me. Sundays or days when I'm feeling lousy are the worst. It's not just loneliness but more—Who cares for me in particular? focuses their attention primarily on me?

Kent poses a question that many single people ask, especially as they approach middle age, when they begin to confront their own aging process. Although Kent has friends who care for him, he knows that none of them can be as responsible to him and for him as a spouse would be. Many married older people do lose their spouse; thus marriage does not guarantee companionship in old age. But that fact does not quite satisfy the doubts from which Kent's concern originates. **14**

Professional Commitment or Job Traps?

The Opportunity: Professional Commitment

Some people make the decision to stay single because they truly want to focus more on their work than on relationships with a spouse and children. Remaining single also gives the individual the flexibility to relocate for a new job or a promotion,

perhaps even across the country, if such a move seems desirable. A cross-country move with a family is much more difficult. Consider this situation:

Stan is a dedicated young lawyer who works in consumer advocacy. His work involves bringing lawsuits against national corporations that produce unsafe or ineffective consumer products. Of his decision not to marry, Stan says, "I am married to my work. I love what I'm doing. With the kind of schedule I keep, it would be irresponsible for me to marry. I'm constantly traveling, and my hours are completely irregular. Besides that, my salary as a consumer advocate is barely enough to feed myself, let alone anyone else."

If Stan were to assume the responsibilities of marriage, he would have to divide his energies between his family and his work. The single life gives him the opportunity to commit himself to his profession as he feels called to do.

The Problem: Job Traps

In the situation above, the young lawyer feels married to his work; it is the major focus of his life. Employers and other workers certainly cannot and should not expect that kind of dedication from single professionals, yet sometimes single people end up feeling trapped by that exact expectation. Ann, an assistant dean of students, is immersed in her career and enjoys it. But she describes the problem of dealing with others' expectations:

I think [my career] takes up a greater portion of my time as a single person than it would for someone who is married. . . . A good 80 percent of what I do is job-related. I think that's one of the myths about the single lifestyle . . . that it must be nice because you can go home and don't have the family there;

14
Have you ever had the desire to belong with one special person? If so, write about the feeling. Explore why you felt the way you did.

you don't have "responsibilities." But if you are a single person in a career, particularly a career where you are with people a lot or people look to you for leadership, people tend to think that you are never off duty. Consequently, you can many times be much more taken up by projects and by people than if you aren't single. (*Love and Lifestyles,* page 88) **15**

The expectation that a single person can absorb unlimited work assignments because he or she is not married is unfair. Single people, like everyone else, have needs for relationships, fun, and solitude.

Employers or other workers also may assume that single persons are not as entitled to pay raises and promotions as married persons are. A complaint heard in a discrimination suit against a college uncovered this situation:

A woman who was a college basketball and volleyball coach was not promoted to athletic director because, as she was told, "Larry has a family to support and needs the job more. You're single, and so it's not as important." The woman coach had been at the college longer, had led her teams to conference titles, and had received the full support of a large segment of the community. She was discriminated against not only as a woman but also as a single person.

A Less Expensive or More Expensive Lifestyle?

The Opportunity: A Less Expensive Lifestyle

A person who is choosing a lifestyle might wonder, Is it more costly to live as a single person or as a married person? The answer, of course, depends not on whether the person is single, but on the standard of living that the person decides is necessary. Lifestyle is a function of one's priorities and values. However, certain factors make single life potentially less expensive, and other factors make it potentially more expensive.

On the less expensive side, a single person obviously does not have to help support a spouse and children. The need to feed, clothe, shelter, educate, get medical care, find recreation, and so on, applies only to an individual, not to a whole family. Furthermore, a single person can opt for a simple lifestyle that might be more difficult with a family. For example, some single persons choose to live in a convenient location without a car and major appliances such as a washing machine because they can get around easily on public transportation or on foot and can wash their clothes at a nearby laundromat. It is more difficult for a family to live without a car or a washing machine.

Another less expensive option for some single people is to share housing with friends or family. Over the past few years, given the tight job market for young people just out of high school or college, many young adults have been moving back in with their parents for a time. Although this option is not considered ideal by most, it can have the advantage of cutting costs dramatically.

So the single life, with economic decisions to be made by and for only one individual, can be a less expensive lifestyle.

The Problem: A More Expensive Lifestyle

Living alone can also be expensive. Like a married couple beginning to furnish an apartment, a single person needs furniture, a radio, towels, and so on. The key difference is that a single person has to pay for these items with one income instead of a potential two incomes that a couple may have.

15
If you were permanently single, do you think you would feel more like Stan or more like Ann about your work? Explain your answer in a paragraph.

Taxes often are higher for single people with no dependents. Insurance rates frequently are higher per person, too, especially for single men. Single people tend to eat out more often than married people or those living in communities.

In order to meet more people, singles sometimes choose to live in rather expensive singles apartment complexes, to join costly health spas, or to spend more money on entertainment than if they were married. What could be a less expensive lifestyle can turn into a high-priced way of life.

For Review

- How can being single allow a person more freedom? a wider circle of friendships?
- What is egocentrism, and how can it be a problem for singles?
- How can solitude be a full and renewing part of the single life?
- How can loneliness be both a problem and an opportunity for single persons?
- What is a question that many single people ask as they begin to face their own aging?
- How can singleness be an opportunity and a problem with regard to one's career?

A Life Full of Possibilities

At some phase of life, most of us live the single life.
- You might wish to examine how singleness, whether permanent or temporary, could contribute to your being fully alive—developing as a person and contributing to the world.
- You might reflect on some of the problems of being single and how you would deal with them.

If being single is a temporary decision for you and someday you would like to marry or enter religious life or the priesthood, you might treat your time of singleness as a chance to learn more about yourself, establish a career, develop wider friendships, and explore life. Whether it is a temporary or a permanent state, being single needs to be thought of as a fruitful way of life, one that is full of possibilities. **16**

Dag Hammarskjöld's personal reflection on individuality offers wisdom for all of us on how to live a fulfilling and generous life, whether single or otherwise:

Don't be afraid of yourself, live your individuality to the full—but for the good of others. Don't copy others in order to buy fellowship, or make convention your law instead of living the righteousness.

To become free and responsible. For this alone [were] man [and woman] created. (*Markings,* page 53)

Hammarskjöld's reflection can lead us to prayer:

Kind God,
As a single person now and for an indefinite time in the future, may I learn to be free and responsible, alive to the possibilities of life on my own. May I use my freedom to be creative, to learn, to form close friendships, to explore, and to be of service. May I take responsibility for making the world a better place and for living joyfully and with love. I ask this in the name of Jesus, who lived his life as a single person. Amen.

16
Write a brief summary of your ideas about the way that being single, either permanently or temporarily, fits into your notion of living fully.

12

Marrying:
Finding a Life Partner

'The relationship is still on'; of asking, 'Is the relationship still on?' It was my way of saying, 'Keep me, I'm good!' (even when sex wasn't always that good), and of reassuring myself, 'See, he still loves me.'

"Important questions were never settled, things like: 'What if I get offered a good job in another state?' or 'What if he decides to go back to school?' or 'The Pill is making me depressed—should I stop taking it?' We'd just end up in bed again, without resolving things. I got to the point where I felt like yelling, 'Sex, schmex! I just want you to talk to me!'

"I told Tom I wanted to move out and think things over. I wanted him to really see me and hear me as a person—something our sexual involvement made it hard for him to do. I wanted perspective—and friendship.

"I must say that—after the initial shock—Tom rose to the challenge. We spent a whole year getting to know each other every way but horizontally. We must have logged 1000 hours just talking. And I knew I wasn't sliding into something through compliance and neediness and emotional fuzziness: I was exercising real sexual intelligence. That gave me new respect for myself—and for Tom.

"We're getting married. It took a while, but now we know we're committed."

As Marsha testifies, communication is the best way for a couple to discover whether they want to get married and tie their destinies together. **4**

Communicating About What?

Many marriage counselors would recommend that a couple considering marriage ask themselves the following questions and spend a lot of time, as Marsha and Tom did, communicating about them.

1. Do we agree about the roles that men and women play in marriage? If a wife needs or wants to work and the husband refuses to take equal responsibility for household chores, trouble is likely. The couple must know what each person expects about roles in the marriage. Compromise is always necessary; that means give-and-take on both sides. In addition, men and women are not static. Changing roles will require adjustments. For instance, a wife may be offered a promotion that requires a move. This change in status will require a commitment to mutual decision making. If the couple has not worked out some understanding before marriage, the relationship could rupture.

2. Do we have the support of our families? When two persons marry, they become part of each other's family. They need time to get to know future in-laws; to build solid, healthy relationships with them; and to anticipate what it will be like to be part of an extended family. Any concerns about disliking future in-laws, finding them too demanding, or feeling judged by them need plenty of discussion and resolution by the couple because the

4
Do you agree or disagree with this statement? *Cohabitation is not a good way to test out the potential for a marriage.* **Explain in writing.**

rest of their lives will be bound with their in-laws' lives to some degree.

3. **Are we too young?** Teenage marriages have a poor chance of lasting. If two teenagers do not have a strong sense of their own identity, marriage between them means that two immature, impressionable persons have entered into a situation demanding maturity, responsibility, and competence. The strain can be too much for the relationship. Furthermore, people who marry before they have had a chance to study, work, travel, or date several people may eventually resent the loss of their young adulthood. This resentment can also cripple a marriage.

4. **Can we both tolerate genuine intimacy?** Intimacy is essential for a lasting marriage. Marriage demands emotional, sexual, spiritual, and intellectual intimacy *at the very least*. However, some people cannot tolerate very much closeness. One who is seriously dating another person should ask these additional questions:
• Do either of us avoid dates that include just the two of us together?
• Do we share significant experiences?
• Can we talk comfortably for long periods of time?
• Can we relax together and not have to talk or do something?
• Are our needs for closeness somewhat similar?

5. **Can each of us accept change in the other?** Change is inevitable. If one person changes and the other cannot accept that change, the relationship is in jeopardy. One should consider how the other person reacts to a change of mind or a new interest.

5
Of the nineteen questions posed on the next few pages, select five that you can answer for yourself and respond to them in writing. For example, Can I tolerate genuine intimacy?

6. **Can each of us stand psychologically on our own two feet?** Marriages have been destroyed when one of the partners is dominated by his or her parents, a boss, or a group of old friends. So a person needs to look carefully at these questions:
• How do our parents (both sets) relate to their other married children?
• Do the parents or boss or old friends of either of us seek control of our time, energy, or resources to the detriment of our relationship?
Marriage counselors report that the problem of being psychologically tied to others in an unhealthy way, particularly to parents and old friends, is more common than people admit it to be. **5**

7. **Do we give each other time and space to be on our own—alone or with our own friends?** Marriage or any healthy relationship relies on each person's retaining her or his own identity. In fact, good relationships enhance each person's identity.

Two full persons share themselves in marriage. Some further questions can help to address this larger issue:

• Do we encourage each other to pursue our respective interests, or are one person's interests always primary?

• Do both of us consider each other's needs important?

• Is either of us jealous or possessive?

• Do either of us resent the demands placed on us by our partner and feel smothered at times?

• Do either of us feel like nothing when the two of us are apart?

If you cannot live without your partner, or vice versa, you should seriously reconsider the relationship; you may not have explored sufficiently the fullness of the persons that you are. Marriage is not the absorption of one person's life by another.

8. What part would children play in our marriage? Children are an important consideration before marriage. Parenthood is intensely demanding. Both persons must be willing to assume such a responsibility. To further clarify this important question, one should ask these additional questions:

• Do we both want to have children?

• How many children would we want?

• Do we agree about child-rearing issues?

• Do we both have the same attitudes about birth control?

• How would we deal with an unplanned pregnancy?

9. What role will sexual expression have for us? Sexual desire varies from person to person. For most of us, passion is not a machine that we can switch on at any time. A woman and a man who

are considering marriage must discuss their expectations about sex.

10. Can both of us confront our problems head-on and then let bygones be bygones? Problems that are allowed to fester can cause havoc in a relationship. If two persons have the ability to air problems, even little ones, as they arise, the relationship will be much better. Once problems have been talked through, it is important to let the anger and frustration end forever.

11. Do both of us show personal integrity? This is a time to observe each other's character traits. If someone cheats, lies, gambles excessively, or manipulates others before marriage, chances are almost 100 percent that they will do so afterward. *One of the worst mistakes that people can make is to*

Student art: "Tulips," acrylic painting by Sarah Anderson, Boylan Catholic High School, Rockford, Illinois

think that marriage will reform someone with little integrity. Marriage usually does not change habitual patterns of behavior.

In particular, people need to take a hard look at substance abuse. Of twenty thousand divorced people surveyed, 44 percent declared that alcohol or drug abuse played a major role in causing the divorce. Here are some useful questions to consider: Do either of us

- have to drink to relax?
- drink when problems arise?
- have to have several drinks each evening?
- get drunk a lot?
- insist that the other person drink?
- find it impossible to stop at one drink?
- drink quickly?
- drive under the influence of alcohol?

These same questions apply to drug use. If the answer is yes to any of these questions, your relationship may face serious problems. **6**

12. Does one of us have to be the boss all the time? Marriage should be a commitment between equals. Partners should ask these questions:

- Do either of us insist on having our own way all the time?
- Do either of us feel ordered around or supervised by our partner?
- Do either of us become furious when losing at sports, cards, and so on?

Consider, too, that someone who does not mind being bossed around may have a problem with self-respect.

13. Do we share similar religious beliefs? Many young adults do not consider this issue sufficiently, but when they begin raising children, it can become a major source of disagreement. Many studies have shown that people who share a common spirituality stand a better chance of sustaining their marriage. These questions need to be answered:

- Do we share similar religious beliefs?
- What role does religious practice play in our relationship now?
- How far will either of us compromise our beliefs, if at all?
- Will religious differences affect our relationship?
- Will differences in religion affect our families?

14. Do we have enough in common upon which to build intimacy? Initially, divergent interests can be fascinating, but lasting relationships rely on common interests more than differences. Answering this question requires honesty because during the time they are considering marriage, two persons may try to be involved in each other's interests without truly wanting to be. Only later does the gap in their interests show up.

15. Can both of us articulate our feelings for each other? Sometimes we need to hear, "I love you." It needs to be said. Some people find that expressing their feelings is very difficult. Before marriage, each partner ought to know her or his own need for hearing expressions of feelings and the ability of the other person to express them.

16. What are our expectations about money and our manner of dealing with financial issues? One person may see no problem in buying on credit, but his or her partner may insist on the principle, If I cannot pay for it now, I do not buy it. Two persons may also have differences about what constitutes a dignified standard of living and how much money and possessions are necessary. Performing an inventory of each person's property or

6
Do you know of anyone with a serious character problem who has been reformed by marriage, or not reformed? Write a description of how marriage has affected that person.

deciding which credit cards to use may not be romantic, but bitter arguments over such matters often can occur later in marriage. If the two persons can work through these practicalities, it indicates that they can handle a basic level of joint decision making. If they cannot settle these basic issues, they probably will not successfully manage more complex dilemmas.

17. How dependable is each of us in our work? People who cut corners, procrastinate, and are lazy in school are likely to be that way at work. They do not suddenly change old habits. As a spouse, a person with such qualities is not likely to carry her or his weight in the relationship.

18. Do we like each other's friends? The types of friendships that a person develops say a great deal about him or her—what the person is like and what his or her values are. Both persons should take a good look at their partner's friends, and pay attention to their feelings of being comfortable or uncomfortable with them.

19. Do our dreams for creating a life together complement each other? While considering marriage, two persons must share their dreams with each other so that they can see how their dreams coincide and conflict. Also, they need to be sure that any notions they have about their dream marriage coincide with the reality they are about to face. The differences in their dreams can be a starting point for negotiating aspects of their marriage. Life is full of compromises and adjustments that couples agree to work on because they believe that their relationship is worth the effort.

Naturally, couples considering marriage will not be able to answer all the questions in favorable

ways because no relationship is perfect. However, if a fair number of the questions seem to have unfavorable responses, the persons may need to conclude that marriage is not the right decision for them.

Besides screening out a potential wrong choice of a life partner, all the communication involved in talking over these questions is a solid foundation for the adventure of marriage that lies ahead for those who do decide to marry. **7**

For Review

- What has research shown about the relationship between the length of time a couple go together and the success of their marriage?
- In terms of the argument for and against cohabitation, what conclusion does the text give on the best way for a couple to discover whether they want to get married?
- List the nineteen questions that a couple considering marriage should communicate about.

7
Envision yourself considering marriage. Imagine that you talk together about these questions. Would it be hard or easy for you to talk? What would make the communication easier? Write your reflections.

Why Marry?

People who choose to marry have decided that at least some of the following purposes of marriage are important to them:

- sharing life with a loving companion
- creating new life
- strengthening individual identities
- calling forth the best in each person
- enabling the couple to reach out beyond themselves in hospitality and compassion
- supporting the journey in faith

Sharing Life with a Loving Companion

The first and most obvious purpose of marriage is the loving companionship of another person—a deep friendship for life. When interviewed for a study published in *Psychology Today*, one man described the companionship of his wife:

"Jen is just the best friend I have. . . . I would rather spend time with her, talk with her, be with her than with anyone else."

A woman in the same study said this about her long and successful marriage:

"Sex . . . was not as important as friendship, understanding and respect. That we had lots of, and still do." **8**

Creating New Life

Another purpose of marriage is the creation of new life. Conceiving children is the most obvious way of creating new life, and becoming parents has always been one of the chief aims of marriage. As Pope John Paul II has said:

The fundamental task of the family is to serve life, to actualize in history the original blessing of the creator—that of transmitting by procreation the divine image from person to person. (*On the Family*, number 28)

By bringing children into the world, a wife and a husband participate in creation with God, the source of all life.

Strengthening Individual Identities

A damaging misunderstanding about marriage is that once two persons marry, they must give up their separate, unique identities. On the contrary, marriage is intended to strengthen the individuals' identities, not to merge them or repress them.

8
Interview your parents or some other married couple to learn their thoughts on the following:
- the purposes of their marriage when they married and now
- how they changed for the better because of their marriage

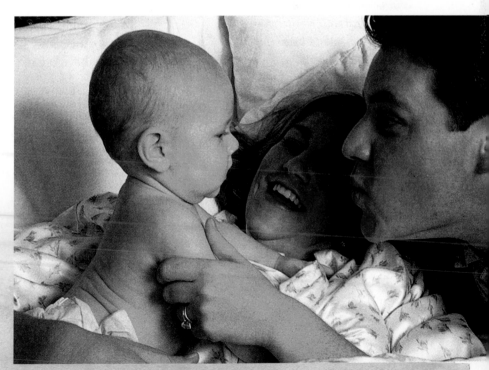

Rather than giving up their identities when they marry, the partners should nourish each other's particular gifts. In her poem "Two Trees," Janet Miles pictures the union of two unique and separate persons:

A portion of your soul has been
    entwined with mine.
A gentle kind of togetherness, while
    separately we stand.
As two trees deeply rooted in
    separate plots of ground,
While their topmost branches
    come together,
Forming a miracle of lace
    against the heavens.

If two persons have had too little time to set their roots into the ground—that is, to develop their individual identities—before they are married, they probably will experience serious problems in their relationship. Marriage can strengthen and nourish the roots of our identity, but those roots first must be planted firmly. **9**

Calling Forth the Best in Each Person

As with all loving relationships, marriage has the potential to draw out the best of each partner. If the wife and the husband care for each other, gradually they can put aside masks that they previously hid behind; they can honestly be themselves. Revealing our true self is liberating.

In the *Psychology Today* study, a man married for thirty years summarized the excitement that a spouse can feel in the growth of a loved one:

"I have watched her grow and have shared with her both the pain and the exhilaration of her journey. I find her more fascinating now than when we were first married."

Marriage can help spouses tap into reservoirs of generosity they never knew they had. Husbands and wives open their hearts and homes and make special meals and careful preparations for in-laws not only because they love them but because they know such service will please their spouses. This man, married for many years and interviewed in the *Psychology Today* study, declared:

"Sometimes I give far more than I receive, and sometimes I receive far more than I give. But my wife does the same. If we weren't willing to do that, we would have broken up long ago."

The give-and-take of marriage constantly calls forth gifts and personality traits that renew the partners. In their marriage, they can discover their best, truest selves. **10**

Student art: "Shadows of Love," acrylic painting by Julie Dibelka, Mercy High School, Omaha, Nebraska

9
Make a list of reasons that some people feel pressured to marry in their teenage years. Write down your thoughts about the effects that early marriage has on young persons' futures and on the development of their identities.

10
Recall times when your own parents or another couple tapped into their reservoirs of generosity or energy in order to serve each other. Describe in writing one example of how marriage brought out the best in them.

Enabling the Couple to Reach Out

Secure in the love that they have for each other, marriage partners are in a position to love beyond the bounds of their relationship. The wife and the husband are freed by their love to reach out to other people in hospitality and compassion.

For Betsy and Al, their life together means openness to all people in their community:

In spite of the rigors of raising several young children, Betsy and Al seem to be very peaceful people—not simply calm but spiritually at peace.

They live in an inner-city neighborhood that has a lot of problems. Kids on the street are hungry and unsupervised, and violent crime is common. So Betsy and Al's small home has become an island of peace for kids or adults who need to put down their burdens for a while.

While talking with Betsy and eating some of her homemade bread, a troubled, restless neighborhood child relaxes. A mother who feels overwhelmed by pressures finds in Betsy some gentle encouragement and a sense of hope. Al is a solid person, a man who loves carpentry and fixing things. He has been behind the move to clean up and rehabilitate some abandoned homes in the neighborhood, and Betsy has begun an after-school program for kids that offers food, fun, and lots of love.

Betsy and Al's life isn't easy; it is full of stress. But the sense of community that they foster with everyone they touch is unforgettable.

Writer Antoine de Saint-Exupéry could have been speaking of Betsy and Al, who share a vision of reaching out beyond themselves, when he wrote, "Love does not consist in gazing at each other but in looking outward together in the same direction."

Supporting the Journey in Faith

For Christian couples, marriage becomes a means of support for their journey in faith. Research has shown that couples who share and develop a common faith are more satisfied in their marriages than couples who lack this dimension in their relationship.

The journey in faith cannot be traveled alone; it needs to be supported and nurtured by a community of common beliefs and values. In marriage and family life, two persons who share their faith find such a community. This is one reason that the ritual of the sacrament of marriage is intended to be a *community* celebration, not a private event. The journey of the couple in love and faith is a challenge that is meant to be shared by other Christians who will be with the couple in their struggles and share in their joys. **11**

For Review

- List and briefly explain the six purposes of marriage given in this section.

11
Talk with a married person who shares and develops a common faith with his or her spouse. Write about the role faith plays in their marriage.

Marriage as a Covenant of Love

The church has always considered marriage a covenantal relationship that mirrors the covenant between God and God's people. A **covenant** is a deeply personal, solemn promise made between persons. Especially in this era of temporary relationships, a pledge of faithful love—a covenant—requires maturity, realism, and preparation. Living out that covenant over a lifetime is possible with the immensely graced love of the sacrament of marriage.

A Symbol of God's Faithful Love

The whole of the Hebrew Scriptures is an account of God's covenant with the Jewish people. God made a covenant with them freely, out of love. But the special people chosen by God went through their ups and downs in history: They alternately clung to God and wandered from God. The Jewish people endured hardship, slavery, and exile from their land; at other times, they experienced triumph, liberation, and prosperity. At times, they were angry at God when life dealt them failure and disappointment, and God was angry with them for their sins and hardness of heart.

But over centuries, the people of God have come to an ever-deeper understanding that God has always been faithful to them, giving them more than they ever could have expected through the good times and the bad. God will never go away and will always be there. The reality of God's faithful, covenantal love for people finds a powerful symbol in the **sacrament of marriage**. In this sacrament, two persons freely give their love to each other for-ever, "in good times and in bad, in sickness and in health."

Marriage also symbolizes the love of Christ for the church. Jesus gave his whole being, his very life, for the people of God, the church. Likewise, in marriage, the wife and the husband are called to give their energies, talents, affection, faith, hope, and love—their lives—for each other. The wonder of marriage is that as long as a woman and a man love each other, they show to the world something of the love that God has for all of us. The God who is love is made visible in the love of the couple. **12**

The sacrament of marriage is more than the wedding ceremony itself; rather, the sacrament is the couple's sharing of their whole life together, the living out of the covenant. The wedding ceremony celebrates and affirms the sacrament that encompasses a lifetime.

12
Do you know any married couples whose love for each other could be seen as a sign of God's love? Write your reflections, giving an example about one of these couples to illustrate your point.

"What God Has Joined Together . . ."

The Catholic Christian tradition has always taken the **permanence of marriage** seriously. So today, when for every two marriages taking place in the United States there is one divorce, the church sees it as essential that engaged persons understand the commitment they are making and prepare well for marriage.

Why the Permanence of Marriage?

The church's belief in the permanence of marriage is based on Jesus' response to a crowd that asked him about divorce. He said that in marriage, "'"the two shall become one flesh." So they are no longer two, but one flesh. Therefore what God has joined together, let no one separate'" (Mark 10:8–9).

Permanence in marriage is necessary for the good of all society, which ultimately contributes to the good of individual persons. If marriages end easily, society suffers from instability. To a large extent, we can see this instability in our society today. Broken marriages cause emotional, financial, spiritual, and interpersonal pain and dislocation.

The prevailing idea that divorce is usually the best solution to a difficult, unhappy marriage may seem commonsensical, but it may not be true. Furthermore, increasing evidence is pointing to the long-term detrimental effects of divorce on children. **13**

Preventing Divorce

The church is not oblivious to the pain of many marriages; it does not want people to live with intolerable marital conditions. But the church's emphasis is on preventing such difficulties through adequate marriage preparation. And when problems do arise, the church encourages married couples to work with all their strength to resolve their problems, relying also on the support and love of the church community. With the support of the church community, a couple is not alone; this is why the sacrament of marriage is a reality for the community as well as for the couple.

Taking Vows: Offering Our Own Integrity

The **marriage vows** during the wedding ceremony are the formal way that the couple make their covenant with each other. A vow is a *solemn* promise. It is not simply an ordinary promise, made in good faith but able to be broken later if circumstances change. A vow has a sacred quality because when we take a vow, we commit our entire being to it. We offer our own integrity as the substance of the vow. If we later break the vow, we break our own integrity.

The Validity of the Vows

The vows of marriage are a sacred matter, so the church tries to ensure that when a couple marry, they know what these vows entail. The vows must be given freely and knowledgeably in order to be **valid**, or true and binding. Consequently, before the promises are given, both persons must have the following:

Freedom from pressures. Many internal and external pressures can weaken a person's ability to consent freely to marriage, making the vows invalid. The pressure may be as blatant as a demand

13
Complete this statement, and then write your thoughts about it: *I believe that divorce is* . . .

by the parents of a pregnant teenage girl that the baby's father marry their daughter. Or the pressure may be felt in a home where quarreling or alcoholism pushes a desperate son or daughter to escape through marriage.

Knowledge and willingness. For marriage vows to be considered valid by the church, both persons also must know what marriage, especially the marriage promises, really means; they must have the capacity and the willingness to fulfill their promises. For example, if either person decides before the marriage that she or he does not want children and will not have them but fails to tell the other person, the vows could be considered invalid because of lack of knowledge by one partner and lack of willingness to fulfill the marriage promises by the other partner.

If Vows Are Not Taken Freely and Knowledgeably

Without sufficient time to discern the essential dynamics of their relationship, a couple may actually say the words of the marriage promises but not really be free enough from internal and external forces or knowledgeable enough to make a valid promise. The church will grant an **annulment** for a marriage that has ended legally in divorce if a church tribunal determines that the marriage vows were invalid from the beginning. In cases where the church does grant an annulment sometime after a marriage has ended, it concludes that at the time of the wedding ceremony, one or both of the persons were not able to make a valid vow. Therefore, the marriage was never a valid sacrament in the eyes of the church.

Annulment is not divorce. A **divorce** dissolves the legal contract of marriage, whereas an annulment acknowledges that as a sacrament, the marriage never existed. Some people confuse these terms, but they describe two distinct realities. **14**

For Review

- What is a covenant? In what way is the sacrament of marriage considered a symbol of God's covenant with the chosen people?
- What is the basis for the church's teaching on the permanence of marriage?
- What two conditions must both persons have at the time of a marriage in order for their vows to be considered valid by the Catholic church?
- Under what condition may an annulment be granted by the church? What is the difference between an annulment and a divorce?

Student art: "Sunflowers," oil painting by Anne Holm, Mercy High School, Omaha, Nebraska

14
Write responses to the following questions:
- **Do you think that divorces should be easily granted?**
- **Do you think that annulments should be easily granted?**

The Engagement: Time to Prepare

The period of **engagement** gives a couple the opportunity to begin a relationship of mutual commitment, even though that commitment has not yet been made permanent in marriage. The word *engagement* implies involvement or activity. Indeed, engagement to marry needs to be a period of active involvement by the man and the woman.

Numerous issues must be settled. Many important questions, which the engaged persons already should have considered in making the decision to marry, were outlined earlier in this chapter. These questions take on more urgency and magnitude as the time to make the marriage commitment nears. Trust needs to be deepened; mutual self-disclosure needs to become more profound. Consequently, an engagement period that adequately prepares a couple for marriage might last for months.

Engagement is also a time of trial; the couple might conclude that they really do not want to marry each other. Engagement serves a valuable purpose if it helps two persons to avoid a marriage that would not be good for them. **15**

The Church's Requirement of Marriage Preparation

A "church wedding" is just that—a ceremony performed in a church building. Most couples, even those who are not actively involved in a parish, want this kind of wedding. But in Catholic teaching, merely being married in a church building is not the same as **marriage *in the church***, which implies being united with the church and its intent for marriage. People who marry in a church building may have wonderful, permanent marriages, but something more than the ceremony's taking place in a church is needed in order to truly be a marriage *in the church*.

So the Catholic church requires that couples who intend to marry in the church, not simply in a church building, attend a **marriage preparation program**, offered by the parish or diocese. The program is intended to help a couple get ready for the serious and deep commitment of marriage, and to realize that marriage is a sacrament in union with the whole church and specifically with their church community.

Although marriage preparation programs vary from diocese to diocese, they all are designed to assist couples in fulfilling their mutual commitments. The courses may be given by the parish or by the diocese, and may even entail making an "Engaged Encounter," a weekend of intensive communication for the couple, modeled on Marriage Encounter.

Many parish or diocesan programs give instruction about such topics as the sacramental nature of marriage, communication skills, goal setting and goal sharing, decision making, development of intimacy, conflict resolution, practical adjustments to married life, sexuality, and children.

Each couple is expected to complete a program several weeks before their wedding ceremony. In

15
List some problems that can arise in a marriage because of basic differences in any three of the following areas: money, recreation, intimacy, sexual expression, in-laws, independence, friends, children, alcohol, decision making.

some dioceses the date of the ceremony cannot be scheduled until the couple completes a preparation program. In cases where the persons have serious obstacles to confront before they can be married, a priest may ask that the couple be counseled by a competent person.

Taking Care of Practical Matters

During the engagement, besides the nineteen questions posed on pages 226–230, the couple needs to address physical and mental health considerations. Both persons should have thorough physical examinations. Each person should know about the medical history of his or her partner and whether hereditary medical problems such as diabetes, congenital defects, Alzheimer's disease, and sickle-cell anemia exist in his or her partner's family. The couple also need to know of any physical or psychological impediment to sexual relations in either person. Genuine love does not gloss over such difficulties and pretend they do not exist: two persons who are about to marry must not be oblivious to each other's medical history.

Athletes prepare themselves for years before they can enter the professional leagues. Lawyers and doctors go through years of education and preparation for their careers. But many people mistakenly believe that they can enter marriage and succeed, simply by going through the most minimal preparation—a few months of dating, blood tests, an application for a marriage license, and so on. Marriage requires far more of us as total persons than do careers in sports, law, or medicine. An engaged couple owe it to themselves, their relationship, and their future family to prepare thoroughly and thoughtfully for their life together. **16**

For Review

- What is the difference between a church wedding and a marriage *in the church*?
- Briefly describe the preparation that is required for couples intending to marry in the Catholic church.

16
Reflect on this question in writing: *Is it fair to say that marriage requires much more of an individual as a total person than do careers in professional athletics, medicine, or law?*

Photo: Athletes train for years to get ready for marathons. Why not put as much energy into preparing for marriage?

The Wedding Celebration

Weddings rank high among life's most moving and joyful occasions for celebration. The pledge of faithful love between a husband and a wife strikes a deep chord in people's hearts, a need to see love made visible in the world. Weddings remind people that love is the central human reality worth celebrating.

The delight in each other that lovers experience when they marry is part of what touches people at a wedding. Beyond that, the act of marrying evokes strong feelings in the family and friends of the couple because it anticipates with hope the reality of a love that will endure the test of time—the struggles and crises as well as the stresses of routine that mark every marriage.

By celebrating their love before the community, the married couple in effect says, "Look, love is here and now. The God who is love is present." The church, in the form of this community, acts as witness and support to the marriage.

What Kind of Celebration?

Weddings can mushroom into major productions. Some families spend fortunes on formal dresses and tuxedos, huge banks of flowers, fountains of champagne, and towering cakes. Indeed, they spend several months ordering food, finding the perfect dress, hiring a photographer, sending out legions of invitations, and rehearsing each move. By the time of the wedding, nerves may be so frayed and the couple so weary that they cannot enjoy the celebration.

An elaborate, costly wedding has no more validity and promises no more happiness for the couple than a simple wedding in which the focus is on the love and commitment of the couple, and where the celebration afterward is an informal affair. What really counts is the love of the woman and the man and the support of the community, not the number of attendants, the size of the ring, or the fanciness of the cake. In fact, a simpler, even homespun wedding may speak more eloquently of the reality and power of God's love in the couple's life. **17**

17
Interview a couple married recently. Ask them about their preparations and the day itself. If they had a chance to prepare the wedding again, would they do things differently? Write up the results of the interview.

The Rite of Marriage

The church encourages a couple to have their wedding ceremony in the context of the Mass. If for some reason that is inappropriate (for example, one of the couple and his or her family are not Catholic and thus would not be receiving Communion), the ceremony can be held within a shorter religious service.

When the ceremony takes place during Mass, it comes after the liturgy of the word—the readings from the Bible and the homily. Some of the prayers of the **Rite of Marriage** have alternate forms, and the readings can vary as well. Any variations can be decided by a couple and their priest. At the heart of the ceremony are the following questions by the priest and the vows by the couple. Addressing the couple, the priest says:

Have you come here freely and without reservation to give yourselves to each other in marriage?

Will you love and honor each other as husband and wife for the rest of your lives?

Will you accept children lovingly from God and bring them up according to the law of Christ and his church?

After responding to each question, the man and the woman in turn each vow their commitment with these words:

I promise to be true to you in good times and in bad, in sickness and in health. I will love you and honor you all the days of my life.

The ceremony highlights the public commitment of the couple to each other. The Christian community needs to hear people say that love is possible, that love exists. The promises that the couple make before the congregation tell all who are present that these two persons have a goal of permanent commitment to foster each other's good and thus the good of society as a whole. Consequently, public weddings are occasions of tremendous optimism for the entire assembled community. The couple, too, need this public witness; they need to feel the support of the community, as their friends and family witness their pledge of faithful love. Then the couple can realize that this community will be there for them when times are tough. **18**

For Review

- What does the text recommend as a consideration in deciding what kind of wedding celebration to have?
- What questions by the priest and statements by the couple are at the heart of the wedding ceremony?

The Love of Two Persons: A True Miracle

The love between two persons is a genuine miracle. As a woman and a man grow into a common vision, share their dreams, come to a profound appreciation and affection for each other, we can only marvel. Such love does not solve all of life's problems, but two people facing the future together are twice as strong, creative, and resilient as one.

With marriage, the love of two persons is celebrated, blessed, and supported in a public way. The origin of such love is a holy mystery, and its results are wonderful and amazing. A marriage gives the community hope in the miracle of human love and reminds people of a tender and ever-faithful God—a God who will never go away and who will always be there.

God of love that lasts forever,
Be with couples who are preparing to marry.
Help them to see each other in depth and in truth.
Give them wisdom and insight into their relationship.
Fire them with your Spirit of generous and passionate
     love.
Instill in their hearts a faithfulness that will last forever.
May their love remind the whole world of how you
     love us.
Amen.

18
If you were planning your own wedding, what one biblical passage would you want read at the service? (For help, you can check the suggested readings for weddings given in the church's lectionary, which is available from your campus ministry office, school chaplain, or parish priest.) Write down the passage, and outline what you would want the priest to say in his homily.

13

Growth in Marriage:
The Blessing of Family Life

The Seasons of a Marriage

"And then they were married, and they lived happily ever after."

Well, not exactly. Anyone in touch with reality knows that marriage does not automatically yield happiness, nor does every marriage last "ever after." A marriage is always a "work in progress," a dynamic relationship with seasons of struggle and satisfaction, sorrow and joy, that call for constant growing and adjusting by the couple. The rich sense of peace that often can be detected in a couple who have been married for many years is the fruit of years spent sharing and supporting each other through the high points and the low points of existence.

This mature love of married life is pictured in Willa Cather's story "Neighbour Rosicky":

Mary sat watching him intently, trying to find any change in his face. It is hard to see anyone who has become like your own body to you. Yes, his hair had got thin, and his high forehead had deep lines running from left to right. . . . He was shorter and broader than when she married him; his back had grown broad and curved, a good deal like the shell of an old turtle. . . .

He was fifteen years older than Mary, but she had hardly ever thought about it before. He was her man, and the kind of man she liked. . . . They had been shipmates on a rough voyage and had stood by each other in trying times. Life had gone well with them because, at bottom, they had the same ideas about life. . . . It was as if they had thought the same thought together. . . . Though he had married a rough farm girl, he had never touched her without gentleness.

For most couples, married life becomes family life. Through the challenges and rewards of sharing life not only with a partner but also with children, married persons can come to a deep sense of the goodness of life and the tenderness of God's love for them.

This chapter focuses on the type of family Cather describes in "Neighbour Rosicky"—mother and father married, living together, and raising their children together. Although this **traditional type of family** is less typical than it used to be, it is still the kind of family most teenagers (92 percent) value as ideal, according to a 1994 Gallup Youth Survey. **1**

However, a traditional family is not the only kind that is wonderful to grow up in. A blended family—in which children from two former marriages combine into a new family with one parent from each marriage—can be healthy and nurturing, as can a family headed by a single parent. And there are other loving family combinations. But this chapter treats the traditional family, which most teens see as ideal, in order to lay out the dynamics of a marriage as it develops over time and through a variety of phases. **2**

In all marriages, especially those that involve children, a great deal of development goes on throughout the years. The couple's development can be seen in their own relationship, their roles as parents, and their individual lives as persons and professionals. These three areas tend to overlap; development in one area usually affects the other areas.

Furthermore, a developmental pattern seems to emerge in most marriages that involve children, a pattern that can be thought of as seven seasons of a marriage. Naturally the length of the seasons and the issues of each season vary from family to family because of the number and spacing of births and many other factors. On the whole, though, a fairly typical pattern can be observed.

Blissful Beginnings: Years One to Two

Most couples report satisfaction in the first two years of marriage. Much of the bliss experienced on the honeymoon remains with them, and the couple feels a great deal of hope. The husband and the wife become each other's primary source of support and affection. In an effort to build an "ideal" marriage, they may even be overly conscious of protecting and fulfilling each other's needs. The couple tries to learn to live with each other's possibly annoying habits.

The spirit of hope and attentiveness smooths over some of the adjustments and compromises that need to be made on a wide variety of issues: who does the laundry, who cleans the house, whose job takes precedence if a move is required, how much time is to be spent together, how

1
Interview an elderly couple you know to find out how they have sustained their long marriage, that is, some of the secrets of their success. Write up the results of your interview.

2
Do you agree with the teenagers who said they value the traditional family as the ideal? Explain your answer in writing.

much time is to be spent alone or with friends, with whose family will the Christmas holidays be spent, and so on. Although these types of compromises are required throughout life, they are particularly obvious during the first two years of marriage.

Any compromises that mark a loss of personal independence are often compensated by the rewards of deeper interdependence. The wife and the husband forego some independence, but they gain daily support, affection, and encouragement. They gain a companion and partner to share their worries and fears with and to help in planning and decision making. **3**

Becoming Domestic: Years Three to Five

The next season, the third to fifth years of marriage, has an intensely domestic focus as the couple settle into the joys and needs of being parents and making a home. The miracle of creating new life and loving a child draws the couple together. Many couples who cannot conceive a child may choose to adopt one or more children. With their innocence, affection, and openness to life, children renew their parents' sense of wonder and hope. Having children can be one of life's greatest joys.

Babies and small children are also needy creatures who require a great deal from their parents. Along with joy and wonder, pregnancy and parenthood bring physical and emotional fatigue. Once a child is born, a round-the-clock routine of feeding, changing, and comforting sets in. Babies turn into toddlers and then into small children, who continue to need lots of nurturing.

After the birth of their first child, the couple is no longer alone; life has to be lived around the needs of another human being. This represents a revolution in the couple's lifestyle. For some individuals, the new domestic focus of their lives is very settling, and they adjust to it easily. For others who are used to a high degree of independence, it can be very unsettling.

Another element of this season of marriage is the redefining of role expectations. For example: Will both partners be involved in child care? Will one parent cease working outside the home to care for children? Will one income be sufficient for family needs? These and many other questions challenge the couple to grow in new ways. **4**

3
Make a list of habits you will probably need to change or at least compromise if you marry. Place a check mark next to the habits you would like to change *before* you marry. Describe in writing how you might alter these habits.

Student art: "Growing Up," pencil drawing by Mandy Rager, Holy Cross High School, Louisville, Kentucky

4
Answer and explain in writing:
- Would you be willing to temporarily give up your future career to be a full-time parent?
- Would you expect your spouse to give up a career to stay at home with your children?

Mike Mallowe, a father of four children, made these remarks about parenting in a *U.S. Catholic* article titled "Is There Married Life after Birth?":

If you are a parent, you have to be a parent all the way. . . . Your responsibility only ends when you do. Then, and only then, can it be over and out. . . .

While it might begin as a commitment, as an expression of enduring, rock-solid love and mutual devotion, a marriage blessed with children automatically becomes a work in progress. It will change, twist, grow, mutate, undergo adversity, experience triumph.

Time of Decision: Years Six to Twelve

The sixth through the twelfth years of marriage may be the most difficult, particularly years seven through ten. At the same time that the partners are growing—professionally, personally, and parentally—the busyness of their lives may be causing them to lose touch with each other. Their growth may be in different directions, or one person may grow while the other stagnates. Some of the sexual fervor of the early years has usually faded by this time.

Careers during this period often are at a pivotal phase. If the wife or the husband has been with a company for seven or eight years, she or he may be at the threshold of a big promotion or a disappointing plateau. A large percentage of workers change jobs during this phase of marriage.

In addition, being parents of school-age children can be fun and creative but also demanding. Children become less dependent than they were as babies but more active and involved in the world and less subject to the parents' control. The hectic pace of keeping up with a household and the busy schedules of all family members can seem like an oppressive daily grind. Sharon Addy describes that sense of drudgery and its effects on her marriage in her poem "Life After Marriage":

When I said "I do" I didn't mean
I would pick up everything
any of us would ever own
or be a hash-slinging,
baby-sitting chauffeur
who runs with the vacuum
between washer loads.

What happened to the soft summer
of our life together
when our twoness
became a oneness
with an eternity of time?

Our oneness became a moreness
and the schedules began
and they race on
chopping life into fragments
leaving me with ragged edges.
Will all our life be scheduled?

Given the strains, it is not surprising that for many couples, this period is one of decision making about their relationship. The honeymoon is long over. The wonder of having a new baby is fading. Many of the routines described in Addy's poem can feel oppressive. Pressures in every aspect of life are more complex. Individuals may find themselves asking, Is this what I want? Do I want to hang in there? Most couples make the transition into the next stage of their marriage, but frequently not without some serious soul searching that strengthens their relationship in the end. **5**

Strength and Renewal: Years Thirteen to Eighteen

The thirteenth through eighteenth years of marriage are free of some of the pressures and strains of the previous season. Frequently a renewal of the marriage is experienced during these years. In a way, the partners become reacquainted. If their children have entered adolescence, the couple might have more time to spend together. Some couples also begin to socialize more. Even if they still have younger children, coping with them can be easier because the couple has had practice by raising their older children.

Being the parents of teenagers can be a tremendously positive experience. Parents learn the delicate balance between guidance and firmness on one hand and letting go and trust on the other. They learn from their adolescent children as those children develop in fascinating ways. Parents can enjoy listening to new ideas and discoveries of the young persons whose world is opening up, and they can get involved in some of the best discussions of their lives. Perhaps, too, parents remember fondly their own struggles to assert their independence twenty or so years earlier.

Being the parents of adolescents can be difficult as well. The adolescent struggle to assert independence and to establish a unique identity may cause great conflict between parents and their children. Families may argue about things like curfews, having an after-school job, household responsibilities, use of a car, drugs and alcohol, and irritating personality traits.

The degree of conflict makes the period more turbulent in some families than in others. But as teenagers grow in making increasingly important decisions and taking more responsibility for their own lives, parents generally appreciate this growth, and family relationships often strengthen over the course of these years.

Two years after a big family blowup, Heather's mother, Connie, told this story of how reconciliation, maturity, and even joy were snatched out of the jaws of anger, profound hurt, and near tragedy:

Heather was, or is, a great kid. She was doing great in school, starred in the school musical, made All-State

5
List as many of your parents' daily activities as you can think of. Then write your reactions to this question: *Do you think that your parents ever ask Sharon Addy's question, "Will all our life be scheduled?"*

band with her clarinet playing, and had lots of friends. How she got mixed up with Raymond I'll never really figure out, but over a couple of months, she was hooked up to this nasty creep. Believe me, I've used a lot stronger language.

So he's twenty-two, she's sixteen. He lies about his age, says he's nineteen, tells her this sorry story about how awful his family is, how he's never been loved. Then he starts this line about being in a band, all the plans they've got, and so on. She's into music and has a heart the size of a football field. God, I get furious just sitting here thinking about it.

He starts manipulating her to, quote, "loan" him some money. When Andy and I find out, we go nuts. Goodhearted Heather defends the jerk. More promises from him about the band. One thing leads to another; we ground her. Then we find out he's twenty-two, and she won't believe us. He has no job, no money, hangs out with a gang.

Next thing we know, Heather's gone—takes off for a couple of days with that @*#! We get the police after him. They bring her back. This is tough-love time. We love her and will fight anyone we think is going to abuse her. We get a restraining order, but he keeps pestering her. They take off again—this time to another state. We're devastated. You can't imagine—just blown out of the water.

Then she comes back, bedraggled, angry, crying continuously, completely broken. Andy and I are crazy: overjoyed she's back, livid, scared to death for her—every emotion in the book. Over the next three days, Andy and I drop everything; we take off from work and talk and talk with Heather, and talk some more. We love her so much. That's why we're so mad and afraid for her.

To make a long story short, she told us she found out that Raymond was just using her. He smacked her around too. Thank God she had enough self-esteem to come home. But she was pregnant. She had the baby, and the baby was adopted immediately.

So where are we now? Well, though I would never, ever want anything like this to have happened, we are really close. I guess all the raw emotion, bitter honesty, our talking, and staying involved with her have paid off. Now I talk to her like a woman, not a girl. Her own compassion for people is immense, but more cautious. What could have been bitterness has turned to wisdom in Heather. I don't know of any mother and daughter who are closer. Like I say, I would never want this to happen, but it did. We love each other more than I thought possible. Andy and I prayed our way constantly through this whole thing. I guess God was really with us because we got the chance to grow together as a family, stronger than we had ever been.

Not all adolescents get into serious trouble or have major crises, but all do challenge their parents in one way or another. Parents, too, do not always understand the pressures and anxieties their teenagers feel. If parents and teenagers can keep talking and struggling together, wisdom, increased love, and maturity can come. **6**

Midlife Transitions: Years Nineteen to Twenty-three

When their adolescent children become young adults and leave home, parents often feel grief over the separation from these significant people who now are on their own. Usually this separation coincides with the onset of a midlife transition for the spouses, which is difficult in itself. For many people, middle age can signal feelings of physical vul-

6
Write an imaginary dialog between you and one of your parents that covers some unresolved issue between you and that parent. Attempt to portray your parent's and your own perspectives as accurately as you can.

nerability and inadequacy. As a person reaches forty years of age, the body cannot perform like it could at age twenty-five or even thirty-five. Individuals may begin to feel that life is passing them by.

Other midlife pressures appear:

- A person at midlife has been working for perhaps twenty years. Realizing that life may be half over, a person begins to ask, Do I want to do this type of work for the rest of my life? Or a person may be forced into early retirement or laid off from a job due to downsizing or a merger. Unemployment at midlife can cause major crises in identity, self-esteem, and family finances.
- A person who has been immersed in achieving within a career may feel an urge to become more home-centered, less driven, or more attuned to relationships.
- A couple may need to help aging parents deal with prolonged illness, selling the family home, moving into elder housing, and eventually passing on.

The midlife period often is marked by restlessness and a search for meaning. A sense that the clock of a life span is running down contributes to the urgency. The implications for a couple's relationship are enormous. One or both persons may feel restless or unfulfilled in the marriage; their search for meaning in life frequently leads to some shift in their way of relating or in their expectations of each other.

This period is even more difficult if the partners have ignored the building of their own relationship in order to devote themselves to their children. Developing mutual interests and other channels for communication is important, otherwise the marriage relationship might become plagued with boredom. As with every crisis or transition, the midlife period presents new opportunities for the couple to deepen and broaden their love. **7**

On Their Own Again: Years Twenty-four to Forty

In the twenty-fourth to fortieth years of marriage, once their children have left home, the couple usually establish new and deeper bonds. If they are creative in using their time together, the partners will use their freedom for travel, hobbies, service to their community, or other pursuits that interest them. Often the persons become grandparents; this

7
Interview a couple whose children have left home. Write about their experience of seeing their children move away and about the adjustments that they had to make as a couple when this happened.

Student art: Untitled, pen and ink drawing by Audrey Marcello, Our Lady of Mercy High School, Rochester, New York

provides opportunities to share affection with a new generation.

During this season, or even before, most couples experience the death of their own parents. When their parents die, the partners come to a fuller realization of what it means to be the older generation, taking their roles as heads of the family. Their own ability to offer wisdom and stability to the next generation is to some extent the fruit of struggling through the painful loss of their own parents and of integrating the meaning of their parents' lives into their understandings of themselves.

Growing Old Together: Years Forty-one and Beyond

The forty-first year of marriage and beyond are marked by the retirement of one or both partners. Retiring from work is frequently traumatic for people because their jobs have been a source of meaning for them. However, retirement is also an opportunity to do things that the couple may have wanted to do for a long time. With so much time to spend together, couples frequently have to learn new patterns of relating. To the extent that they have developed mutual interests before retirement, the transition in their relationship will require less adjustment.

Generally, retired couples also have to face the physical, emotional, and financial problems of aging. Because the partners are a major source of support and affirmation for each other, the terminal illness or death of a spouse is the most difficult element in their older years, especially if the period of disability or suffering is long. In spite of the difficulties of growing old together, a couple may come to an appreciation of each other and an integrity in their shared life far greater than they have known in earlier years.

If they have been open and flexible in their approach to life, a couple can find after years together that each season of their marriage—even the tough ones—has had its own significance and joy.

For Review

- What is the traditional type of family?
- Briefly summarize the seven seasons of a marriage and the challenges and adjustments they require.

Ongoing Adjustments in Married Life

A couple need to make numerous adjustments—to each other and to changing circumstances—as they progress through the seasons of their marriage. Over time, the choices they make in these adjustments shape their marriage.

From "I" to "We"

The need to move from independent action to a willingness to compromise in marriage has already been mentioned briefly, but the topic requires more comment. This move toward thinking as a couple, rather than simply as individuals, is the move from "I" to "we," and it is never accomplished all at once or in the first year or so of marriage. Even if the couple make compromises in the initial stage of marriage, they will have to keep making compromises throughout their life together because, as the years pass, the desires and needs of each person change and emerge. Take this situation as an example:

For years, busy with their family's needs, Alice and Herman did not have time to do many of the things that they wanted to do. Now that their children have left home, Alice wants to see new places and meet new people. Herman simply wants the peace and quiet of home.

One night during dinner, Alice proposes that she and Herman take a cruise in the Caribbean. This trip has been her secret dream for years. Herman is startled because he was just about to ask Alice if she liked his plans for landscaping the front lawn. He shares his ideas, knowing that they cannot afford to go on the cruise and do the landscaping.

Alice did not share her dream of traveling before because conditions would not have allowed it anyway, and Herman's ambitions for his lawn took a back seat to his commitments to raising his children. Now these desires in each person have been permitted to emerge because of a change in circumstances. Alice and Herman need to ask themselves not simply what "I" want to do but what "we" can do that will come closest to meeting both persons' needs and desires. **8**

Changes in Sexual Expression

Sexual expression changes throughout a marriage, at times assuming more importance than at other times. These changes require the partners to be sensitive and responsive to each other's expectations. As in other facets of marriage, frank and open communication about sex is essential to creating and fostering intimacy.

Sexual intercourse, besides being open to the conception of children, can be a powerful unifier for a couple. It can bring joy and renewal to two persons who have committed their lives to each other, but it does not exist apart from the rest of a marriage. Sexual intimacy can deepen the affection that makes other kinds of intimacy so meaningful in a marriage—the sharing of ideas, feelings, difficulties, and fun. Those kinds of intimacy likewise complement and build sexual intimacy.

Sexual expression that is satisfying for both partners takes time to learn. It calls for a willingness to be attuned to the other person and not to be focused solely on one's own satisfaction. Theologian

8
Watch a TV program that features a married couple, such as a soap opera or a situation comedy. Then, in a brief written report, answer the following questions:

- What image of marriage and family life did this program portray?
- What behaviors in the characters contributed to that image?

and writer Christine Gudorf remarks in an article in *U.S. Catholic:*

Sex—good, frequent, mutually pleasurable—is as vitally important to the vocation of marriage as reception of Eucharist is to membership in the church community. . . .

Within good marital sexual communication, some basic guidelines that should be explicitly agreed upon are that sex should be mutually pleasurable and that when sex is not mutually pleasurable, both partners share responsibility for making and keeping sex pleasurable.

At times love requires self-control, for instance, when one partner desires sex at a time when the other is not physically or emotionally able to respond. Also, a partner who is always sexually unresponsive needs to look honestly at the reasons for this and try to discover with the other what will make their sex life more satisfying for them both.

Financial Issues

Chapter 4 of this course discussed money and possessions as part of a lifestyle. In marriage, financial issues influence the relationship in many ways.

- In a financially limited situation, a couple may have to alter their habits of eating, recreating, or shopping. They may not be able to have some of the conveniences they have hoped for or to live in the area they would like.
- If a couple decide that one of the spouses will leave a job to raise their children, both persons must be willing to share the financial sacrifices that come with a reduction in income.

Control of money is a type of power. Consequently, a husband and a wife should thoroughly discuss who will pay bills, balance accounts, make major purchases, and so on. Ideally both persons should have an equal voice in all financial decisions, so that they share the responsibility and power. **9**

Changing Roles

With the changes in societal expectations of female and male roles over the last few decades, women and men are faced with many conflicting values. A woman may hear the following messages from the surrounding culture:
- Be an exciting and devoted wife.
- Focus on getting to the top in a career.
- Be a great mother.
- Stay independent.

A man may hear these messages:
- Be a real man.
- Be sensitive.
- Take charge at home and at work.
- Be a nurturing partner and parent.

9
Under the categories *social, financial,* and *emotional,* list all the adjustments you can think of that you would have to make in each category if you married at the end of this school year.

Responding to these conflicting messages seems at times to require superhuman capabilities. As formerly well-defined sex roles have begun to change, considerable pressure has been exerted on men and women to excel in all areas of life. Women are expected to be mothers, career professionals, homemakers, seducers, and creative socializers. The pressure on men to diversify their roles does not seem to be as great, but more men are realizing that if they expect women to balance a career and child rearing, they must help. Men are also discovering new sides of themselves when they take a more active role in nurturing children and in homemaking. Even so, trying to become adept at a variety of roles can place a lot of demands on men and women.

While avoiding attempts at "superwoman" or "superman" status, wives and husbands do need to allow each other the freedom to go beyond traditional expectations. If a wife and a husband are to have equal dignity and a special kind of friendship, they should flexibly adjust the roles that each plays in the marriage, based on individual talents and interests. Decisions that affect both persons should be made together, as equal partners. **10**

Coping in Crisis

- Two Teens Die in Fiery Crash
- Local Lawyer Arrested for Cocaine Use
- Gas Explosion Leaves Family Homeless

Headlines like these appear in newspapers all the time. Behind every headline is a tragic story of a family in crisis: Young people are killed in car accidents, and the sudden tragedy throws their families into prolonged anguish. Spouses and parents are arrested for crimes and even go to prison, with tremendous financial and personal ramifications for their families. Freak accidents uproot families from their homes and deprive them of all their belongings.

Other kinds of crises do not appear in the headlines:

- A parent loses a job and cannot find work.
- A family member becomes addicted to alcohol or another drug.
- A marriage exists on the verge of fracturing.
- The mental illness of a family member requires long, perhaps lifetime, treatment.
- A baby is born severely handicapped.

Many families must cope with one or even several major crises in their life together.

Such crises obviously require major adjustments, skills, and loyalty of the family members and support from their friends. Amazingly, it seems that many marriages and families survive and become stronger through crises in spite of pressures that

10

List ten household chores that must be taken care of in a family. Circle the chores that you do not know how to do well, and put an X next to any chore that you would not want to do (some of these may be the same). Then answer this question: *What would I do if my spouse and I did not agree on who would take care of the household responsibilities that neither of us wanted to do?*

seem unbearable to many observers. A mystery seems at work in these situations, perhaps the same mystery that sustains other, more fortunate families through years of day-in and day-out routine and difficult adjustments. From a Christian perspective, the mystery of God's presence—grace—sustains a couple even when they are not aware of it, as they experience the large and small deaths of marriage and family life.

Anna Erhart and her husband felt and recognized the grace of the sacrament of marriage after finding the strength to deal with the terrible chronic disease of their two adopted sons, as she described in a *U.S. Catholic* article:

Sometimes grace is concrete, clearly present to us, and felt as it grows in us. Grace is experienced as the strength to love and commit oneself to another person even when you know that commitment will bring pain.

In marriage, for those of us who work hard at it and are incredibly lucky, the grace that each spouse brings to the marriage is multiplied and bestowed on the spouses in the form of strength—strength to love not only each other but together love others as well. **11**

For Review

- What does it mean for a couple to move from "I" to "we" in their marriage?
- Explain the need to adjust to changes in sexual expression in a marriage.
- What adjustments around male and female roles do husbands and wives need to make?
- From a Christian perspective, what sustains couples and families through crises?

11

In writing, briefly recount a crisis that happened to a family you know or to your own family. Tell how the family coped with the crisis, and describe what you see as the long-term effects of the crisis on the family.

Three Stances Toward Relationships

Throughout a couple's lifetime together, three basic, positive stances toward the relationships in their life are essential to their marriage:

- faithfulness to each other
- hospitality to new life
- openness to community

Faithfulness to Each Other

Faithfulness, or fidelity, is more than the avoidance of sexual involvements outside of marriage. Faithfulness means that development of the relationship is of the highest priority to both the wife and the husband. Both of them have faith that even deeper love is possible and probable. Couples who believe in each other and the possibilities for their relationship are easy to identify. Here are some indications of a couple's faithfulness:

They spend time together. They set aside time to be with each other—not necessarily to do anything in particular but simply to be present to each other.

They support and affirm each other. They take seriously their marriage promise to support each other in bad times and in good times, in sickness and in health.

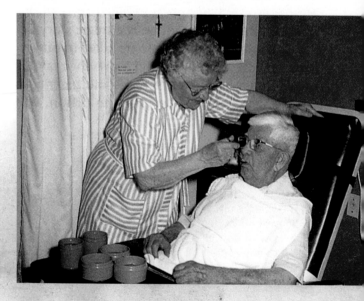

They trust each other. They give each other room to make friends, even friends of the other sex, and to pursue interests that may not be shared between them.

They develop many types of intimacy with each other. A faithful marriage relationship implies that the partners seek to grow ever more intimate with each other—emotionally, spiritually, recreationally, intellectually, sexually, and so on.

They see their relationship as one of constant rediscovery. People may wonder, How can I stay married faithfully without eventually becoming bored? Although some boredom is natural at times, faithful husbands and wives continue to discover a different person in their partner if they are both growing. On this subject, the U.S. bishops say:

> An enduring marriage is more than simply endurance. It is a process of growth into an intimate friendship and a deepening peace. So we urge all couples: Renew your commitment regularly, seek enrichment often, and ask for pastoral and professional help when needed. ("Follow the Way of Love") **12**

One aspect of faithfulness that may be misunderstood is the importance of confronting a serious personal or marital problem such as alcoholism or other addiction, physical or mental abuse, infidelity, or grossly irresponsible behavior. A person may be under the mistaken impression that faithfulness requires her or him to bear with these problems and not to disturb the relationship by confronting the partner.

Actually, looking the other way when faced with such problems indicates not faithfulness but *lack of faith.* Avoiding confrontation is a way of abandoning responsibility for the relationship. Bringing up

Babies are bits of stardust blown from the hand of God. Lucky the woman who knows the pangs of birth for she has held a star.

these problems and assisting a spouse through counseling or treatment is faithfulness. Perhaps a time will come in the marriage when the good of the family requires a separation of husband and wife. Meanwhile, faithfulness means insisting that serious problems be dealt with honestly.

Hospitality to New Life

Children as Honored Guests and Blessings

For a married couple, **hospitality to new life—** that is, the sense of welcoming any children who might be born from their love—bears some resemblance to the hospitality offered to any **honored guest.** The couple extend to their children comfort, nourishment, shelter, respect, and the freedom to be themselves, because they see their children as

---

12
In writing, describe a married couple you know who are faithful in many of the ways described here.

Student art: "Mother and Child," tempera painting by Stephanie Beier, Notre Dame Academy, Toledo, Ohio

guests whose presence they treasure, not as burdens and not as their property. This hospitality comes from generosity but also from a sense of expectancy, as the couple ask themselves:

- What will this child be like?
- How will this child change our life and help us grow?
- What discoveries and dreams are ahead for this child?

As with hospitality extended to other visitors, the welcoming of children as honored guests means that the couple are willing to let their perhaps very comfortable life be unsettled for a while. They may even have to endure financial or emotional hardship or give up certain freedoms.

Every child is worth the sacrifice for the parents because every child is a **blessing.** Couples who adopt children are particularly aware of what a blessing they are receiving. One father says of his eleven-year-old daughter, whose birth was unplanned:

Jenny came later in our marriage, as a "surprise." We weren't expecting to have another child, but now I can't imagine a world without Jenny in it. She's wonderful, and she's brought so much to us.

Children who are born with mental or physical handicaps are blessings just as other children are, although they may challenge a family to be generous in extraordinary ways. One man, recalling his brother who was born mentally retarded and who had lived at home with their family into his teenage years, remarks:

We all pitched in and helped out with caring for Bobby. He couldn't understand what we said, and he couldn't walk or take care of himself at all. But he was the happiest, friendliest guy; he made everybody feel good just being around him. I know this sounds hard to believe, but we thought of Bobby as an angel sent to our family. **13**

The church has always promoted the vision of welcoming new life in marriage, and in the Hebrew Scriptures, the perspective that children are blessings is expressed many times. For instance:

You shall be happy, and it shall go well with you.
Your wife will be like a fruitful vine
   within your house;
your children will be like olive [tree] shoots
   around your table.

(Psalm 128:2–3)

13
Recall a family you know who seem to live out the description of hospitality to new life given in this section. Explain in writing how you have seen them welcome their children as honored guests and blessings.

The Contemporary Mentality

The church's teaching that children are always blessings to be welcomed into life often conflicts with the contemporary Western mentality. This mentality seeks more to control all life through technology than to welcome the mystery and the spiritual riches of new life. Increasingly, many North American couples choose not simply to delay having children but to avoid having them at all. For many of these couples, it seems that their lives are too full and too busy to welcome another life.

In some cases, the choice not to have children stems from a lack of hope, a sense, as one man expressed it, that "this world is too violent to bring a child into." But a sense of despair in the face of a dangerous world only engenders more hopelessness because it keeps a couple from imagining and working at a better future. Having a child in the midst of a hazardous world can be a sign of a couple's commitment to work toward a society and a world that are more hospitable to life.

The Church's Stand for Life

A historic encyclical by **Pope Paul VI**, *On the Regulation of Birth (Humanae Vitae)*, issued in 1968, reaffirmed church teaching that every act of sexual intercourse must remain open to the possibility of new life. The church is concerned about the factors that motivate people not to welcome children into the world. In Pope John Paul II's document titled *On the Family*, he articulated why the church is opposed to **artificial birth control, sterilization,** and **abortion,** and especially to government attempts to require these methods as measures of population control:

The church firmly believes that human life, even if weak and suffering, is always a splendid gift of God's goodness. Against the pessimism and selfishness which cast a shadow over the world, the church stands for life: In each human life [it] sees the splendor of that "yes," that "amen," who is Christ himself. To the "no" which assails and afflicts the world, [the church] replies with this living "yes," thus defending the human person and the world from all who plot against and harm life. (Number 30)

Natural Family Planning

The most natural method of regulating conception is abstinence from sexual intercourse. Though God created sexuality as a source of communion and joy, sensitivity to each other and to the whole

family's situation may require a couple to abstain from sexual intercourse at times.

In recent years, **natural family planning (NFP)**, an approach to regulating conception that relies on knowledge of the woman's natural rhythms of fertility and infertility, has been refined by researchers. By charting the woman's cycle of fertility, a couple can use the method either to attempt to prevent or to achieve pregnancy. This approach is affirmed by the church as consistent with its stand of openness to life. In the church's view, the respect for the natural rhythms of the woman's body makes this method an acceptable way to prevent pregnancy in cases where it must be avoided for health or other compelling reasons.

To prevent pregnancy, abstinence from sexual intercourse is required during and just before the woman's fertile time of each month. Unlike artificial methods of birth control, natural family planning depends on cooperation between the spouses; it encourages dialog, shared responsibility, mutual respect, and self-control for the good of the relationship. This approach also avoids some of the health hazards of methods like the birth control pill and long-term drug implants. **14**

A married couple's hospitality to any children—whether their births are planned or unplanned—widens the circle of their love. All children, planned or unplanned, deserve that generous welcome.

Openness to Community

Besides widening the circle of their love to include children, married couples also are called to widen their love to include friends. A family cannot be an isolated unit, relying only on its members for support and extending love only to its own inner circle. Rather, married couples need to be open to the community of Christians and other friends. Particularly in our society, where so many couples live away from their families of origin and traditional sources of help are often lacking, people need to have a community of friends that they can turn to for support and companionship.

Help with Children

If a couple have children, they might need help from friends or family in caring for them during emergencies or while they go out together. In addition, parents benefit from the support of other parents, who can offer practical help and wisdom. An African proverb says, "It takes a whole village to raise a child." The U.S. bishops agree:

Student art: "The Park," acrylic painting by Orsolya Mate, St. Peter's High School, New Brunswick, New Jersey

14
Research natural family planning and prepare a brief written report on it.

You cannot raise your own children alone. All families—even those with two parents—need a wider circle of aunts and uncles, grandparents, godparents and other faith-filled families. ("Follow the Way of Love") **15**

Friendship

On a personal level, men and women sometimes need a listener, someone who can allow them to express sides of themselves for which their spouses may not have an understanding or an interest. In a study of friendships in marriage, a woman married for thirty years summed up the importance of having friends outside of the marriage relationship:

"No two people can be everything for each other, nor should they be, nor should we have such impossible expectations. Friendship is really a way to get some of the other things that you don't get from the particular person you love and married." (*Just Friends,* page 142)

Couples need friends who will care for them. These friends take off some of the pressure for marriage to provide all the intellectual, emotional, spiritual, and recreational needs that each partner has.

Service to Others

Families also show their openness to community by involving the whole family in service. The U.S. bishops offer thoughts on how a family can give life to the world:

You also give life as a family by doing such simple things as taking a grandparent out of a nursing home for a ride, bringing a meal to a sick neighbor, helping to build homes for poor people, working in a soup kitchen, recycling your goods, working to improve the schools or joining political action on behalf of those treated unjustly.

Such activity builds stronger family bonds. It enriches both the receiver and the giver. It releases the "formidable energies" present in families for building a better society. ("Follow the Way of Love")

For Review

- What does faithfulness in marriage mean, and what are five indicators of fidelity between husband and wife?
- What is hospitality to new life? What are two ways of seeing children that indicate a hospitable attitude toward them?
- Explain the church's perspective on welcoming new life in marriage, and describe the contemporary mentality that is in conflict with the church's view.
- What is natural family planning, and why does the church support it?
- Why is openness to community needed for married couples? In what ways can they open their family to community?

Photo: **A mother and daughter work together at an outdoor soup kitchen.**

15
List all the people who have "raised you": aunts, uncles, adult friends of your parents, and so on. Next to each name, describe what unique contribution that individual made to your growing to be the person you are.

A KWIK HISTORY OF FAMILY LIFE

The Healthy Family

Marriage partners who are faithful to each other, welcoming to new life, and open to community are well on their way to building a healthy family. Living in a **healthy family** feels good; it is an ideal environment for an individual to grow into a happy, caring, self-respecting person.

A hazard of discussing the healthy family is that we might become too critical of our own family of origin. The healthy family is an ideal. We should consider ourselves blessed if the family we have grown up in has even *some* of the characteristics of a healthy family. Parents, like their children, are limited human beings who do the best they can with whatever talents, knowledge, and feelings they have. So the purpose of presenting the ideal is not to make us more critical of our own parents and families but to help us see ways that we ourselves can grow as potential spouses and parents.

No family is perfect, but healthy families show many of the following characteristics:

Open communication. In healthy families, the members feel listened to and are able to listen. They can talk honestly about their feelings with everyone in the family. Independent thinking is encouraged. Television and video games are not the centerpiece of family life because too much of that type of entertainment crowds out more interesting ways of being together. Family members can reconcile conflicts in fair ways. Furthermore, family problems are not pushed out of sight but are confronted openly. As one man put it, "Trying to hush up a problem is like whispering into an empty closet; it is loud and harsh and someone is bound to hear it eventually."

Affirmation. Healthy families tend to give affirmation generously to each individual. Family members take an active interest in what the other family members are doing. For example, if Eric is competing in a swim meet, other members of the family try to attend. If they cannot be there, they let Eric know they are interested by asking how things went. Or if the mother of the family gets a promotion at work, the family takes her out to dinner or buys her a congratulatory cake. They seek some tangible way of saying, "Fantastic!"

Trust. In a trusting family, the husband and the wife believe in each other, and the children are given the chance to grow without fear of making mis-

takes. For instance, if the children attempt to bake a cake and it flops, this mistake can be treated by their parents as a chance for the children to figure out what went wrong rather than as a reason to blame someone. Trust builds self-esteem and esteem for others.

A sense of tradition. Having some family rituals or traditions is a way of binding a family together. For example, periodic family reunions reinforce a family's sense of identity. Or a family may celebrate Christmas in the same way every year: Decorations are brought out and put in the same places. The same relatives come over for dinner. Even the menu is the same. Every year, Uncle Jake tells about the time that Seth, when he was five, ate all the fudge and became ill. Seth might groan and say to himself, "Not again!" but these stories and traditions are reminders of who the family is and where they have been. Traditions give us a sense of roots. **16**

Shared leisure time. Shared leisure time may be one of the least common features of modern family life. Parents and children usually tend to be overscheduled with meetings, lessons, sports, and so on. But healthy families take time for leisure to-

gether. They know that leisure time spent as a family fosters talk and appreciation of one another, that being together without stress allows the members to lower their guard and be themselves. One of the best times for leisure is the shared family meal. It can be a time to talk, plan, laugh, and celebrate together. Experienced in this relaxed way, shared meals support health in a family.

A sense of right and wrong. Studies of moral development indicate that we acquire our sense of right and wrong primarily through our family. In healthy families, children are held responsible for their behavior. Parents teach their children why certain actions are right or wrong, and they confront wrong behavior directly. Both in the way the members treat each other and in the way they respond to others beyond the family, healthy families can be a kind of school in honesty, respect for other people, and service to those in need.

A sense of responsibility. Families function best when all members take responsibility to help the family, to contribute in some way to the common good: Someone is in charge of feeding the dog. One person cooks, and another does the dishes. People do not leave the family room in a mess

16
Describe the following items in writing:
- **one or two rituals or traditions of your family**
- **one or two rituals that you would like to start if you have your own family**

with the assumption that someone else will clean it up. Everyone seems to take ownership for the family's well-being. Taking responsibility enhances self-esteem, and because responsible family members feel that they have an influence on the world of their family, they are empowered for responsible participation in the world beyond their family. **17**

A shared religious vision. A family that shares a religious vision of life is united by a common set of beliefs and religious practices and also by deeply important values about the meaning of life. Most religions, certainly Catholic Christianity, encourage families to love one another, and they help families to celebrate important passages in their members' lives, such as baptisms or marriages. Involvement in a parish community sustains families, drawing them out of themselves in generosity and enabling them to receive the support that every family needs from friends who share religious values with them. A family's shared religious vision and active participation in a worshiping community also deepen each member's faith—a faith that will strengthen them in times of crisis or suffering.

Perhaps you can recognize your own family in many of the traits of a healthy family. Because we are limited creatures, though, our families are not ideal in every respect. But one of life's mysteries is that vital, generous, fascinating human beings can come forth even from terribly unhealthy backgrounds—abusive, alcoholic, or otherwise painful situations. Against tremendous odds, some people not only survive but transcend their background, transforming the pain and suffering of their upbringing to some positive purpose. They carry the emotional scars of their childhood with them, perhaps causing major difficulties for them in life. But the scars ultimately do not define them. Such people remind us of the greatness of the human spirit and the power of good to triumph over evil and life over death.

For Review

- List and briefly explain the characteristics of a healthy family.

17
List the responsibilities that you have in your family. For each one, explain your attitude toward that responsibility. Then reflect in writing on what you and your family have gained from your taking on these responsibilities.

Toward a "Civilization of Love"

We would have to have our head buried in the sand not to know that family life has undergone many changes during the last several decades. Families led by a single parent are more numerous. Many marriages end in divorce. Families are pulled in many directions by all kinds of pressures. A pessimist might say that the future of the family is bleak. A naive optimist might try to ignore the evidence and wish away the problems.

But young realists need to look squarely at the social and cultural trends that influence the family and, if they wish to marry, to begin thinking about how the family they create will nourish life. Our society's future depends on the existence of healthy families in which children can grow to be self-respecting, loving, free, and responsible persons. Healthy families grow from healthy couples.

Pope John Paul II, in his 1994 "Letter to Families," connected the salvation of humankind with the family:

Through the family passes the primary current of the civilization of love, which finds therein its social foundations. . . .

. . . The history of salvation, passes by way of the family. . . . The family is placed at the center of the great struggle between good and evil, between life and death, between love and all that is opposed to love. To the family is entrusted the task of striving, first and foremost, to unleash the forces of good, the source of which is found in Christ, the redeemer.

With all human beings, we can pray for our families:

God, you gave us families to love us into life,
    and we are grateful for them.
We treasure each person in our family,
    even though at times we are less than ideal
        together.
Make your presence felt with our family,
    bringing goodness and love
    from our pains and struggles,
    as well as from our happy times.
To all husbands and wives, please give
    vision, generosity, forgiveness, and courage—
Vision, so they can see how you are present
    and working in their family,
Generosity, so they can love with great hearts,
Forgiveness, so they can heal
    the inevitable wounds
    of family life,
And courage, for the long haul.
Amen. **18**

18
Write a reflection about or a prayer for your family, focusing on each of your family members in turn and then on your family as a whole.

Student art: "Siblings," oil painting by Kate Tusa, Mercy High School, Omaha, Nebraska

On the Way to Marriage

You are, by statistical average, seven to nine years away from marriage—if you do marry. Although marriage may seem relatively remote now, as you move into young adulthood, relationships will probably point toward the possibility, or at least the question, of marriage. Increasingly, dating and "going out" with one special person may be a way of discovering what you are looking for in someone you would spend your life with, and of exploring how you relate to a person you may one day marry.

Partners for Life

What is it like to find your life partner, the person with whom your whole meaning, life history, and destiny will always be intertwined? When a man and a woman come together, pledging themselves in marriage, they promise to be there for each other, loving year-in and year-out, through good times and hard times. Picture a couple married faithfully for many years. In "A Marriage Prayer," John Shea, a priest and storyteller, paints a picture for us that might be familiar:

> He said he would never go away
> and she said she would always be there
> so they got an apartment
> with a bedroom set that cost too much
> and ate spaghetti and Chianti
> with breadsticks and butter.
> His sky-the-limit potential
> ceilinged at forty
> and she got pregnant
> a respectable three times.

The best was
when she would park the kids at her mother's
and meet him after work
for drinks and dinner.
They would find out
who they were living with
and then go on as always.
The night of their first daughter's wedding
they wondered about it all.

.   .   .   .

Once
when they were going to see
her mother in the nursing home,
she knew she loved him
and cried.
He told her not to worry.
On the dresser in their bedroom
they have photos of their grandchildren
holding hands with Mickey Mouse at Disney World.
They never thought their love a fire
so it did not burn out,
this man who would never go away
and this woman who would always be there. **1**

(*The God Who Fell from Heaven,* page 97)

Finding That One Special Person

How could the couple in the poem above have found each other? And how could they be so sure of their commitment that they could pledge to "never go away" and "always be there"? In this era of high divorce rates and tentative, temporary commitments, young people may feel anxious about the possibility of a permanent, loving marriage for themselves. Yet, in a 1994 Gallup Youth Survey, 88 percent of teenagers want to get married someday, and 84 percent want to have children.

The Top Ten Qualities

How do you know this person is the one; how do you know it will last? To consider this question, it is helpful to look at the experience of people who have been there. In a study of married couples, researchers asked them what they valued most in a mate. The ten characteristics valued by both women and men in the study were the following, in order of their rank:

1. good companion
2. considerate
3. honest
4. affectionate
5. dependable
6. intelligent
7. kind
8. understanding
9. interesting to talk to
10. loyal

1

How do you react to this picture of a couple married for many years? How does it compare with your ideal of a marriage? Write your thoughts in an essay.

People who have these traits are prized as life-long partners. They "wear well" because over the long haul, they are a joy to live with and love. **2**

Paths to Marriage

If you were to interview a dozen married couples about what paths they took in arriving at their decision to marry each other, you would probably come up with quite a variety of answers. Some men and women wed each other after a whirlwind romance, a brief and usually intense time. Although this way of marrying has produced some wonderful marriages, statistically it does not stand a good chance of long-term success. In 1985 researchers at Kansas State University reported that marriage has the best chance when the couple have gone together at least two years before marriage, and the poorest chance when they have gone together less than six months.

Some people end up marrying the first person they ever loved, a "childhood sweetheart." Others do not find the right life partner until later in life, well into their thirties or even forties. Typically, men and women explore several relationships before they finally find the person whom they marry. This has the benefit of letting them discover what they really want and do not want in a marriage partner. **3**

Cohabitation: Common Sense?

In the last few decades many people have argued that **cohabitation,** or living together before marriage, is just common sense: it helps people "train for marriage" and avoid the mistake of marrying someone with whom they are not compatible. However, research studies in the mid-1980s concluded that this practice does not improve the chances of selecting a compatible mate. Couples who had not lived together in a "trial marriage" had higher marital adjustment scores one year after marriage than those who had cohabited before they married. Marital communication and overall marital satisfaction were higher for couples who did not live together until after they married.

Researchers have speculated on the reasons for these findings. An explanation recorded in *U.S. Catholic,* from the experience of a twenty-two-year-old woman, Marsha, can give us some insight into the dynamics of cohabiting:

"My own parents divorced 15 years ago, so I was determined not to jump into marriage. That's why I moved in with Tom—so we could develop our relationship and get to know each other first.

"It went from beautiful to miserable in about four months. I was knocking myself out to please him, feeling insecure whenever the arrangement seemed the least bit shaky. And I was using sex in a way that was false to myself. Intercourse was my way of reiterating,

2
List the top ten qualities you predict you would value most in a marriage partner someday.

3
Interview a married couple whom you consider to be happy together. Use these and other questions:
- How did your dating begin?
- How did you know your relationship was becoming serious?

- Do you think that a long period of going together before marrying helps a marriage?
- How important is it to date a variety of people?

Summarize the results in writing.

14
Religious Life:
Dedicated to God

Who Are the Religious?

Many of the world's religions have members who dedicate their lives solely to the service of their deity. For example, Hindu holy men wander India, praying and performing acts of self-sacrifice, and Zen Buddhist monks and nuns gather in communities to seek enlightenment.

In the Catholic Tradition

In the Catholic Christian tradition, people who choose to live in communities where members vow solely to serve God are commonly called **religious.** They publicly profess the evangelical counsels—poverty, chastity, and obedience—as a way of life consecrated to God.

Certainly all Christians are called to *be religious*—that is, to live out their faith in the way that God calls them to. But in addition, *religious* is the most familiar term for sisters, brothers, and priests who belong to **religious orders**—groups officially recognized by the Catholic church as offering a way of life for those called to profess the evangelical counsels. These groups are also called **religious congregations** or **religious communities.**

Christian religious communities began a few centuries after the Resurrection of Jesus. Men and women went into the deserts of northern Africa and the Middle East to pray, fast, and meditate on the word of God. Most of the time they banded together, even if somewhat loosely, and followed a rule of life formulated by one among them who was recognized for his or her holiness. From those beginnings to the present, hundreds of religious communities have been founded, with many still in existence today.

Immense Variety

Today, members of religious orders are nuclear physicists and spiritual directors, administrators of

facilities for emotionally disturbed youth and missionaries in poor countries, people who spend their days in silent prayer and teachers in Catholic schools. Coming from many different backgrounds, Catholic sisters, brothers, and priests in religious orders serve God in immensely varied ways. The majority of priests, incidentally, are **diocesan**—that is, ordained for service in a certain diocese—rather than being members of a religious order like the Jesuits or the Augustinians. **1**

Spreading the Good News of Jesus Christ and promoting life and human dignity are central to the meaning of religious life, just as they are central to the vocation of all Christians. However, religious life is specific and distinct as compared with other Christian lifestyles because a religious takes vows to serve God alone as he or she follows a **rule of life** unique to each religious congregation. That rule of life gives substance to the vows by specifying how an individual religious will fulfill the mission or purpose of her or his congregation.

For Review

- Define *religious orders*.
- When and where did the first Christian religious communities begin?

The Essentials: Community, Prayer, and Service

A religious order's rule of life usually gives instructions about the essential elements of religious life: community, prayer, and service.

Community: Supporting, Challenging, and Strengthening

Support and Challenge

Community life is intended to support and challenge each member of the religious community. Religious, like everyone else, need the support and affirmation of other people. For instance, a sister who ministers in a women's prison can easily become discouraged by the enormity of the problems those women face. When she comes home from work, her community can provide her with concerned listening, practical advice, and words of encouragement and humor. Just as important, the sister's community can challenge her to remember that God is present in each of the women to whom she is ministering. In this way, the sister is reminded of the sacredness of each prisoner's life.

Most religious congregations were founded to serve the human community and the church in specific ways. Historically, some congregations opened hospitals, schools, or centers for prayer. But no matter what the work of the individual religious orders, their founders realized that the members would need community, and they focused a lot of attention on building community.

1
List the names of three religious whom you know personally. After each name, write an explanation of why that individual came to mind right away. What is noteworthy about that person?

Photo: Br. Tim Tomczak, Sr. Barbara Clarke, and Fr. Ted Parker, All Saints Parish in Harlem. The men are members of the Crosiers. Sister Barbara is a member of the Franciscan Handmaids of the Most Pure Heart of Mary.

Art (facing page): A 1901 painting by Giovanni Gagliardi depicts John Baptist de La Salle in a classroom of the Christian Brothers' first school in Paris. Here the pastor of the parish visits the school.

De La Salle:
The Strength of a Community of Teachers

Religious community founders knew that the work they were inspired to undertake would profit from the strength of a community of people banded together to do it.

For example, **Saint John Baptist de La Salle**, the founder of the Brothers of the Christian Schools (often called the Christian Brothers) and the patron saint of teachers, recognized the practicality of such a community. When he realized that most of the poor boys who roamed the streets of seventeenth-century Reims, France, were in need of a practical education and religious instruction, he wanted to open a school. If poor and middle-class boys were being educated at all, it was by "writing masters," poor men who were only marginally literate themselves. De La Salle realized that the only way he could guarantee properly managed schools would be to form the poor, untrained writing masters into a religious community—a group living together who were trained as teachers, motivated by the Good News, and supportive of one another in their work of teaching. The resulting community life gave these young teachers support, discipline, a sense of purpose, a role in church ministry, and the strength to carry it out. The schools that De La Salle founded were successful largely because of the brothers' life in community.

The biblical writer of the Book of Ecclesiastes understood the strength that comes from community life:

Two are better than one, because they have a good reward for their toil. For if they fall, one will lift up the other; but woe to one who is alone and falls and does not have another to help. . . . A threefold cord is not quickly broken. (4:9–12) **2**

Prayer:
Focusing on the Center of Life

Keeping Faith That Love Will Lead to Good

As the mainstay of a person's faith in God and sense of mission, prayer is another essential element of religious life. In her book on religious women, laywoman Marcelle Bernstein wrote:

Nuns deal with more of life's harsh realities than most lay people ever see. Alcoholics, homicides, drug addicts, deserted wives, delinquent children, prostitutes—this is the list of a hardened professional caseworker. The Daughters of Charity of Saint Vincent

2
Write down what for you would be the advantages and disadvantages of living in a religious community.

de Paul, for example, have operated Marillac House in Chicago [since the 1940s]. From a settlement house in East Garfield Park, they have gone out day after day to serve an area with the highest crime, VD, illegitimacy, illiteracy, and poverty rates in the whole of the United States. (*The Nuns,* page 136) **3**

A casual observer of these sisters in their work might wonder, How does a sister who works day in and day out in such a tough and depressing world keep her faith that God is present there and that love will finally lead to good? The answer is found to a large degree in prayer, which helps a sister in a difficult situation to focus on God, the center of existence.

Deepening the Relationship with God

Prayer may take many forms: the Eucharist, paraliturgical services, meditation, shared reflection, and so on. Prayer is a central experience in religious life. According to the Rule of the School Sisters of Saint Francis,

In prayer we encounter the living God. Prayer is the forming experience that nourishes and unifies every aspect of our lives. . . . We are opened to be transformed in Christ.

. . . [Prayer's various forms are] authentic to the degree [that] they assist us in making ordinary life experiences lead to deepening of relationship with the Living Presence who is the Center of Life.

Prayer helps religious to renew their sense of the Holy Spirit at work in them.

Members of religious orders must stay in communication with God, who enriches their faith

and gives them strength for the important work they have undertaken. They may begin to perceive that even their work itself is prayer. With deeper faith and strength for their mission, religious can fulfill the purpose of Christian life as described by **Saint Bernard of Clairvaux** to his fellow monks more than eight hundred years ago: "Brothers, the whole object of our lives is to love and to make ourselves lovable." **4**

Service: Meeting Needs in the Human Community

The love that Saint Bernard called "the whole object of our lives" results in **service**, the third essential element of religious life. Religious serve in a myriad of ways.

3
Answer this question in writing: *Is Marcelle Bernstein's statement about nuns consistent with the popular perception of them? If so, how so? If not, why not?*

4
Write a brief description of how life experiences might become part of a person's prayer life.

Founded in Response to Specific Needs

Religious communities frequently were founded to meet specific human needs. For example, De La Salle's Christian Brothers had a particular focus—the education of poor boys. The Missionaries of Charity, founded by **Mother Teresa of Calcutta**, shelter those who are dying, and care for homeless poor people.

A contemporary U.S. example of a community begun to respond to the needs of the times is the Little Sisters of Jesus and Mary, founded in the late 1960s by Sr. Mary Elizabeth Gintling. Her small group of sisters and large staff of volunteers operate Joseph House Village in Salisbury, Maryland. The village offers counseling, medical assistance, education, and housing for people who are trying to get on their feet but lack the resources to do so. As Sister Mary Elizabeth described in an article published in the *St. Anthony Messenger,* she wanted "to have a place for people who don't have a home, those who are falling between the cracks, or those who are picked up by police and have no place to go." **5**

An Openness to Changing Needs

If a need exists in the human community, a religious congregation is probably trying to meet it. Accordingly, as needs in the human community change, so do the methods of serving that are used by religious orders. Many congregations allow their members a great deal of flexibility in choosing how they will serve, as long as their ministries reflect the mission of Jesus and the spirit of the congregation's founder.

Community, prayer, and service are the essential elements of religious life. If a religious neglects or ignores any one of these elements, her or his life will feel off balance. The sense of mission will be out of focus for that individual, and life will seem burdensome. A supportive and challenging community, a rich and faithful prayer life, and dedicated service enliven and empower a religious to further Jesus' mission.

For Review

- Name the three essentials of religious life.
- Why is community important to religious life?
- In what way is prayer essential for religious?
- Name two specific ways that religious congregations have served human needs.

5
Create a list of the services performed by religious in and around the city or town in which you live.

Religious Vows: Commitment to the Evangelical Counsels

When two people marry, they make a solemn covenant by taking vows pledging themselves to each other. The substance of their vows is the offer of their own integrity. As tough times come along, the sacredness of their vows becomes an anchor for the marriage, without which the two persons could drift apart.

For similar reasons, religious publicly make solemn **religious vows.** Through these vows, men and women are consecrated to God—dedicated in a solemn, sacred way—committing themselves to the religious lifestyle of community, prayer, and service. In the words of a Vatican text on religious life, this consecration is not simply a choice made by a human being but a gift from God:

Consecration is a divine action. God calls a person whom he sets apart for a particular dedication to himself. At the same time, he offers the grace to respond so that consecration is expressed on the human side by profound and free self-surrender. The resulting relationship is pure gift. It is a covenant of mutual love and fidelity, of communion and mission, established for God's glory, the joy of the person consecrated and the salvation of the world. (*Essential Elements,* number 5)

The vows made by a religious are a public statement that says: "This is my chosen lifestyle. I am committed to be a religious and to live according to the way of Jesus as well as I can with God's help." Once the commitment is made, a religious can wholeheartedly get on with living religious life, somewhat like a newly married couple can get on with living their life together.

Traditionally, religious take three vows, pledging themselves to follow the **evangelical counsels** of poverty, chastity, and obedience. They are called "evangelical" because they are Gospel-oriented, aimed at striving for the charity of the Gospel.

The vows help to define or give shape to religious life and to the ways a religious will answer the call to love that is given to all Christians. Married people answer this call to love chiefly by loving their spouses and committing themselves to each other and to their families for their entire lives. The vows that religious take commit them to a more open, or less specifically focused, way of loving. Religious are free from concerns specific to marriage and family, but through their vows, they take on a commitment to listen for God's call to love and to follow that call no matter where it leads them during their entire lives.

The Vow of Poverty: Sharing a Simple Life

In North American culture, to say that people live in poverty implies that they are destitute or malnourished. But the **vow of poverty** taken by religious has more to do with having little than with being destitute. In fact, the root of the word *poverty* comes from a Latin word meaning "little." Religious take a vow to have few material possessions so that they can avoid the distractions that accompany ownership. Money and possessions can make slaves of our spirit. The more people have, the more they tend to protect and worry about their possessions. Even more important, piling up possessions is not in the spirit of Jesus' command to share with those in need. By taking the vow of poverty, religious commit themselves to live simply and to share their resources with others.

Conscious Decisions About Possessions

Members of a religious order work for their daily bread in solidarity with all other workers. The congregation makes conscious decisions about how best to use the fruits of their labors, which should go to serve the human community. The vow of poverty is a reminder to religious that their lives should be like that of Jesus, who journeyed from place to place, spreading the Good News and sharing his few possessions with people in need.

Life with the Eskimos

One example of this spirit of poverty is found in the ministry of Sister Ann, a missionary deep in the Northwest Territories of Canada, just below the Arctic Circle at the Yellow Knife–Arctic Copper wasteland border. Shortly after she arrived among the Inuit, or Eskimo, people, Sister Ann realized that her ministry would include far more than teaching religion. Life in the Northwest Territories is a daily struggle to survive:

"Sweat and grit is what it takes to work in the North Country," Sister affirms. Continuing, Sister tells of one such survival emergency. "Once while I was instructing Catechism to a group of Indian children, a distraught Eskimo mother burst into my one-room hut shrieking that her little boy had wandered off and now was lost. Most of the village men were on a trapping expedition and there was only one older white man I could turn to for help. Together we donned our snowshoes and began our trek into the snow-covered hills in search of this little one. Just as a blizzard began to stir up, we found the little boy—thanks be to God!" . . .

The people of the "Nor" country never saw a Sister before Ann arrived. Her life, like her people's, is simple and brave. She lives in a hut as they do, with their hand-made snowshoes, and shares in every aspect of their rugged existence. As one Eskimo mother has put it, "Snow Sister tells about Jesus and lives like him here with us." (*Vocation Info,* pages 123, 125)

Sister Ann exemplifies what the vow of poverty is about—living simply and sharing possessions, time, and talents with others. Sharing is a recognition that the goods of this earth are meant to serve everyone's needs. **6**

6
Think about the vow of poverty as it is described here. Then answer these questions in writing:
- **Would any aspects of the vow be beneficial for you?**
- **Which aspects of the vow would you find difficult?**

The Vow of Chastity: Loving All of Humankind

All Christians are called to love God and their neighbors; all Christians—married, single, religious, and ordained—are called to practice chastity (recall the description of chastity on pages 119–121). But in the religious life, the **vow of chastity** has a particular meaning. It is a promise to love in a way that frees the religious sister, brother, or priest to respond to all of humankind, especially those people most in need. This vow includes the pledge to be **celibate**, to abstain from genital sexual behavior, which is proper to marriage. However, the meaning of the vow goes beyond this limited sense of abstaining; it is well expressed in the Rule of the School Sisters of Saint Francis:

Because we are "grasped by Christ Jesus" (Phil. 3:12) we consecrate all our energies to the building of the reign of God. In our celibate living we witness to the unconditional love God has for every person and to the call to love as Jesus loves. We realize that the search for, and experience of, aloneness with God opens us to the fullness of relating with others. Vowed chastity is rooted in our intimacy with God and in a deepening love and compassion for others.

The Freedom to Respond to Needs

The vow of chastity is a choice to love other people while free of the single commitment to one particular person. Married couples, on the other hand, must be committed first and foremost to love each other and their children. This arrangement has practical consequences. A married couple must provide a stable home environment, adequate education, and security for their family. They must nurture their mutual relationship so that their love will grow as the years pass. This requires work, money, time, and energy. Religious, on the other hand, need to be free to respond to needs regardless of where or when they arise. Like the Apostle Paul, who went where he was needed and faced danger to preach the word of God, religious should have the same freedom, the freedom that comes with chastity. **7**

Student art: "Trinity," scratch board by Michael A. Pipitone, Boylan Catholic High School, Rockford, Illinois

7
Think back to some TV programs or movies you have seen that depicted women religious. Write a reflection about how they typically are represented on television or in the movies and whether these representations are accurate.

A Pledge to Build Community

The vow of chastity is a pledge to build community. Religious must be loving people who are great friends, nurturers, and unifiers. They live in community and should strive to create community wherever they go and in whatever work they do. Naturally, religious need friendship and community support, too. But instead of centering their intimate personal relationships on a family of their own, religious develop relationships within their religious communities and within the other communities to which they belong (hospital staff, close friends, colleagues, and so on).

Reliance on God

The vow of chastity also urges religious to stay in close communication with God, who provides the strength and the courage to live celibately. A religious has to rely on the affection and affirmation of a loving God. Thus, prayer is a way of being sustained in a celibate lifestyle. **8**

The Vow of Obedience: Listening to God's Will

Obedience has its root in a Latin word meaning "to hear." To a religious, the **vow of obedience** pledges him or her to listen for the call of God, what God wills in a particular situation, and to follow it.

An Attitude of Openness

Remember that listening, as a skill among human beings, requires an open attitude—a willingness to put aside our own agenda, to not assume we know what the other is going to say, and to try

sincerely to understand what is in the mind and heart of the person we are listening to. Listening to God's call, trying to discern God's will, requires a similar attitude with respect to God.

Learning God's Will in Human Ways

How can a person hear God's call? The call from God does not come through a divine voice that gives specific directions. Rather, Christians—including religious—usually learn what God is calling them to in very human ways. The will of God

Write down your thoughts about whether the explanation of the vow of chastity given here matches the popular understanding of religious celibacy. Then write a dialog in which you debate with yourself about your own ability to lead a celibate lifestyle. In the dialog, have one side of yourself argue yes and the other side argue no.

is shown to religious through the church, through the Bible, in their constitutions and community decisions, in the signs of the times, and especially in the needs of the human family.

The religious vow of obedience requires that members of religious orders take the initiative to seek the will of God with regard to their service and lifestyle. In practice this means that the religious members make decisions by first listening to the sources mentioned with an open attitude, and then praying that God will lead the group to a correct decision and response. Obedience is an active, searching process, not a passive, closed, or rigid mentality. This process of obedience applies both to the community as a whole and to each individual member. **9**

All members of religious congregations—whether sisters, brothers, or priests—take the vows of poverty, chastity, and obedience. Some take other vows particular to their congregation's mission or spirit. In addition, religious priests, like diocesan priests, receive the sacrament of holy orders, which empowers them to lead in celebrating the sacraments.

For Review

- What are the evangelical counsels? Why do religious take vows professing their commitment to them?
- Explain the vow of poverty.
- For religious, what does the vow of chastity mean?
- What does listening have to do with the vow of obedience? How do religious listen to the will of God?

9
Have you ever opened your mind and heart to try actively to seek what was right, without having your mind made up in advance? If so, write about what you did.

Three Types of Religious Congregations

Over many centuries, three types of religious congregations have been founded:
- contemplatives
- mendicants
- service congregations

All these religious orders have community, prayer, and service dimensions, and all require their members to take the traditional vows of poverty, chastity, and obedience. Communities in each category have developed distinct manners of living religious life, although they have also adapted their lifestyles to changing needs and circumstances.

Contemplatives: The Search for God

The first religious orders that formed in the church were **contemplatives.** As the name suggests, their way of life centered primarily on contemplation, meditation, or communion with God. Some well-known contemplative orders are the Carmelites, the Trappists, the Poor Clares, and largest of all, the Benedictines.

The Gospel of Mark tells of Jesus going into the desert or the hills to pray (for example, Mark 1:45 and 6:46). Some early Christians imitated Jesus by going into the desert to encounter God. Eventually they banded together in groups to share their faith stories, to celebrate the Eucharist, and to counsel one another. Because any group needs some guidelines so that its life goes smoothly, various holy men and women composed rules for their communities.

Thomas Merton on Seeking God

Besides regulating communal life, the contemplatives' rules help the women and the men to focus their entire attention on God. Trappist Thomas Merton, perhaps the best-known modern contemplative, once wrote about the focus on God that is the key to contemplative life:

We come to the monastery to *seek* God. . . .

The end which we seek is not merely something within ourselves, some personal quality added to ourselves, some new gift. It is God. . . .

. . . While living by the labour of his hands, [a monk] remembers that [the] highest and most fruitful activity is the spiritual "work" of contemplation. (*The Monastic Journey,* pages 14, 37)

Merton knew well the frenzy of work and the search for power because his young adulthood had been spent in their pursuit. When he had exhausted himself, looking in vain for meaning, Merton turned at last to God. Just as he had previously poured himself into his writing and party going, he now poured all his energy into the work of a monk—contemplation. Merton's reflection and writing have inspired millions of people—Christian and non-Christian alike.

Photo: **Our Lady of New Melleray Monastery in rural Dubuque, Iowa, is home to a community of Trappist monks.**

Saint Benedict: Founder of Western Monasticism

Merton was not the first person to become a monk after being saturated with life's illusions. That pattern of coming to the contemplative life goes back to early Christianity. Many sixth-century followers of **Saint Benedict**, the founder of Western monasticism, were men and women who were tired of the meaninglessness of their lives. So they joined Benedict, a man who, in imitation of Jesus, had gone into the hills to pray. He had left his life in sophisticated but corrupt Rome and the wealth that he would have inherited. Eventually Benedict wrote a rule to give guidance to the dozens of men and women—the first Benedictines—who gathered around him and his sister, Scholastica, in the Italian mountains. Today most Western monastic orders follow the **Rule of Benedict.**

Prayer, work, and rest. The Benedictine Rule orders every day so that time is given to prayer, work, and rest. The monks pray seven times each day from very early morning until night. They pray together the Divine Office, which is composed of psalms, special hymns, prayers, and readings from the Bible. In between these communal prayers, the monks are to work or study. Benedict strived for a simple, well-ordered lifestyle for his followers that would balance prayer and work—*ora et labora,* in Latin.

Contributions to Western civilization. Benedictine monasteries were like small towns. Monks were farmers, healers, librarians, carpenters, masons, cooks, and artists, so each monastery filled its own needs. Besides being islands of contemplation in a busy and often violent world, the monasteries served the human community by preserving learning in their libraries, opening schools (from which the European universities evolved), and experimenting with agricultural techniques that eventually were taught all over Europe. The Benedictines had a great impact on the progress of Western civilization.

A tradition of hospitality. Service was essential to the Benedictine way of life. In his Rule, Benedict was especially careful to tell his monks that hospitality was a priority: "All guests that come should be received as would the person of Christ. . . . And let them be shown every proper courtesy, especially those of the household of the faith . . . and strangers."

Contemplatives Today

Today many contemplative orders have monasteries and convents in North America. We do not hear about many of them because they continue the tradition of Benedict by living lives of prayer, quiet community, and unobtrusive service. Some are involved outside their monasteries, and others

Photo: **Trappistine nuns of Our Lady of the Mississippi Abbey in Iowa are modeling for their neighbor farmers how to treat the land well.**

live an entirely **cloistered** existence—that is, secluded from the outside world. Trappist monasteries dot the map of the United States in such places as Ava, Missouri; Moncks Corner, South Carolina; and Gethsemani, Kentucky. Convents of Poor Clares are scattered throughout North America. Benedictines operate high schools and colleges, continuing the tradition of the monastery schools. Carmelite monks and nuns live in monasteries and hermitages, some offering retreats to people seeking silence and solitude in the midst of their busy lives.

Here is an example, summarized from an article in *The National Catholic Reporter,* of monastic communities that are quietly pursuing life with God while being deeply committed to the world around them:

In Iowa, two monastic abbeys several miles apart have dedicated themselves to sustainable agriculture—farming that restores and enhances the land, rather than depletes it. The Trappist monks of Our Lady of New Melleray Abbey and the Trappistine nuns of Our Lady of the Mississippi Abbey are trying to make their land more productive while getting away from the use of chemicals and diversifying their crops. In their experiments in farming, they are modeling for their neighbor farmers how treating the land well enhances productivity in the long run. These monks and nuns are following in a long tradition of monastic innovation in agriculture: the Cistercian Order, of which the Trappists and Trappistines are a branch, were leaders in agriculture since the Middle Ages in Europe. **10**

Mendicants: Zeal to Spread the Good News

Seven hundred years after Western monasticism began, two men were inspired to initiate a new form of religious community—the mendicants. **Saint Francis of Assisi,** Italy (1181–1226) founded the Order of Friars Minor, known today as the Franciscans, and **Saint Dominic de Guzman,** of Spain (1170–1221) founded the Order of Preachers, now named the Dominicans. Although the men had never met each other, their inspiration to found a new kind of religious community was similar.

In Francis and Dominic's time, heresy and clerical corruption were beginning to divide the church in France and in other areas of Europe. The forces of Islam had conquered most of the Middle East and were gaining a foothold in southern Europe. Monasteries that provided stable centers of Christian faith had long been established, but combating heresy and spreading the word of God to nonbelievers required mobile preachers who would travel the countryside. Both Francis and Dominic, responding to the urgent needs of their era, were inspired to found communities of such preachers.

A Simple Life of Spreading God's Word

The new orders were called ***mendicants,*** a term that means "beggars." Instead of farming like the contemplative monks, the mendicants fed and clothed themselves by begging from those to

10
List the aspects of contemplative life that appeal to you and the aspects that do not appeal to you. Then compile a list of questions that you would ask a monk or a contemplative sister if you had a chance to meet one.

whom they preached. If they were to remain mobile, they had to depend on the goodwill of people. Ownership of property such as a monastery would have tied them down. Both Francis and Dominic took seriously the words of Jesus: "'Go into all the world and proclaim the good news to the whole creation'" (Mark 16:15), and "'Carry no purse, no bag, no sandals. . . . Whatever house you enter, first say, "Peace to this house!" . . . Remain in the same house, eating and drinking whatever they provide, for the laborer deserves to be paid'" (Luke 10:4–7).

The commitment to a simple life of spreading the word of God is reflected in the Rule that Saint Francis gave to his friars (which means "little brothers"):

The friars are to appropriate nothing for themselves, neither a house, nor a place, nor anything else. As *strangers and pilgrims* (1 Pet. 2:11) in this world, who serve God in poverty and humility, they should beg alms trustingly. . . .

Wherever the friars meet one another, they should show that they are members of the same family. . . .

A friar should certainly love and care for his spiritual brother . . . tenderly.

For the task of preaching, Francis recommended simplicity and brevity:

In their preaching . . . they should aim only at the . . . spiritual good of their listeners, telling them briefly about vice and virtue, punishment and glory, because our Lord himself kept his words short on earth.

Prayer was to center on the Eucharist and the Divine Office, but Francis believed that a good friar also prayed throughout the day.

Franciscan and Dominican sisters, brothers, and priests continue in the many communities around the world that follow the traditions of these founders. Although most of these religious are not beggars in the same way that Francis and Dominic were, they work in ways consistent with the spirit of these two great men. The primary purpose of the two orders has remained the same—to spread the Good News. But as times have changed, Dominicans and Franciscans have fulfilled their mission by running hospitals, schools, retreat centers, universities, and parishes. In this respect, the distinction between the mendicant orders and the service congregations (see pages 279–282) has blurred.

The Franciscan Mission to Russia

With the fall of communism in the early 1990s in the former Soviet Union, the small communities of Catholics there needed priests to serve them. In the true spirit of mendicant friars, U.S. Franciscan Fr. Silas Oleksinski responded. The priest, whose family originally came to the United States from Ukraine (one of the former Soviet republics), has

The Franciscans will set up friaries in five locations where communities of Catholics already exist in Russia and the former Soviet republics.

"We'll try to be present to the people, and to each other in fraternity. . . . I see a wonderful opportunity to witness to the basic commitment we have to Jesus. . . . If we live the gospel, if we preach and share the gospel, God will take care of us."

This was the mission of the mendicants of Francis and Dominic's time, and their successors are carrying on that spirit today. **11**

Service Congregations: Ministry to Human Needs

Many of the contemplative and mendicant orders of earlier centuries gradually evolved into orders that provided crucial human services for the church and society. But in the last four hundred years, many new religious orders have been founded specifically as **service congregations.** These congregations engage in a wide variety of ministries.

moved to Russia to minister to Catholics there. In a 1992 *St. Anthony Messenger* article, he said, "'When I read the letter [asking for volunteers] from the [Franciscan] minister general I said, "This is it!" It struck a chord within me.'"

Among Christians in Russia and other former Soviet republics, the overwhelming majority are members of the Russian Orthodox church, which was allowed to function in a limited way under communism. Father Silas, aware of the sensitive nature of relations between the Orthodox and the incoming Roman Catholics, explains the Franciscan Russia mission this way:

"We don't come to offend the Orthodox Church. . . . We treat them as a sister Church. . . . Our primary purpose is to go there as Franciscans, to share in the journey of life with our brothers and sisters. We're not there to implement a program of evangelization that will convert the Russian Orthodox to Roman Catholics. It will happen with some people, but that's not our goal."

For instance, the Society of Jesus, or the Jesuits, founded by **Saint Ignatius Loyola,** is currently the largest men's order. They run schools, colleges, and universities, and they serve as missionaries all over the world. The Daughters of Charity, founded by **Saints Vincent de Paul** and **Louise de Marillac,** is the largest religious order of women; they work in hospitals, orphanages, settlement houses, schools, and clinics. Some orders are specifically missionary in character, such as Maryknoll, the Society of the Divine Word, and the Medical Mission Sisters. Other orders work primarily in education, such as the Marist Brothers and

■

Photo: **A priest of the Greek Orthodox church in a village in Greece. The Greek Orthodox church, like the Russian Orthodox church, is part of the branch called Orthodox Christianity.**

11
Imagine that you are the founder of a religious community of mendicant preachers and that you have ten followers whom you are going to send out in five teams. Decide what places you want to send them to and what issues you

want them to preach about. In writing, assign each team its duties, with an explanation of why you selected these assignments.

the School Sisters of Notre Dame. Many congregations, such as the Sisters of Mercy, the Sisters of Charity, and the Sisters of Saint Joseph, are involved in hospitals, schools, missions, and social work. The founders of these congregations were extraordinary individuals, many of whom played significant roles in shaping their own time and the eras that came after them.

A Modern Founder: Mother Cabrini

Saint Frances Xavier Cabrini (1850–1917), known to her community as Mother Cabrini, was a founder of a relatively modern (nineteenth century) service congregation. Few people who knew her growing up in Italy would have wagered that the frail Italian girl would do all that she did in her lifetime and later become the first U.S. citizen to be declared a saint.

While still in Italy, Cabrini heard about the hard life that Italian immigrants led when they first came to the United States. She sought to join a religious community that worked with those poor immigrants. Because no such order existed, Cabrini founded one herself—the Missionary Sisters of the Sacred Heart. Her conviction to serve humankind was evident in the astounding accomplishments of her short life. She crossed the Atlantic Ocean thirty-seven times and opened orphanages, schools, hospitals, and clinics in North and South America, Spain, France, and England.

A delightful description of Mother Cabrini and her band of "daughters" appeared in a New York newspaper article in May 1889, shortly after the arrival of the missionaries in the United States:

"This week young ladies with radiant faces dressed in plain black religious hoods and robes were seen coursing the overcrowded streets of Little Italy. . . . They left no stones unturned, climbing the dark narrow hallways of poverty to the top floors, descending murky cellar-ways into filthy basement flats. . . . They are the pioneers of a congregation called the Missionary Sisters of the Sacred Heart, and in the short period of a month have already founded a school and orphanage. . . .

". . . The Directoress . . . is 'Madre Francesca Cabrini,' a diminutive, youthful lady with great eyes and an attractive smiling face. . . . She knows the universal language of the human spirit."

This simple, intelligent, courageous, loving, faith-filled woman typified many of the founders of religious congregations, who set a standard that continues to inspire the religious who follow them.

Sister of the Street People

Sister Mary Scullion, a member of the Sisters of Mercy, cofounded Project HOME in 1989 to provide poor people in Philadelphia with affordable housing, addiction recovery programs, mental health services, education, and health care. In an article in the *Philadelphia Inquirer* featuring her work, she says enthusiastically, "'These are *be-yoo-tee-ful* people.'"

Sister Mary is patient and loving, but she gets angry, too. She can be fierce. In the 16 years she has worked with the homeless, Sister Mary has seen some of them come to horrible ends. They have frozen to death and died of heat stroke. They've been run over by cars, hit by buses, set on fire and beaten with two-by-fours by skinheads.

She has also seen—with her leadership—the virtual disappearance of "bag ladies" from Philadelphia streets. She has set up a half-dozen residences around

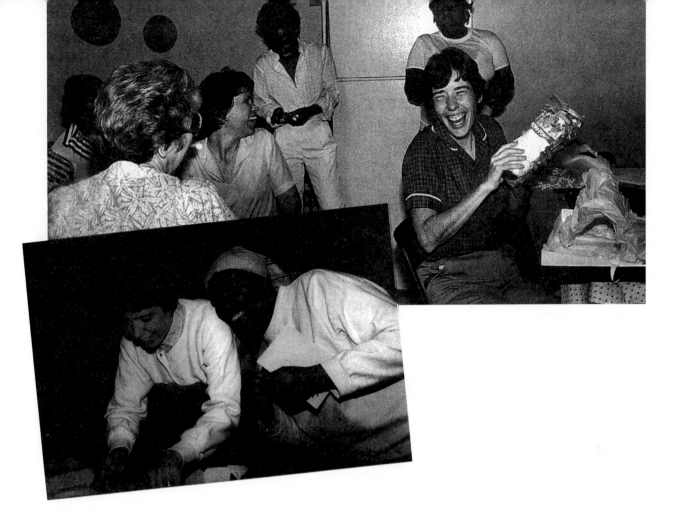

the city for homeless men and women. And she has seen miracles happen.

Yet, when admirers marvel, she demurs.

"I'm the one who's been privileged," she says, "to work with these men and women."

A Brother's Work for Christian Unity

Jeffrey Gros, a De La Salle Christian Brother, serves as associate director of the U.S. Catholic bishops' Secretariat for Ecumenical and Interreligious Affairs. He began his career as a teacher of biology and chemistry, but soon became absorbed in trying to bring unity to the many Christian denomina-

tions that have divided the one church of Jesus Christ. So he earned a PhD in theology and has become a key person in the movement to unite the churches. Over the years, Brother Jeffrey has written dozens of articles on ecumenical issues and participated in international gatherings where members of diverse Christian communities have struggled to overcome matters that divide, among others, Baptists, Episcopalians, Catholics, Methodists, Lutherans, and Orthodox Christians. He states:

My interest in ecumenism, which Vatican II defined as "promoting the restoration of unity among all Christians," started in childhood. I grew up in Memphis,

Photos: **Sr. Mary Scullion** *(on the right in top photo, on the left in bottom photo)* with some of the homeless women she serves through Project HOME in Philadelphia, Pennsylvania.

Tennessee, where Catholics are about 5 percent of the population. To be a Catholic there is to be someone in a minority who looks around and sees that everybody else is Baptist. . . .

. . . The various Christian churches recognize the differences that they have. . . . We look for the day when Orthodox and Catholic, Catholic and Protestant, will worship at the same altar table, confess the same faith, and recognize the same leadership and, indeed, be part of the same church. After all, what does it mean to be a Roman Catholic? And what does it mean to be a Southern Baptist? These designations were not found in the Bible. . . .

. . . *Will we all be called simply Christians, or will we still have our own designations?* Well, who knows the future to which the Holy Spirit is calling us? (*Catholics USA,* pages 268, 272, 273)

In the meantime, Brother Jeffrey continues talking and praying with non-Catholic Christians striving for common understanding and appreciation of their unity in Christ. **12**

For Review

- According to Merton, what is the key to contemplative life?
- Why were the mendicants founded, and how did they differ from the contemplatives?
- For Saint Francis, what did it mean that his friars were to live a simple life?
- List five service congregations and the ministries they perform.

Discovering a Call to Religious Life

- How do I know if I have a call to religious life?
- How do I know if I love someone enough to get married?

What is common to both of these questions is that neither can be answered with absolute certainty. The calls to both religious life and marriage are filled with mystery, and in many ways both calls are matters of the heart.

12
If you were asked to found a religious congregation to meet a pressing need in the human family, what would that need be? Describe it in writing and explain what you would want your congregation to do in response.

Photo: **Br. Jeffrey Gros with bishops of the Anglican church (called the Episcopal church in the United States) and bishops of the Roman Catholic church, in Canterbury, England.**

Positive Signs

Great mystery surrounds any call. However, a call to religious life requires a clear assessment of whether several positive signs are present:

- an attraction to religious life based on proper motives
- an ability to meet the requirements of religious life
- an inner sense of being called by God to religious life

An Attraction to Religious Life

An attraction to religious life may be based on the service of a particular order: missionary projects in poor countries, teaching, working with homeless people, and so on. Or the attraction may be to community life or prayer. Often an attraction to religious life originates in a relationship with a religious who exemplifies a lifestyle that seems to be meaningful and happy for her or him. Some-times a person feels drawn to religious life through a pivotal experience, such as serving for a year or more with a lay volunteer program. These programs—begun by religious orders, dioceses, and other groups in recent decades—offer many opportunities for laypeople to give short-term service.

Proper motives that attract a person to religious life could be any of the following:

- a desire to help people who are in need
- a sense that growth in love of God and neighbor can happen in a religious community
- a belief that the vowed life has value in the modern world

On the other hand, a longing for psychological or financial security, a desire to escape loneliness, or a wish for socially recognized status are improper motives for a person to consider religious life.

An Ability to Meet the Requirements

A person who is considering religious life also needs to determine whether he or she has the ability to meet the requirements of that life. Naturally, the requirements will vary among individual religious congregations, but most requirements fall into three categories:

1. Flexibility. Community life can be a wonderful experience, but the members have to be flexible and tolerant. Few communities exist in total harmony; people disagree and have their quirks. So religious must be able to make allowances for other people and not be too set in their ways.

2. Intellectual and physical qualities. Each religious congregation has its own set of intellectual

Student art: "Avia," oil painting by Craig DeAmbrose, Marist High School, Chicago, Illinois

A KWIK HISTORY OF RELIGIOUS LIFE

and physical requirements, depending on the work of the congregation. For instance, teaching orders would expect that their members have the potential to earn a college or perhaps advanced degree and to teach. Some medical missionary orders require that persons be professionally trained before entering and that they be healthy enough to adapt to a new, physically demanding environment.

3. **The ability to live as a celibate.** To be a healthy religious, a person must be able to live out the vow of chastity, which entails celibacy in religious life. People who would feel constant anguish about not having a spouse and children of their own should probably follow the call to marriage rather than be continually frustrated. Or if seeking sexual gratification is frequently present in a person's consciousness, she or he will find celibacy extremely difficult.

An Inner Sense of Being Called by God

If an individual is aware of the previously mentioned signs toward a religious vocation, then the person needs to pray and to look inward to determine whether he or she has an inner sense of God's call to religious life.

Having an inner sense of God's call does not mean feeling spiritually superior to others; in fact, feeling superior would not be a good sign. Religious life is challenging, but congregations are composed of imperfect human beings who, with the grace of God, do the best they can to fulfill their commitments. They have not joined religious life because they feel that they are better than others but because they have recognized that in the midst of their imperfect human condition, God has invited them to a particular, vowed lifestyle of community, prayer, and service. This lifestyle is their way of responding to the Christian call to love. **13**

Religious Formation

Before making a vowed commitment to religious life, a period of preparation is necessary and required by the church. This period is also a way of

13
Talk with a religious whom you know. Find out how that person discerned that she or he was being called to religious life. Write up what you learn from your discussion.

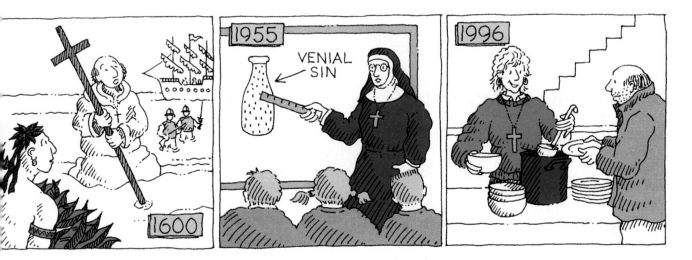

further discerning whether an individual has a permanent vocation to be a religious. Each order has its own program of **religious formation**, but usually three steps are involved: the novitiate, professional training, and vows.

1. **The novitiate.** A beginner at a sport or a job is called a novice. In religious life as well, beginners are called **novices,** and their one- or two-year program of training is referred to as the **novitiate.** (Some religious communities also offer preliminary programs of associate membership or postulancy before the novitiate.) A novice studies basic theology and spirituality, the history and particular rules of the order, and other facets of religious life. Novices work closely with spiritual directors, who help them to work out questions about their relationships with God and the community. At the end of the novitiate, the religious take temporary vows (poverty, chastity, obedience, and any other vows particular to a community) by which they commit themselves to live in the community for one year.

2. **Professional training.** Religious are active in many professions—as psychiatrists, professors, social workers, nurses, carpenters, priests, catechists, and so on. If a religious has not had professional training before joining a community, she or he will receive it after the novitiate, and then enter into the work of the community.

3. **Vows.** After the vows taken at the end of the novitiate, religious take annual vows for several years before making the final commitment of perpetual, or lifetime, vows. Usually religious are counseled by spiritual directors and make special retreats in order to be sure that they are ready to commit themselves permanently to religious life.

For Review

- Explain the three positive signs of a call to religious life.
- What are the usual steps in the formation of a religious?

Small Numbers, Big Results

Members of religious congregations make up only a tiny percentage of Catholic Christians. However, over the many centuries since the foundation of the first monasteries, religious have provided leadership for the church in learning, in education, in health care, in social service, in liturgy, and in forming Christian communities.

Over the last several decades, the number of religious has declined, and the average age of members has steadily become older. These changes have caused many congregations and orders to take measures to continue the work and spirit of their order through the involvement of laypeople. **Lay volunteer programs** (mentioned earlier in the chapter) and **associate** or **affiliate programs** orient their lay associates to the spirituality of the religious order, provide support for the associates, and unite them with the religious in the ministry of the community. And groups of canonically recognized lay affiliates who follow a modified version of a religious order's rule have been around for centuries.

Among the dozens of lay volunteer and associate groups springing up in recent decades are the Sisters of Charity of Nazareth Ministry Corps, Jesuit Volunteer Corps, Marianist Voluntary Service Communities, MercyCorps, Lasallian Volunteers, and Maryknoll Associates.

All these programs extend the work of religious communities and may give rise to new forms of religious community for the future. A few lay volunteers end up joining religious communities. Almost all learn more about service, God, and themselves. Laura Thomas, who went to India as part of the Sisters of Charity of Nazareth Ministry Corps, reflects on her experience:

The last two months I've been caring for abandoned babies and children with the Missionaries of Charity in Jamshedpur. . . .

I am here in India, and I think I've been loving God. Working with the poor. . . . Living a simple life. . . .

I came to India because I thought that this was how I could love God. I knew India was a right thing, but my understanding was all wrong. Really I didn't come here to love God like I thought, coming here wasn't even my decision. God brought me here, India has been God's gift to me. I now understand the reason I am in India is to learn how to let God love me.

Though religious orders may be smaller in number than they were a few years ago, they are inviting, supporting, and training other members of the church to carry on the spirit and ministry of their communities. They are giving life to the church today.

Perhaps society needs religious today more than it ever has before. We need models of community

and service who help us to realize our radical dependence on God:

- In a world that seduces us to consume and to buy, we need persons vowed to poverty, who can remind us that life and happiness are more than having a lot of possessions.
- In a world where people are treated like objects, we need persons vowed to chastity, who can show us how to love all human beings as sisters and brothers.
- In a world that emphasizes the utmost importance of our personal wants, we need persons vowed to obedience, who can show us how to listen to what God wills for the whole human family. **14**

In a spirit of thanksgiving and openness, we can pray:

Holy Friend, our God,
Over many centuries, you have called forth women
    and men
    to serve your people as vowed religious.
Some have quietly prayed for us in monasteries.
Others have gone out preaching the Gospel.
Many have educated, healed, housed,
    clothed, and inspired us.
For what has been, we give thanks.

Help us now to be open to a call to religious life
    or a call to work with religious to build a better
        world,
    a world inspired by the Good News of Jesus
        Christ.
For what is and what can be, we give thanks. Amen.

■
Photo (facing page): **A member of the Lasallian Volunteers teaches in a school. These volunteers work in association with the De La Salle Christian Brothers.**

■
Photo (above): **A priest from a religious order celebrates the sacrament of reconciliation with a person seeking God's healing forgiveness.**

14
Write your reflections in writing:
- **After studying religious life, do you feel the need to consider further whether you have a call to that life?**
- **If so, what questions do you still need to ask yourself?**

15

Ordained Ministry:
To Celebrate, Guide, and Serve

Called to a Special Ministry

Baptism calls every Christian to minister to others. The lifestyles that have been discussed so far in this course—single life, marriage, and religious life—are full of potential for ministry of various kinds. Another life path, this one to a particular kind of service in the Roman Catholic church, is **ordained ministry.**

In the sacrament of ordination, or holy orders, certain men are called from the Catholic community and anointed to be priests, bishops, and deacons. They spend their lives ministering to the church in a special way that is vital to the life of the whole community.

A Tradition of Sacramental Ministry

The tradition of ordained ministry in the church is ancient. Catholic teaching traces it to Jesus' call to the twelve men who would become his **Apostles.** In Matthew's account of Jesus' invitation to Peter and Andrew, the first two Apostles, we read:

As he walked by the Sea of Galilee, he saw two brothers, Simon, who is called Peter, and Andrew his brother, casting a net into the sea—for they were fishermen. And he said to them, "Follow me, and I will make you fish for people." Immediately they left their nets and followed him. (Matthew 4:18–20)

After Jesus called them, the twelve he chose became his disciples—his followers throughout the three years of his active ministry. During this time, Jesus sent them forth to represent him and to proclaim and heal in his name.

The Catholic church draws its understanding of the specific ministry of the ordained from the scriptural accounts of the Last Supper:

Then he took a cup, and after giving thanks he said, "Take this and divide it among yourselves; for I tell you that from now on I will not drink of the fruit of the vine until the kingdom of God comes." Then he took a loaf of bread, and when he had given thanks, he broke it and gave it to them, saying, "This is my body, which is given for you. Do this in remembrance of me." And he did the same with the cup after supper, saying, "This cup that is poured out for you is the new covenant in my blood." (Luke 22:17–20)

In the tradition of the church, it was at this first Eucharist that the specific ministry of the ordained —that is, **leadership in the sacramental life of the church**—was established. The **Eucharist** is the central celebration of the Christian community, the sign of unity and love that draws the people of God together with one another and with God in Jesus. So, as leaders of the community, ordained ministers are called specifically to lead the Christian community in celebrating the Eucharist and the other sacraments.

The call to ordained ministry continues to be offered today. In one of his speeches, Pope John Paul II talked about the need for new ordained ministers:

The Divine Redeemer wants many of you, more numerous than you may think, to participate in the ministerial priesthood in order to give the Eucharist to humanity, to forgive sins, to guide the community. Christ counts on you for this marvelous mission. Priests are necessary to the world because Christ is necessary. (*Message for World Day of Prayer for Vocations,* number 3)

As discussed in chapter 14, some ordained persons are also members of religious orders. In this chapter it is worthwhile to take some time to consider what the lifestyle of ordained ministry entails.

Called as Leaders, Mediators, and Servants

The specific, unique ministry of the ordained person is a sacramental one. Priests, bishops, and to some extent, deacons preside at celebrations of the sacraments. Furthermore, like all baptized Christians, ordained ministers are called to spread the Good News of Jesus Christ. But over the centuries ordained ministers have taken on other roles as well—the roles of leader, mediator, and servant.

Leaders:
Carrying on the Work of the Apostles

In the church's tradition, ordained ministers, as **leaders,** carry on the work of Jesus' Apostles, the first persons called to leadership in the church. Jesus designated Peter to be the head of the new Christian community. The other Apostles were to provide leadership to the church, too, but Peter was first among them. Soon after Jesus' death and

Photo: **Pope John Paul II brings a message of hope and challenge to the world.**

Resurrection, missionaries such as Barnabas and the Apostle Paul spread out across the Roman Empire to preach the word of God, to heal, and to form local Christian communities.

Soon many local communities were thriving—the churches of Jerusalem, Rome, Antioch, Philippi, and Ephesus, to name a few. As a local church grew in size, one of the founding Apostles selected a leader, or bishop, to head that Christian community. Evidence exists that some of the Apostles moved to the larger cities and exercised leadership there. For example, Peter led the community in Rome. (On the basis of Peter's residence and martyrdom there, the bishop of Rome—later called the pope—traditionally has held the central position of authority and leadership in the Roman Catholic church.)

In the earliest days of the church, an Apostle worked with the local church to determine who in that community was most suited for leadership as a bishop. After all the founding Apostles died, the communities selected their own bishops, usually with the advice of a bishop from another local church.

Ordination in the early church meant that a person was expected to lead the Christian community, and this characteristic is still true for bishops, priests, and deacons in the church today.

Mediators:
Putting People in Touch with God

Ordained ministers traditionally have been seen as **mediators**, helping the members of the Christian community to be in touch with God. Ordained ministers carry the Christian community's concerns to God, praying on the people's behalf and offering sacrifice to God for them. But the ordained also speak to the community on God's behalf, reminding them of God's word and helping them discern how that word applies to their lives.

Fr. Jack Carroll, pastor of a parish in the Diocese of Paterson, New Jersey, expressed in an interview in *U.S. Catholic* his sense of how important it is to be a mediator between God and his parishioners:

"The greatest thing I can do for the people of my parish . . . is to give them a love for Jesus and an understanding of how much he loves them. . . .

"If I can bring them close to Jesus, make him more real to them, let them know he's always close to them, impress on them how much he loves them . . . I want them to see that in me, and then I hope it will be a little bit contagious, that they'll want to pursue a loving relationship with Jesus. If I do that and nothing else, I'll have done my job."

Servants: Becoming Like Jesus

In the church's tradition, the ordained ministry has always included the expectation that leaders should follow the model of Jesus, who came "not to be served but to serve, and to give his life as a ransom for many" (Mark 10:45). Above all, bishops, deacons, and priests need to be **servants**, people who spend their lives and energies for others. At the Last Supper, when Jesus performed the servant's role of washing the feet of each Apostle, he gave an example of the loving service that his followers must give to the community (John 13:1–15).

Fr. Clifford Norman exemplifies the servant role of the ordained ministry. His story was told in a 1992 issue of *Catholic Digest.*

Since 1976 Father Norman has run an orphanage in Colon, Mexico, for boys and girls, most of whom have been abused and discarded by their parents. Known for his great compassion for unwanted children, Father Norman has enlisted the help—financial and labor—of people in his home diocese of Pueblo, Colorado, to expand the work of the orphanage so that it can care for some two hundred children, tots to teens, in three facilities.

Of his work, he says, "I thrive on challenge. The more difficult things are, the more interesting they become." When a visitor says to this boundlessly energetic man, "I don't know how you keep up," Father Norman just smiles and shrugs. "It's love," he says. "That's all there is to it." **1**

In recent decades, especially since Vatican Council II in the early 1960s, the church has renewed and broadened its understanding of priesthood, re-emphasizing the meaning it had in the early church. Particularly in the first century, the whole Christian community was seen as sharing in Jesus' priestly function. By virtue of their baptism, all Christians were to act after the model of Jesus, the High Priest, who most clearly revealed God to human beings. But this understanding was somewhat obscured over the centuries of the church's history.

Today, however, Catholic Christians are rediscovering the sense that they, along with the clergy, are called to roles of leadership, mediation, and servanthood. Many aspects of the roles that for many centuries were considered exclusive to the clergy are now being shared with the laity, the laypeople. Thus the *essential* role of bishops, deacons, and priests—their leadership in sacramental ministry—has been able to stand out even more clearly.

For Review

- What is the essential, specific role of ordained ministers in the Catholic church, and from where in the Scriptures does Catholic tradition derive that role?
- Explain how the tradition of ordained ministers as leaders originated and has continued.
- In what ways are ordained ministers to be mediators and servants?

1
Give an example in writing of the service you have seen or experienced from an ordained minister.

Bishops: Successors of the Apostles

Supervisors, Shepherds, and Teachers

The word *bishop* has its origin in the Greek word *episkopos,* meaning "overseer." This defines well the role of bishops. Beginning with the first century of the church, **bishops** were selected to head local churches, now called **dioceses.** Bishops have inherited the authority of the Apostles to appoint deacons and priests to serve the Christian community. Bishops themselves serve the church by supervising the activities of their dioceses while taking part in the roles of the ordained ministry outlined in the first section of this chapter. Perhaps you have experienced the sacramental ministry of a bishop by receiving the sacrament of confirmation. **2**

These words from the ordination ceremony for a bishop express the union of leadership with service that is held up as an ideal for bishops:

You, dear brother, have been chosen by the Lord. Remember that you are chosen from among men and appointed to act for men and women in relation to God. The title of bishop is one not of honor but of function, and therefore a bishop should strive to serve rather than to rule. Such is the counsel of the Master: the greater should behave as if he were the least, and the leader as if he were the one who serves. Proclaim the message whether it is welcome or unwelcome. . . . Pray and offer sacrifice for the people committed to your care and so draw every kind of grace for them from the overflowing holiness of Christ. . . .

As a father and a brother, love all those whom God places in your care. Love the priests and deacons who share with you the ministry of Christ. Love the poor and infirm, strangers and the homeless. Encourage the faithful to work with you in your apostolic task; listen willingly to what they have to say. Never relax your concern for those who do not yet belong to the one fold of Christ; they too are commended to you in the Lord.

The responsibilities of bishops are complex and demanding. Bishops are to be not only administrators but also shepherds, caring tenderly about the concerns of the thousands of members of their dioceses.

2
List all the official activities you are aware of that the bishop of your diocese performs. Then summarize how your bishop provides leadership to the local Christian community.

■
Photo: **By anointing the young person on the forehead with sacred oil, a bishop confers the sacrament of confirmation.**

In addition, because of their very public role as leaders and teachers in the church, bishops look into difficult social and moral issues to try to articulate for the faithful and the world what guidance the Bible and the tradition of the church can give about those issues.

- The U.S. Catholic bishops have issued pastoral letters such as *The Challenge of Peace* (1983), *Economic Justice for All* (1986), and, on family issues, *Follow the Way of Love* (1993).
- The Canadian Catholic bishops have offered their perspective on the future of Canada's socioeconomic order in *Ethical Choices and Political Challenges* (1983).
- The Federation of Asian Bishops Conferences, in a statement *Journeying Together in Faith with the Filipino Migrant Workers in Asia* (1993), denounced "the economic system, which through its primacy of money and market, constitutes a violent aggression on the rights of the Asian

poor to live with human dignity as sons and daughters of God."
- The bishops of Zambia, Africa, in their letter *Hear the Cry of the Poor* (1993), advocated justice for the suffering people of their country. They concluded: "We are indeed at a critical moment in the life of our new democracy. There is a great danger that government policies, if not combined with clear social concern, will bring about a situation of 'economic apartheid' in Zambia." **3**

All over the world, Catholic bishops offer a Gospel perspective on the urgent needs of humankind.

A Bishop for Our Times: Oscar Romero

In the Central American country of El Salvador today, people, especially the poor, regard **Oscar Romero** as a saint. From 1977 until his assassination in 1980, Romero was the archbishop of San

■

Photo: Archbishop Oscar Romero greets his beloved Salvadoran people after a Sunday Mass in 1980.

3
Write your reaction to this statement: *Bishops should not make official statements on subjects like nuclear weapons, world economic imbalances, and disarmament.*

Salvador, the country's capital and major archdiocese. (Romero was killed in the same year that North American missionary Jean Donovan, described on pages 210–211, was murdered for working with El Salvador's refugees.)

When Romero was appointed archbishop, the country was in the midst of a popular revolutionary movement to free the society of oppressive rule by the rich and the military. For decades, most of the people had been treated as virtual slaves; the masses of peasants were landless, hungry, and uneducated. A few rich families, supported by the government, held most of the land for their own profit, using the military and paramilitary death squads to support them by terrorizing the peasants into submission.

Known to be a cautious conservative, Romero nonetheless became convinced that he had to defend the poor people in their struggle to obtain their rights. After the murders of several priests and laypeople who were working with poor Salvadorans, Romero took an increasingly courageous stand against the torture, kidnapping, and murder of people who had shown any sympathy with the movement for justice. The peasants became the archbishop's own friends, and soon he was known worldwide as "the voice of those who have no voice," a fearless advocate for the poor people of his country.

Attempts were made to silence Romero by threats against his life, but in his homilies he continued to speak "dangerous" words of truth. At the regular Sunday Mass held in the Cathedral on the day before his death, he made an appeal, carried by radio across the whole country, to the army, the National Guard, and the police to end the repression:

"Brothers, each one of you is one of us. We are the same people. The peasants you kill are your own brothers and sisters. When you hear the voice of a man commanding you to kill, remember instead the voice of God: 'Thou Shalt Not Kill!' God's law must prevail. No soldier is obliged to obey an order contrary to the law of God. There is still time for you to obey your own conscience, even in the face of a sinful command to kill.

"The Church, defender of the rights of God, of the law of God, and of the dignity of each human being, cannot remain silent in the presence of such abominations.

"The government must understand that reforms, steeped in so much blood, are worthless. In the name of God, in the name of our tormented people whose cries rise up to Heaven, I beseech you, I beg you, I command you, *Stop the repression!*"

■ *Photo:* **The burial place of Archbishop Romero draws thousands of people each year who revere his memory and acknowledge his continuing presence in the hearts of the Salvadoran people.**

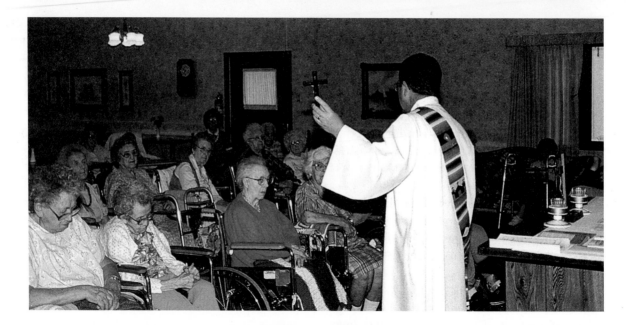

On the following day, 24 March 1980, Romero celebrated Mass in the chapel of a hospital for poor cancer patients. During the homily, the archbishop spoke these prophetic words:

"Whoever out of love for Christ gives himself to the service of others will live, like the grain of wheat that falls and only apparently dies. If it did not die it would remain alone. . . . Only in undoing itself does it produce the harvest."

At the end of the homily a shot rang out; a short time later Romero was dead, killed by an assassin. He had joined the long line of bishop-martyrs who, from the time of the Apostles, died for preaching the law of love—the word of God. **4**

For Review

- What are some of the roles of bishops?
- How was Oscar Romero a model of courage and pastoral concern?

Deacons: From the Earliest Years

Ministers of Charity, of the Word, and of the Liturgy

Deacons have served in the church from its earliest years. In fact, the first martyr, **Saint Stephen**, was a deacon. He had been elected with six others by the Christian community of Jerusalem to help the Apostles; these deacons distributed food to widows and poor members whose needs might otherwise have been overlooked. Deacons and deaconesses were important in the early church's ministry because they had significant roles in preaching, in the liturgy, and in service to poor members of the community.

Over the centuries the role of deacons and deaconesses declined, with the diaconate—or period of serving as a deacon—becoming only a stage in the preparation for the priesthood. Since the idea of

---

■
Photo: **Elderly and infirm people experience the ministry of a deacon, who leads a communion service at a nursing home.**

4
Describe in writing your reactions to the excerpts from the two homilies given by Archbishop Romero. Can you think of any issues about which you wish your bishop would speak as forcefully?

restoring the **permanent diaconate** was approved by Vatican Council II, many men have become permanent deacons. Others are deacons temporarily, as a step in the process of preparing to become priests. Men already married may become permanent deacons; in fact, most permanent deacons are married and support their families with full-time secular jobs. However, single men may not marry after they have been ordained as deacons, nor may a married deacon remarry if his wife dies.

Permanent deacons go through a three- to four-year training period that includes studies in theology, preaching, the Scriptures, and counseling, as well as practical experiences in ministry. After they are ordained, deacons usually attend classes to deepen their spirituality and to enhance their skills in ministry. Today deacons serve in the following areas:

- *Charity.* Just like the first deacons of the early church, today's deacons are involved in serving poor people and other persons on the margins of society. For example, deacons might minister to prisoners, inner-city homeless people, elderly shut-ins, or people in nursing homes.
- *Preaching.* Deacons may proclaim the Gospel at Mass and preach the homily. Their responsibilities often extend to other ways of proclaiming the word, such as religious education and campus ministry.
- *Liturgy.* Deacons have official functions at liturgies. They distribute the Eucharist and may officiate at baptisms, marriages, wakes, funerals, and burial services. Consecrating the Eucharist and performing the sacrament of reconciliation is reserved for priests, however.

One Deacon: A Visible Presence in His Community

Deacons have been a familiar feature in African American churches, mostly Protestant, for hundreds of years. So the permanent diaconate has been welcomed by African American Catholics as something they are already comfortable with. Dwight Alexander, of New Orleans, is an African American Catholic deacon interviewed for an article in *St. Anthony Messenger:*

Dwight is one of the newest [deacons in the archdiocese], ordained about a year. "There is an extreme urgency that the presence of an ordained minister be very visible in the black community," says 47-year-old Dwight, who is a construction worker. "My becoming an ordained minister in the Catholic Church gives the people I meet every day something to think about," he says. He speaks of the young people whom he visits regularly in the prisons of the City of New Orleans. "My being visible in the way that I live, knowing that I have a family, like they want to" allows the youth to see they have a chance to live a different life, he adds. **5**

For Review

- When did the ministry of deacons begin, and in what ways do they serve in the church today?

5
Interview a deacon or a priest. Ask him about the satisfactions and frustrations in his ministry, his views on obedience to the bishop, and any other questions of interest to you. Write a brief summary of your interview.

Priests: Helping Bishops Care for the People

Catholic Christians usually are more familiar with the work of **priests** than with that of bishops and deacons. However, the **priesthood** as it is understood today was the last of the three forms of ordained ministry to emerge in the Christian community. In the early church the dioceses were similar in population size to our parishes. Bishops were able to preside at the Eucharist and other liturgies. But eventually, as the church spread out into small towns and Christian communities in cities became larger, bishops found it harder to supervise effectively. They needed help in their task of guiding the church. With this growth came another level of ordained ministry—the presbyters, or elders. The modern word *priest* comes from *presbyter*. Organizationally, presbyters as well as deacons worked under the local bishop. The role of presbyter evolved into what we now know as the priesthood.

Diversity Is the Word

Like bishops and deacons, priests are to be sacramental ministers, leaders, mediators, and servants of the people of God. Most commonly, diocesan priests (priests who are not members of religious orders) work in parishes, presiding at sacramental celebrations, preaching, teaching, and coordinating the ministries done by others in the parish. Diocesan priests also work in other ministries besides parishes; for example, they teach in and administer schools, work in social service agencies, write for diocesan newspapers, serve in hospitals and prisons as chaplains, and minister on college campuses.

Priests belonging to religious orders minister under the supervision of their congregation, doing the work of their own religious community. But by the sacrament of ordination, they also are empowered to fulfill the role of sacramental minister.

The actual functions of a priest in a local community vary greatly. In many small towns and villages throughout the world, a priest might be the only educated resident. Consequently, he may become a civic leader or a health and welfare agent, in addition to performing his priestly duties. However, the sacramental role is key for all priests.

Even in large cities, parish priests often assume many roles. Fr. Donald J. Winkels, a diocesan priest, described the duties of a parish priest:

If one word could describe the ministry of the parish priest, it would be "diversity."

The scope of his daily concern would include the celebration of the Eucharist, the care of the sick, administrative responsibilities, programs of sacramental preparation, meetings with parish council and committees, community concerns, spiritual direction, reconciliation and healing, teaching and homily preparation and time for prayer, study, and recreation.

Over and above these [concerns] are the "surprises," the unscheduled needs that can emerge any-

time, and can be anything from the highly unusual to the very inspiring. All are opportunities for service and often are the most effective ministry of the day. In all this, diversity is the word.

Handling such diversity is difficult. The expectations placed on priests sometimes make it seem they are called upon to be all things to all people. **6**

Building Up the Christian Family

A pastor cannot possibly perform all the functions of ministry that are needed in a parish. Sharing ministry with parishioners is the key not only to the priest's own sense of balance but also to building up a sense of family and nurturing the gifts of the people. For instance, one parishioner in what was formerly a declining inner-city parish in Philadelphia recalled how the pastor built a sense of community and shared ministry with the people:

Father Bud had the remarkable ability to get things to start happening among people. He often worked behind the scenes, encouraging a parishioner to get someone else involved in a project or to reach out to a member who needed to be brought into the community. He loved us and believed in us so much that we found ourselves wanting to pass that on. We used to say, "Father Bud has 'calling power.' When he calls, you listen." And he passed that calling power on to his parishioners.

Pretty soon lots of people were taking the initiative of calling others to get involved in the liturgy, offering retreats for the rest of the parish, or simply befriending the lonely or abandoned folks who usually found their way to our parish. With all these connections between people, our lives were really being knit together. Eventually we turned our focus outward as well; the parish took on a regular ministry to homeless people, with a soup kitchen, free medical clinic, and lots of other supports. We even turned abandoned houses into low-cost rental units for poor single moms and their kids.

When Father Bud celebrated Sunday Mass with us, it was not simply a ritual that we were going through. It was a celebration of our life together in Jesus, with all its difficulties and joys. Since Father Bud was transferred, the spirit of family and of reaching out beyond our parish has stayed alive and grown. **7**

For Review

- How did the role of priests evolve in the church?
- Why is *diversity* a good word to describe the ministry of a parish priest?
- How can a parish priest help build up the Christian family?

Student art: "Our Lady of Lourdes Church on a Snowy Night," batik by Jodi Wieczorek, Mercy High School, Omaha, Nebraska

6
Write your reflections on this question: *Why is it necessary that priests display by their actions what they preach in their words?*

7
Think of a priest whom you admire. List the qualities that make this priest admirable and write a reflection on how this priest can be a model for your own life.

Qualifications for the Priesthood

Persons who are considering the priesthood need to examine themselves to determine whether they have the qualities necessary to become a priest. If they find that they do have the following qualities, then through prayer and discussion with a spiritual guide or counselor, they may become aware that God is calling them to the priesthood.

An Attraction to the Priesthood

First an individual needs to have an attraction to the lifestyle of the priesthood based on proper motives. Perhaps a friendship with a priest gives a person an initial attraction to the lifestyle. Proper motives would include a desire to serve the Christian community, to preach the word of God, and to enter into leadership in the sacramental ministry of the church.

An Ability to Live as a Priest

Living as a priest entails promises of obedience and celibacy. Someone considering the priesthood needs to assess whether he can faithfully fulfill these promises.

Obedience. Priests place themselves at the service of the church by submitting to the authority of the diocesan bishop. Although assignments usually are made after close consultation between the bishop and the priest, a priest may be asked to assume duties for which he does not feel a great fondness. Someone who cannot promise obedience to a bishop should probably consider a different vocation.

Celibacy. Celibacy is required of priests for many of the same reasons that it is required of religious. Celibacy ideally allows the priest the freedom to love inclusively—that is, with a love that extends to the wider human community and without the limitations of a commitment to a wife and family—and to move when required. Celibacy can result in intense loneliness. Nevertheless, loneliness is part of every person's life—married, single, or celibate. Fr. John Reedy, writing in *Notre Dame Magazine,* remarked:

Commitments [to either marriage or celibacy] do not erase the yearning for the kind of intimacy that can come from a unique sharing of one's life, with all its hopes and fears and hurts, with one other person

Student art: "The Dark of Night—to the Light of Day," acrylic painting by Kate Tusa, Mercy High School, Omaha, Nebraska

who accepts this trust and returns it. I'm not so naive as to believe that all marriages provide such intimacy. But married or celibate, most of us feel the need for it. . . .

Ideally, the [priest] should find such intimacy in his relationship with God. . . .

. . . Every life has its difficulties. Mine also has had satisfactions which have enabled me, with God's support, to accept the difficulties and to find a deep, underlying happiness beneath the routine.

Priests can and should develop all types of intimacy with friends, except sexual intimacy. Just like everyone else, priests rely on the support of close friends and loved ones, but they vow that no one relationship will claim the attention and responsibility that they have pledged to give to God. **8**

Sufficient Intellectual Ability

Candidates for the priesthood must have sufficient intellectual ability to complete their course of study, which usually includes an undergraduate degree and four years of theological and ministerial training. Some priests are brilliant scholars, but brilliance certainly is not required. Indeed, the patron saint of parish priests, **Saint John Vianney**, was barely able to finish his studies. What made him a saintly, wonderful priest was his great love for God and for those he pastored. **9**

For Review

- List and explain the qualifications necessary to become a priest.

Sharing the Richness of Human Life

Bishops, deacons, and priests hand on the heritage of Jesus and the Catholic faith. Their sacramental ministry offers them a unique opportunity to enter into the richness of human existence and to help people realize how God is present in their lives. Fr. Robert Stamschror summarizes how ministering through the sacraments is a great blessing:

No life is without its problems, but I'm quite happy. The priesthood has been a blessing for me, especially because people share so much of the richness of their lives with me. As a priest, I am a part of and celebrate some of the most important and touching times in people's lives: At baptism, I wonder at the creation of new life. At the Eucharist, I share with my community the love of God. In the Mass of the Resurrection [funeral Mass], I am allowed to share in people's grieving, I try to console them, and we celebrate the new life of resurrection. Then, in reconciliation, I share in the pain of guilt and the relief of forgiveness and healing. I cannot imagine any other profession that so totally permits a person to partake of the richness of human life—its suffering and joy, despair and hope, blindness and creativity. I feel continually blessed. **10**

With the whole church, we can pray the prayer from the special Mass for priests:

Lord our God, who in governing your people
make use of the ministry of Priests,
grant to these men
a persevering obedience to your will,
so that by their ministry and life
they may gain glory for you in Christ.

(*The Roman Missal*)

8
Answer in writing:
- **What characteristics do you have that would qualify you for the ordained ministry?**
- **What obstacles might prevent you from following a call to ordained ministry?**

9
Complete each part of the following statement in writing. If my best friend announced that he was going to be a priest
- **my greatest joy would be** . . .
- **my concern would be** . . .
- **I would feel** . . .

10
In writing, summarize your beliefs and feelings about the lifestyle of the ordained ministry.

Epilogue:
A Dream for Your Future

The Power of Dreams

Dreams have fascinated, inspired, driven, and energized people for thousands of years. In religious writings, in the arts and literature, and in civic speeches, references to dreams have a remarkably moving power. This is true for both the sleeping kind of dream that comes from deep in our unconscious and the waking kind that emerges from our heartfelt longings for a full life.

This course has provided you an opportunity to get in touch with your waking dream and envision it—that is, to create an image of the kind of life and future you long for.

Destinations and Dreams

Life is not terribly different from taking a trip. Our destination—our dream, or the goals we have for life—allows us to focus on what sort of education we will need, what kinds of friends we will have, and so on. A **dream** is essential. Your destination determines what sort of preparations you will need to make and the experiences you will have, just as a life dream helps you to focus on what you must do to attain that dream.

Of course, travelers can find that despite their best efforts at preparation, they may not always reach their destination—perhaps because of an accident, a sickness, or a flight cancellation. Or they even may find upon arriving at their longed-for destination that they are not so happy there. In fact, travelers sometimes discover that a completely different destination than the one they originally had envisioned—a place they just stumble upon along the way—is what really satisfies them.

A Dream That May Change with Us

Dreams, like travel plans, can be altered. The dreams of our youth will be subjected to the mighty forces of personal crises, changing societal conditions, and fluctuations in personal interests

and preferences. Each of us needs a dream to give us focus, to mobilize our energies toward something outside of ourselves. In reality, as we move through years of experience, this dream will be shaped, reshaped, tempered, refined, and in some cases tossed out in favor of an alternative dream. But we have got to have a dream; we perish without a dream. Our dream, the vision of the future that we want to bring about, gives our life direction and meaning. **1**

United with Jesus' Dream

The end of this course is a good time to reflect on what our own dream is for our future, and whether and how well it is united with Jesus' dream for us. Jesus' dream, as we have seen in this course, is that all people become fully alive—loving, serving, empowered and empowering, creating, learning, sharing, sacrificing, healing, nurturing, befriending. In Jesus' dream, every person would flourish under the **Reign of God**, living out God's will of justice and peace for all human beings and for all creation.

Moment by Moment, Day by Day

Dreams, however, do not magically come true. In the real world, despite the affectionate kisses of a beautiful princess, a toad does not become a handsome prince. Winners of million-dollar sweepstakes may be very lucky, but they at least had to mail in their entry forms. Our dream is realized—it "comes true"—moment by moment, day by day, in the way that we take on the choices and challenges at hand.

Focusing on our dream for the future does not remove us from the present moment; rather, it calls us to live more deeply in the present by making choices consciously. In reality, the present moment is all that we have. It was Jesus who encouraged people to see a dream's potential in small beginnings in the present:

"With what can we compare the kingdom of God, or what parable will we use for it? It is like a mustard seed, which, when sown upon the ground, is the smallest of all the seeds on earth; yet when it is sown it grows up and becomes the greatest of all shrubs,

1

In one sentence, write your dream, the goal toward which you want to direct all your life's energy.

and puts forth large branches, so that the birds of the air can make nests in its shade." (Mark 4:30–32)

Jesus urged people to open their eyes so that they might see clearly that the dream they did not even understand yet was already in their midst: "'In fact, the kingdom of God is among you'" (Luke 17:21).

Sr. Thea Bowman, whose thoughts were quoted on pages 94–95, understood the significance of the present moment for bringing about our life's dream. We may have only a little time left in life,

as she had, or our future may be very uncertain, or what we can do may seem very small in the world's eyes. But every moment of our life can lead to our dream if we treat the present as a precious gift. As Sister Thea said in an interview a few months before her death:

"I don't know what my future holds. . . .

". . . When I first found out I had cancer, I didn't know what to pray for. I didn't know if I should pray for healing or life or death. Then, I found peace in praying for what my folks call 'God's perfect will.' As it evolved, my prayer has become, 'Lord, let me live until I die.' By that I mean I want to live, love and serve fully until death comes. If that prayer is answered, if I am able to live until I die, how long really doesn't matter." **2**

And So, We Hope

Dreams provide us with a goal to live for now; hope gives us energy and stamina to "just keep on keeping on," in Sister Thea's words. Jim Wallis, a leader in the Christian movement for peace and justice, has described hope as "the very dynamic of history . . . the engine of change . . . the energy of transformation . . . the door from one reality to another" (*The Soul of Politics*, page 238). He cites examples of "impossible" situations made possible by the actions of people who hoped in spite of the evidence, such as the multiracial elections in South Africa in 1994 after decades of apartheid rule. Wallis concludes, "Hope is believing in spite of the evidence and watching the evidence change. And hope is a sign of transformation" (page 240).

2
What present moments could you be living more fully? Write your reflections in a one-page essay.

In the fifth century, Saint Augustine pointed to the transforming power of hope, how "impossible" situations become possible: "Hope has two beautiful daughters. Their names are anger and courage; anger at the ways things are, and courage to see that they do not remain the way they are." **3**

God wants us to hope. That is why Jesus rose from the dead. That is why God sent the Holy Spirit to dwell within us, to light our way and fire our will.

You Are Important

Imagine a clear, calm pond. In your mind, toss a small stone into the water. Immediately, ripples spread out in an ever-widening circle, changing the face of the pond.

The world is large. Several billion people inhabit our planet. Nevertheless, small pebble that each of us is, you affect the world and its future. Your decisions and actions spread ripples of effects far beyond what you can see.

The value of your life cannot be measured. You are important because you are made in God's image, created to love because God is love.

The diary of a very remarkable woman, **Etty Hillesum**, contains a striking message with which to end this course, a message of hope and the worth of each person. Etty Hillesum was a young Jewish graduate student living in Amsterdam, the Netherlands, during World War II when the Nazis invaded and began deporting Jews to the death camps. In the midst of this situation, before she was deported and executed at Auschwitz, she wrote

3
Reflect on what Augustine said about hope's "two beautiful daughters." In a paragraph, tell whether you have experienced that kind of hope, and if so, how it affected you.

Student art: "The Pathway to Life," tempera painting by Christina Ampudia, Academy of the Sacred Heart, Hoboken, New Jersey

in her diary, which was published almost forty years after her death:

I find life beautiful and I feel free. The sky within me is as wide as the one stretching above my head. I believe in God and I believe in man and I say so without embarrassment. Life is hard, but that is no bad thing. If one starts by taking one's own importance seriously, the rest follows. It is not morbid individualism to work on oneself. True peace will come only when every individual finds peace within himself; when we have all vanquished and transformed our hatred for our fellow human beings of whatever race—even into love one day, although perhaps that is asking too much. It is, however, the only solution. I am a happy person and I hold life dear indeed. (*An Interrupted Life,* page 151) **4**

In the Spirit of wonder of Etty Hillesum and with all who believe in the Creator God, we can pray from the Psalms:

Yahweh . . .
You created my inmost being
and knit me together in my mother's womb.
For all these mysteries—
for the wonders of myself,
for the wonder of your works—
I thank you.

(Psalm 139:1,13–14)

Student art: "New Horizons," watercolor painting by Johanna DeBacco, Pope John XXIII High School, Sparta, New Jersey

4
Compose a prayer of thanks for all the good gifts that God has already given to you.

ndex

Italic numbers are references to photos.

Acknowledgments *(continued)*

All scriptural quotes in this book are from the New Revised Standard Version of the Bible. Copyright © 1989 by the Division of Christian Education of the National Council of the Churches of Christ in the United States of America. All rights reserved.

The second quote by Jon Kabat-Zinn on page 10 is from an interview reproduced in *Healing and the Mind,* by Bill Moyers, edited by Betty Sue Flowers and David Grubin (New York: Doubleday, 1993), page 117. Copyright © 1993 by Public Affairs Television and David Grubin Productions.

The quote on page 10 is from *The Song of the Bird,* by Anthony de Mello (Garden City, NY: Image Books, 1984), pages 32–33. Copyright © 1982 by Anthony de Mello. Used by permission of Doubleday, a division of Bantam Doubleday Dell Publishing Group, and Fordham University.

The quote on page 16 is from *That Hideous Strength: A Modern Fairy-Tale for Grown-ups,* by C. S. Lewis (New York: Macmillan, 1946), pages 287–288.

The Robert Frost poem on page 20, "The Road Not Taken," is from *Selected Poems of Robert Frost,* with an introduction by Robert Graves (New York: Holt, Rinehart and Winston, 1963), pages 71–72. Copyright © 1962 by Robert Frost.

The quote by Socrates on page 29 is taken from *The Great Thoughts,* compiled by George Seldes (New York: Ballantine Books, 1985), page 391. Copyright © 1985 by George Seldes.

The quote on page 31 is from *Self-Renewal: The Individual and Innovative Society,* by John W. Gardner (New York: Harper and Row, 1965), pages 10–11. Copyright © 1963, 1964 by John W. Gardner.

The excerpt by Molly Dee Rundle on page 35; the poem "For Every Woman," by Nancy R. Smith, on pages 113–114; the poem "Unique," by Mary Paquette, on page 191; and the poem "Two Trees," by Janet Miles, on page 232 are all from *Images of Women in Transition,* compiled by Janice Grana (Winona, MN: Saint Mary's Press, 1991), pages 48, 49, 65, and 58, respectively. Copyright © 1976 by The Upper Room, Nashville, Tennessee.

The quote on page 39 is from *The Language of the Night: Essays on Fantasy and Science Fiction,* by Ursula K. Le Guin, edited by Susan Wood (New York: Berkley Books, 1979), page 187. Copyright © 1979 by Susan Wood.

The excerpts on pages 41, 101, and 101–102 are based on *It's Our World, Too!* by Phillip Hoose (Boston: Little, Brown and Company, 1993), pages 49–55 and 94–100; 68–74; and 102–109; respectively. Copyright © 1993 by Phillip Hoose.

The excerpt on page 43 is from "Letter to a Daughter: Taking Pains," *Christian Century,* 2 March 1994, pages 216–217. Copyright © 1994 by the Christian Century Foundation. Reprinted with permission.

The Lao-Tzu excerpt on page 44 is quoted from *Freedom and Destiny,* by Rollo May (New York: W. W. Norton and Company, 1981), page 165. Copyright © 1981 by Rollo May.

The excerpt on page 45 is from *Freedom and Destiny,* by Rollo May, page 177. Used with permission.

The excerpt on page 47 is from *Power and Innocence: A Search for the Sources of Violence,* by Rollo May (New York:

W. W. Norton and Company, 1972), page 19. Copyright © 1972 by Rollo May.

The excerpt on page 48 is from *The Grapes of Wrath,* by John Steinbeck (New York: Penguin Books, 1976), pages 554–555. Copyright © 1937, renewed 1967 by John Steinbeck. Used with permission of Viking Penguin, a division of Penguin Books USA.

The excerpts on pages 49, 49–50, and 53 are from *Working,* by Studs Terkel (New York: Pantheon Books, 1972), pages 422–424; 294–295; 489, 491, 493, and xxiv; respectively. Copyright © 1972, 1974 by Studs Terkel. Reprinted by permission of Pantheon Books, a division of Random House.

The excerpts by Pope John Paul II on pages 54 and 78 are from *On Human Work* (Washington, DC: United States Catholic Conference [USCC], 1981), numbers 6 and 14. Copyright © 1981 by the USCC.

The excerpt on page 56 is from *Spiritual Fitness: Everyday Exercises for Body and Soul,* by Doris Donnelly (San Francisco: HarperSanFrancisco, 1993), page 83. Copyright © 1993 by Doris Donnelly.

The excerpt on page 57 is from *Work and Play,* by Alasdair Clayre (New York: Harper and Row, 1974), page 176. Copyright © 1974 by Alasdair Clayre.

The excerpt on page 58 is from *Of Human Hands: A Reader in the Spirituality of Work,* edited by Gregory F. Augustine Pierce (Minneapolis: Augsburg Fortress and Chicago: ACTA Publications, 1991), pages 77 and 79. Copyright © 1991 by Augsburg Fortress. Used with permission. All rights reserved.

The excerpt on page 71 is from "Needing and Wanting Are Different," by Jimmy Carrasquillo, *Newsweek,* 16 November 1992, page 82.

The excerpt on page 72 is from "How Much Is Enough?" by Alan Durning, *Utne Reader,* July–August 1991, page 73. Copyright © by the Worldwatch Institute. Used with permission.

The excerpt on page 73 is from "Too Old, Too Fast?" by Steven Waldman and Karen Springen, *Newsweek,* 16 November 1992, page 84.

The excerpt on page 74 is from "Is There Too Much Stuff in Your Life?" by Mike Mallowe, *U.S. Catholic,* December 1992, page 14.

The self-evaluative questions on page 75 are from "Are You a Shopaholic?" *USA Today,* April 1991, page 11.

The statistic on credit card spending on page 75 is taken from *Utne Reader,* July–August 1991, page 72.

The excerpt on pages 75–76 is from "Betting: When It Becomes a Problem," by Michelle Ingrassia, *Newsweek,* 14 June 1993, page 74. Copyright © 1993 by *Newsweek.* All rights reserved. Used with permission.

The statistics on compulsive gamblers and the quote on teen gambling on page 76 are from "The Rise of Teenage Gambling," by Ricardo Chavira, *Time,* 25 February 1991, page 78.

The excerpt on page 77, the quote from Saint Cyprian on page 78, and the excerpt on page 79 are from *Economic Justice for All: Pastoral Letter on Catholic Social Teaching and the*

U.S. Economy, by the National Conference of Catholic Bishops (NCCB) (Washington, DC: USCC, 1986), numbers 75, 34, and 172, respectively. Copyright © 1986 by the USCC.

The prayer by Terra Ryan on page 83, by J. C. on pages 98–99, by Liliana Ramirez on page 103, by Adelaide Juguilon on page 136, by Peter Murray on page 141, and by JulieAnn DeSantis on page 161 are from *Dreams Alive: Prayers by Teenagers,* edited by Carl Koch (Winona, MN: Saint Mary's Press, 1991), pages 25, 34, 59, 66, 75, 29, and 27, respectively. Copyright © 1991 by Saint Mary's Press. All rights reserved.

The excerpts on pages 87 and 100 are from *Words by Kids, 1994: Family Life: Ties That Bind* (Boston: Wang Center for the Performing Arts, 1994), pages 17 and 7–8. Copyright © 1994 by the Wang Center for the Performing Arts. Used with permission.

The excerpt on page 88 is from *Body Theology,* by James B. Nelson (Louisville, KY: Westminster/John Knox Press, 1992), page 125. Copyright © 1992 by James B. Nelson.

The excerpts on pages 88–89, 93, 116, and 117 are from *Take Time to Play Checkers,* by Misti Snow (New York: Viking Penguin, 1992), pages 74, 217, 142, and 143, respectively. Copyright © by Alison Brown Cerier Book Development. Used with permission.

The quote on pages 91–92 is from *Night,* by Elie Wiesel (New York: Bantam Books, 1960), pages 61–63. Copyright © 1960 by MacGibbon and Kee. Copyright © renewed 1988 by the Collins Publishing Group. Reprinted by permission of Hill and Wang, a division of Farrar, Straus and Giroux.

The excerpts on page 94 are from *When Bad Things Happen to Good People,* by Harold S. Kushner (New York: Avon Books, 1981), pages 81 and 58–60. Copyright © 1981 by Harold S. Kushner.

The excerpt on page 95 is from an interview with Thea Bowman by Patrice J. Tuohy, "Sister Thea Bowman: On the Road to Glory," *U.S. Catholic,* June 1990, pages 20, 22. Used with permission.

The excerpt on page 103 is from *The Ecology of Commerce,* by Paul Hawken (New York: HarperCollins, 1993), page 17. Copyright © 1993 by Paul Hawken; originally from Gordon Sherman's 1986 commencement address, California School of Professional Psychology.

The excerpt on pages 106–107 is from *Human Sexuality: A Catholic Perspective for Education and Lifelong Learning,* by the USCC (Washington, DC: USCC, 1991), page 7. Copyright © 1991 by the USCC.

The first full excerpt on page 107 and the excerpt in activity 16 on page 119 are from *What I Wish My Parents Knew About My Sexuality,* by Josh McDowell (San Bernardino, CA: Here's Life Publishers, 1987), pages 124 and 30. Copyright © 1987 by Josh McDowell.

The second excerpt on page 107 is from *Reclaiming the Connections: A Contemporary Spirituality,* by Kathleen Fischer (Kansas City, MO: Sheed and Ward, 1990), page 75. Copyright © 1990 by Kathleen Fischer.

The poem by Jorge Manrique on pages 107–108, and the poem "How Do I Love Thee?" by Elizabeth Barrett Browning on page 123 are quoted from *The World's Love Poetry,* edited by Michael Rheta Martin (New York: Bantam Books, 1960), pages 166–167 and 285. Copyright © 1960 by Bantam Books.

The excerpt on page 112 is reprinted as quoted in *Sexuality and the Sacred,* edited by James B. Nelson and Sandra P. Longfellow (Louisville, KY: Westminster/John Knox Press, 1994), page 337. Copyright © 1994 by Westminster/John Knox Press.

The excerpt by Sojourner Truth on page 113 is quoted from *The Norton Anthology of Literature by Women,* by Sandra M. Gilbert and Susan Gubar (New York: W. W. Norton and Company, 1985), page 253. Copyright © 1985 by Sandra M. Gilbert and Susan Gubar.

The John Updike quote on page 115 is from the *New York Times Book Review,* 20 June 1993, as quoted in *Overview,* June 1994, page 3.

The statistics on sexual assault reporting on page 115 are from "Teens Are Victims of Sexual Assault," *Youthviews,* 1994, page 2.

The information about the Spur Posse on page 116 is from "Hanging with the Spur Posse," *Rolling Stone,* 8–22 July 1993.

The second quote on page 116 is from "Girls Who Go Too Far," *Newsweek,* 22 July 1991, page 58.

The excerpt on page 118 is from "On the Bus," by Tim Rasmussen, *New York Time Magazine,* 27 March 1994, page 59. Copyright © 1994 by the New York Times Company. Reprinted by permission.

The excerpts on pages 119–120 are from "Chastity as Shared Strength," by Mary Patricia Barth Fourqurean, *America,* 6 November 1993, pages 10 and 12. Used with permission.

The excerpt on page 121 is from *Love and Sexuality: A Christian Approach,* by Mary Perkins Ryan and John Julian Ryan (New York: Holt, Rinehart and Winston, 1967), page 77. Copyright © 1967 by Mary Perkins Ryan and John Julian Ryan.

The prayer by F. J. on page 125 and the prayer by Donna Webb on page 174 are from *More Dreams Alive: Prayers by Teenagers,* edited by Carl Koch (Winona, MN: Saint Mary's Press, 1995), pages 79 and 39. Copyright © 1995 by Saint Mary's Press. All rights reserved.

The second excerpt on page 134 is from *Following Jesus,* by Segundo Galilea, translated from the Spanish by Helen Phillips (Maryknoll, NY: Orbis Books, 1981), page 31. Copyright © 1981 by Orbis Books.

The first poem on page 135, "Romping," by John Ciardi, is from *I Marry You: A Sheaf of Love Poems* (New Brunswick, NJ: Rutgers University Press, 1958), page 27. Copyright © 1958 by Rutgers, The State University.

The second poem on page 135, "As Once, So Were We," is from *The Writer's Reader,* by Raymond Hamilton (Santa Fe, NM: Institute of American Indian Arts Museum, 1966), as quoted in *Earthsongs,* by Wayne Simsic (Winona, MN: Saint Mary's Press, 1992), page 67. Copyright © 1992 by Saint Mary's Press. All rights reserved.

The excerpt by Karen DeFilippis on pages 136–137 is from *Womenpsalms,* compiled by Julia Ahlers, Rosemary Broughton, and Carl Koch (Winona, MN: Saint Mary's Press, 1992), pages 98–99. Copyright © 1992 by Saint Mary's Press. All rights reserved.

The excerpt by David on page 145, the excerpt by Walter Winchell on page 149, and the fourth excerpt on page 149 are from *Among Friends: Who We Like, Why We Like Them, and What We Do with Them,* by Letty Cottin Pogrebin (New York: McGraw-Hill, 1987), pages 349, 37, and 44, respectively. Copyright © 1987 by Letty Cottin Pogrebin.

The second excerpt on page 145 is from *I and Thou,* second edition, by Martin Buber (New York: Charles Scribner's Sons, 1958), page 75. Copyright © 1958 by Charles Scribner's Sons.

The excerpts on pages 148, 156, and 259 are from *Just Friends: The Role of Friendship in Our Lives,* by Lillian B. Rubin (New York: Harper and Row, 1985), pages 40, 25–26, and 142, respectively. Copyright © 1985 by Lillian B. Rubin. Reprinted by permission of HarperCollins Publishers.

The Aesop fable on page 149 is quoted from *The Norton Book of Friendship,* edited by Eudora Welty and Ronald A. Sharp (New York: W. W. Norton and Company), page 531. Copyright © 1991 by Eudora Welty and Ronald A. Sharp.

The excerpts on pages 150, 154, 155, the first excerpt on page 192, and the third excerpt on page 192 are from *Worlds of Friendship,* by Robert R. Bell (Beverly Hills, CA: Sage Publications, 1981), pages 16, 22, 143, 111, and 107, respectively. Copyright © 1991 by Sage Publications. Reprinted by permission of Sage Publications.

The poem "Friendship," by Kathryn Crossley, on page 152 is reprinted from *St. Anthony Messenger,* August 1993, page 56. Used by permission of the author.

The Langston Hughes poem on page 159 is reprinted from *The Norton Book of Friendship,* page 189; originally published in *The Dream Keeper and Other Poems* (New York: Alfred A. Knopf, 1932), no page. Copyright © 1932 Alfred A. Knopf and copyright © renewed 1960 by Langston Hughes. Reprinted by permission of the publisher and by Harold Ober Associates.

The excerpt on pages 163–164 is from *Speaking Out: Teenagers Take On Race, Sex, and Identity,* by Susan Kuklin (New York: G. P. Putnam's Sons, 1993), pages 53–54. Copyright © 1993 by Susan Kuklin. Reprinted by permission of G. P. Putnam's Sons.

The excerpt on page 176 is from *Ordinary People,* by Judith Guest (New York: Viking Press, 1976), pages 225, 227. Copyright © 1976 by Judith Guest.

The excerpt on page 177 is from *The Annotated Alice: Alice's Adventures in Wonderland and Through the Looking Glass,* by Lewis Carroll, edited by Martin Gardner (New York: Bramhall House, no date), page 94. Copyright © by Martin Gardner.

The excerpt on page 182 is from *Rolling Thunder,* by Doug Boyd (New York: Random House, 1974), pages 105–106. Copyright © 1974 by Robert Briggs Associates. Reprinted by permission of Random House.

The statistic on the median age of first marriage on page 188, the quote on page 190, and the quote on page 202 are from *13th Gen: Abort, Retry, Ignore, Fail?* by Neil Howe and Bill Strauss (New York: Vintage Books, 1993), pages 156, 154, and 155, respectively. Copyright © 1993 by Neil Howe and Bill Strauss. Reprinted by permission of Vintage Books, a division of Random House.

The second excerpt on page 192 is from *Among Friends,* by Letty Cottin Pogrebin, page 338; originally published as

"Some of My Best Friends Are . . . Men," by Rita Mae Brown, *Ms.,* September 1985, no page.

The statistics on singleness on page 207 are from the U.S. Bureau of the Census, *Statistical Abstract of the U.S.,* 1994, page 55.

The divorce rate given on page 207 is from the *1994 World Almanac and Book of Facts* (Mahwah, NJ: World Almanac, 1993), page 954. Copyright © 1993 by Funk and Wagnalls.

The excerpts on page 210 and 295 are from *Salvador Witness: The Life and Calling of Jean Donovan,* by Ana Carrigan (New York: Simon and Schuster, 1984), pages 67 and 96, and 157. Copyright © 1984 by Ana Carrigan.

The first quote on page 212 and the second quote on page 216 are from "The Art of Flying Solo," by Jean Seligmann and others, *Newsweek,* 1 March 1993, page 73.

The excerpt on pages 212–213 is from *Dorothy Day: Selected Writings,* edited by Robert Ellsberg (Maryknoll, NY: Orbis Books, 1983), pages 69–70. Copyright © 1983, 1992 by Robert Ellsberg and Tamar Hennessey. Used by permission of the publisher.

The quote by Samuel Johnson on page 214 and the third excerpt on page 216 are reprinted from "One's Company," by Barbara Holland, *Utne Reader,* January–February 1993, page 106.

The first three excerpts on page 215 are from *The Habit of Being,* by Flannery O'Connor, edited by Sally Fitzgerald (New York: Farrar, Straus and Giroux, 1979), pages 163, 164 and 92–93. Copyright © 1979 by Regina O'Connor. Reprinted by permission of Farrar, Straus and Giroux.

The first excerpt on page 217 is from *Loneliness,* by Clark E. Moustakas (Upper Saddle River, NJ: Prentice-Hall, 1961), pages 102–103. Copyright © 1961, 1969 by Clark E. Moustakas. Reprinted with the permission of Prentice-Hall, a division of Simon and Schuster.

The second excerpt on page 217 and the excerpt on page 221 are from *Markings,* by Dag Hammarskjöld, translated from the Swedish by Leif Sjöberg and W. H. Auden (New York: Alfred A. Knopf, 1976), pages 85 and 53. Translation copyright © 1964 by Alfred A. Knopf. Reprinted by permission of Alfred A. Knopf, New York, and Faber and Faber, London.

The excerpt on pages 219–220 is from *Love and Lifestyles: Building Relationships in a Changing Society,* by Mary Judd (Winona, MN: Saint Mary's Press, 1981), page 88. Copyright © 1981 by Saint Mary's Press. All rights reserved.

"A Marriage Prayer," on pages 223–224 is from *The God Who Fell from Heaven,* by John Shea (Allen, TX: Tabor Publishing, 1979), page 97. Copyright © 1979 by Tabor Publishing, Allen, TX 75002. Used with permission.

The statistics on page 224 are from a Gallup Youth Survey on teens wanting to marry, as quoted in *Youthviews,* September 1994, page 2.

The statistics from studies on cohabitation on page 225 are taken from *The Sexual Challenge* (Washington, DC: USCC, 1990), page 9. Copyright © 1990 by the USCC.

The excerpt on pages 225–226 is from "Unmarried Couples Shouldn't Live Together," by Juli Loesch, *U.S. Catholic,* July 1985, pages 16–17. Reprinted with permission from *U.S. Catholic,* published by Claretian Publications, 205 West Monroe Street, Chicago, IL 60605.

The statistic on alcohol and drug abuse on page 229 is reprinted from *Church,* Winter 1993, page 32.

The first two excerpts on page 231 and the second and third excerpts on page 232 are from "Marriages Made to Last," by Jeanette Lauer and Robert Lauer, *Psychology Today,* June 1985, pages 24 and 26. Reprinted with permission from *Psychology Today* magazine. Copyright © 1985 by Sussex Publishers.

The excerpts by Pope John Paul II on pages 231 and 257 are from *On the Family* (Washington, DC: USCC, 15 December 1981), numbers 28 and 30. Copyright © 1982 by the USCC.

The excerpt by Antoine de Saint-Exupéry on page 233 is quoted from *Gift from the Sea,* by Anne Morrow Lindbergh (New York: Vintage Books, 1978), page 81. Copyright © 1955, 1975 by Anne Morrow Lindbergh.

The excerpts from the English translation of the Rite of Marriage on page 240 are reprinted from *The Rites of the Catholic Church,* volume 2 (New York: Pueblo Publishing Company, 1976), pages 726–727. Copyright © 1969 by the International Committee on English in the Liturgy (ICEL). Used with permission. All rights reserved.

The excerpt on page 243 is from "Neighbour Rosicky," in *Obscure Destinies,* by Willa Cather (New York: Alfred A. Knopf, 1930), pages 23 and 24. Copyright © 1930, 1932 by Willa Cather and renewed 1958, 1960 by the Executors of the Estate of Willa Cather. Reprinted by permission of Alfred A. Knopf.

The statistics on teens valuing the nuclear family on page 244 are from a Gallup Youth Survey, as quoted in *Youthviews,* May 1994, no page.

The first excerpt on page 246 is from "Is There Married Life After Birth?" by Mike Mallowe, *U.S. Catholic,* October 1994, pages 6 and 8.

The poem on page 246, "Life After Marriage," by Sharon Addy, is from *Marriage and Family Living,* May 1985, page 37.

The excerpt on page 252 is from "Why Sex?" by Christine Gudorf, *U.S. Catholic,* November 1992, pages 6 and 13.

The excerpt on page 254 is from "I Knew My Marriage," by Anna Erhart, *U.S. Catholic,* February 1992, page 9.

The excerpt on page 255 and the first and third excerpts on page 259 are from "Follow the Way of Love," by the NCCB, *Origins,* 2 December 1993, pages 438 and 439.

The excerpt by Pope John Paul II on page 263 is from "Letter to Families," as quoted in *Origins,* 3 March 1994, pages 649 and 658.

The excerpt on pages 267–268 and the quote by Bernard of Clairvaux on page 268 are from *The Nuns,* by Marcelle Bernstein (New York: J. B. Lippincott, 1976), pages 136 and 47. Copyright © 1976 by Marcelle Bernstein.

The second excerpt on page 268 and the excerpt on page 272 are from *Response in Faith: Rule of Life,* by the School Sisters of Saint Francis (Milwaukee, WI: School Sisters of Saint Francis, no date), numbers 8 and 3, and 13. Copyright © by the School Sisters of Saint Francis. Used with permission.

The quote on page 269 is from "A Woman of Vision, A Place of Hope," by Mary Elizabeth Gintling, *St. Anthony Messsenger,* August 1994, pages 11–14.

The excerpt on page 270 is from "Essential Elements in Church Teaching on Religious Life," *Origins,* 7 July 1983, number 5.

The excerpt on page 271 is from *Vocation Info,* edited by Jeremiah J. McGrath (Stockbridge, MA: Marian Press, no date), pages 123, 125. Copyright © Congregation of Marians, Stockbridge, MA 01263. Reprinted with permission. All rights reserved.

The excerpt on page 275 is from *The Monastic Journey,* by Thomas Merton (Kansas City, KS: Sheed Andrews and McMeel, 1977), pages 14 and 37. Copyright © 1977 by the Trustees of the Merton Legacy Trust.

The excerpt on page 276 is from the Rule of Saint Benedict, an unpublished manuscript, with an introduction by Basilius Steidle (Canon City, CO: Holy Cross Abbey, 1967), page 226. Copyright © 1952 by Beuroner Kunstverlag, Beuron.

The information on Trappists and Trappistines on page 277 is summarized from "Monks, Sisters Cultivate Farming Tradition," by Dawn Gibeau *National Catholic Reporter,* 5 November 1993, no page.

The excerpts on page 278 are from *Saint Francis of Assisi: Writings and Early Biographies,* edited by Marion A. Habig (Chicago: Franciscan Herald Press, 1973), pages 61–63. Copyright © 1973 by Franciscan Herald Press.

The excerpts on page 279 are from "What's Next?" by John Bookser Feister, *St. Anthony Messenger,* March 1992, pages 36–37. Used with permission of *St. Anthony Messenger.*

The first excerpt on page 280 is from *Immigrant Saint: The Life of Mother Cabrini,* by Pietro Di Donato (New York: Mc-Graw-Hill, 1960), pages 77–78. Copyright © 1960 by Pietro Di Donato.

The excerpt on pages 280–281 is from "Sister Mary of the Streets," by Ginny Weigand, *The Philadelphia Inquirer,* 22 November 1992. Reprinted with permission from *The Philadelphia Inquirer.*

The excerpt on pages 281–282 is from *Catholics USA: Makers of a Modern Church,* by Linda Brandi Cateura (New York: William Morrow and Company, 1989), pages 268, 272, and 273. Copyright © 1989 by Linda Brandi Cateura.

The excerpt by Laura Thomas on page 286 is from *Open Hearts, Helping Hands: Prayers by Lay Volunteers in Mission,* compiled by Carl Koch and Michael Culligan (Winona, MN: Saint Mary's Press, 1993), pages 15–16. Copyright © 1993 by Saint Mary's Press. Originally published in *SC News,* a newsletter published by the Sisters of Charity of Nazareth, February 1992. Used with permission.

The excerpt by Pope John Paul II on page 290 is from the *Message for World Day of Prayer for Vocations,* 28 April 1985 (Chicago: National Catholic Vocation Council, 1985), number 3.

The excerpt on pages 291–292 is from "A Day in the Life of a Parish Priest," by Gerald M. Costello, *U.S. Catholic,* October 1994, page 31.

The excerpt on page 292 is based on "Father Clifford and His Minor Miracles" by Alan Gottlieb, *Catholic Digest,* pages 1–8; originally published in *The Denver Post,* 2 May 1992.

The excerpt on page 293 is from the English translation of *Ordination of Deacons, Priests, and Bishops,* in *The Rites of the*

Catholic Church, volume 2, page 69. Copyright © 1975 by the ICEL. Reprinted with permission. All rights reserved.

The excerpt on page 294 from *Journeying Together in Faith with the Filipino Migrant Workers in Asia* is quoted from *Catholic International,* December 1993, page 570.

The excerpt on page 294 from *Hear the Cry of the Poor* is quoted from *Catholic International,* October 1993, page 478.

The excerpt by Oscar Romero on page 296 is quoted from "Since Death Came to the Archbishop," by Jack Wintz, *Catholic Digest,* June 1985, page 32; originally published in *St. Anthony Messenger,* March 1985.

The excerpt on page 297 is from "Deacons: In the Footsteps of St. Stephen," by John Bookser Feister, *St. Anthony Messenger,* December 1994, page 18. Used with permission of *St. Anthony Messenger.*

The excerpt on pages 298–299 is from *Priest: A Way of Life,* by the Diocese of Winona (Winona, MN: Immaculate Heart of Mary Seminary, no date), no page. Used with permission of the Diocese of Winona.

The excerpt on pages 300–301 is from "Why I'm Still a Priest," by John Reedy, *Catholic Digest,* February 1981, pages 66–67; originally published in *Notre Dame Magazine,* July 1980. Copyright © 1980 by the University of Notre Dame. Used by permission of *Catholic Digest.*

The final excerpt on page 301 is from the English translation of *The Roman Missal* © 2010, ICEL. Used with permission. All rights reserved.

The excerpt by Thea Bowman on page 305 is from "Lord, Let Me Live Till I Die," by Fabvienen Taylor, *Praying,* November–December 1989, pages 19–20.

The second and third excerpts on page 305 are from *The Soul of Politics: A Practical and Prophetic Vision for Change,* by Jim Wallis (Maryknoll, NY: Orbis Books and New York: New Press, 1994), pages 238 and 240. Copyright © 1994 by Jim Wallis.

The quote from Saint Augustine on page 306 is quoted from *Context,* 1 February 1992, page 3.

The first excerpt on page 307 is from *An Interrupted Life: The Diaries of Etty Hillesum, 1941–43,* translated by Jonathan Cape (New York: Pocket Books, 1981), page 151. Copyright © 1981 by De Haan/Uniebock b.v., Bussum. English translation copyright © 1983 by Jonathan Cape.

The psalm on page 307 is from *Psalms Anew: In Inclusive Language,* compiled by Nancy Schreck and Maureen Leach (Winona, MN: Saint Mary's Press, 1986), page 188. Copyright © 1986 by Saint Mary's Press. All rights reserved.

Photo Credits

Cover: Tom Wright

George Ancona, International Stock Photo: pages 93, 101
Laurie Bayer, International Stock Photo: page 170
Bettmann Archive: pages 112, 294
Mark Bolster, International Stock Photo: pages 50, 56
F. Bouillot, International Stock Photo: page 126
Cleo Freelance Photography: pages 69 right, 221, 224, 244
Mimi Cotter, International Stock Photo: pages 21, 36
James Davis, International Stock Photo: pages: 117, 140, 188, 238
Tony Demin, International Stock Photo: page 146
Gail Denham: pages 10, 44, 131, 204, 216, 225, 227
Gregory Edwards, International Stock Photo: page 161

Chad Ehlers, International Stock Photo: page 19
Barry Elz: International Stock Photo: page 148
Warren Faidley, International Stock Photo: pages 90, 118, 304
Harvey Finkle: pages 281 top, 281 bottom, 295
Robert Fried Photography: pages 64, 73, 191, 215, 230, 279, 298
Frost Publishing Group: page 48
FSPA Archives: page 95
Dawn Gibeau, *National Catholic Reporter:* page 276
Frank Grant, International Stock Photo: page 171
Jeff Greenberg, International Stock Photo: page 166
Photo on page 282 is courtesy of Jeffrey Gros
Dan Habib, Impact Visuals: page 246
Richard Hackett, International Stock Photo: page 158
Jack Hamilton: pages 31, 34, 71, 74, 108, 111, 160, 175, 184, 193, 195, 202, 211, 217, 259
Cliff Hollenbeck, International Stock Photo: page 239
Mike J. Howell, International Stock Photo: page 32
Shirley Kelter: page 210 right
Gabe Kirchheimer, Impact Visuals: page 257
Lasallian Volunteers: page 286
Phil Lauro: pages 135, 165
Michael Manheim, International Stock Photo: page 38
Maratea, International Stock Photo: page 182
Roger Markham Smith, International Stock Photo: page 89 left and right
Marquette University Archives: page 212
Tom McCarthy, Rainbow: page 231
Dan McCoy, Rainbow: page 237
Mary Messenger: pages 87, 96, 120
John Michael, International Stock Photo: pages 15, 233
Mark Newman, International Stock Photo: page 149
Stock Noble, International Stock Photo: page 124
Dario Perla, International Stock Photo: page 156
Richard Pharaoh, International Stock Photo: page 8
Gene Plaisted, The Crosiers: pages 70, 86, 103, 266, 271, 291, 293
Frank Priegue, International Stock Photo: page 234
Stan Ries, International Stock Photo: page 256
E. Rousset, Limet, France: page 267
Scala, Art Resource, NY: page 54
L. J. Schneider Photography, International Stock Photo: page 130
James L. Shaffer: pages 12, 18, 27, 58, 59, 69 left, 113, 121, 167, 168, 176, 177, 179, 196, 209, 226, 240, 247, 250, 252, 253, 254, 262, 268, 269, 273, 274, 275, 278, 284, 287, 290, 296
Skjold Photographs: pages 24, 35, 39, 51, 61, 190, 218, 241
Catherine Smith, Impact Visuals: page 22
Bill Stanton, International Stock Photo: pages 99, 154, 180, 305
Scott Thode, International Stock Photo: pages 72, 127, 129, 157
Jay Thomas, International Stock Photo: pages 11, 23, 65
Bill Tucker, International Stock Photo: page 83
UPI Bettmann: pages 189, 210 left
Elliott Varner Smith, International Stock Photo: page 26
Jim West, Impact Visuals: page 203
Dusty Willison, International Stock Photo: page 151